DR E. W. THORNTON

WOMEN, STRESS, AND HEART DISEASE

WOMEN, STRESS, AND HEART DISEASE

Edited by

Kristina Orth-Gomér
Karolinska Institute, Stockholm

Margaret Chesney
University of California, San Francisco

Nanette K. Wenger
Emory University School of Medicine, Atlanta

 LAWRENCE ERLBAUM ASSOCIATES, PUBLISHERS
1998   **Mahwah, New Jersey**   **London**

Lawrence Erlbaum Associates, Inc., Publishers
10 Industrial Avenue
Mahwah, New Jersey 07430

Cover design by Kathryn Houghtaling Lacey

Library of Congress Cataloging-in-Publication Data

Women, stress, and heart disease / edited by Kristina Orth-Gomér,
Margaret Chesney, Nanette K. Wenger.
   p.   cm.
   Includes bibliographical references and index.
   ISBN 0-8058-2124-4 (cloth : alk. paper).
   1. Heart diseases in women—Risk factors. 2. Women—Health and
hygiene. 3. Stress (Psychology). 4. Stress (Physiology). I. Orth-
Gomér, Kristina. II. Chesney, Margaret. III. Wenger, Nanette
Kass.
RC682.W65 1998
616.1′2′0082—dc21   97-44966
                                                  CIP

Books published by Lawrence Erlbaum Associates are printed on acid-free paper,
and their bindings are chosen for strength and durability.

Printed in the United States of America
10 9 8 7 6 5 4 3 2 1

To Gösta Tibblin, M.D.,
who unsparingly shared time and effort
to support good science on women by women

Contents

Preface

This volume reflects the attempt to describe and discuss an area that has not attracted much attention until very recently. Although we are beginning to become aware of the importance of heart disease in women, the specific origins of and risk factors for heart disease in women are rarely considered in great detail. This is particularly true for behavioral and psychosocial factors. Therefore, we felt that the proceedings of the international conference on "Women, Stress, and Heart Disease" held in Stockholm at the Swedish Society of Medicine in September 1994 should be extended to a more comprehensive review of behavioral risk factors and diagnostic and prognostic factors, which are of particular interest for female heart disease. The speakers at the conference have devoted much time and energy after the conference to complete and update their knowledge and evidence on clinical aspects, on hormonal aspects, and physiological aspects of female heart disease. In this context, it is important to note that even if, for simplicity, we often use the general term *heart disease*, we are always referring to the most common of the female heart diseases, coronary heart disease.

Under the term heart disease we may include the underlying coronary artery atherosclerosis as well as the metabolic and hemodynamic characteristics of the coronary disease process. We also include the various clinical manifestations of stable and unstable angina pectoris and acute myocardial infarction. As described in the first chapter, the Framingham study reported angina pectoris to be more common as a first manifestation of coronary heart disease in women than in men. From the Framingham study, it was also reported that angina pectoris in women was a less ominous sign, which had a better prognosis in women than in men. This early observation is not entirely true. In a recently completed community-based study of all women aged 65 years or under, living in the greater Stockholm area, who were hospitalized for acute clinical manifestations of coronary heart disease, 38% were found to have an acute MI and 62% were found to suffer from severe angina pectoris, requiring hospitalization. Of the patients with angina pectoris 24% had evidence of a previous MI either from their clinical history or from their electrocardiogram. In a substantial proportion of the women with angina (47%) their acute chest pain was characterized as unstable angina pectoris, defined as newly debuted severe angina pectoris, which had deteriorated during the last 4 weeks before admission, with an increase in pain intensity and pain duration, or with pain at rest or very low physical exertion (Orth-Gomér et al., 1977). This unstable form of coronary disease can be seen as an early stage of the infarction process and is sometimes referred to as an impending infarction. Thus a major proportion of those women, who were admitted to a coronary care unit and hospitalized for acute coronary disease, have a serious and life threatening illness, which necessitates powerful clinical diagnostic resources and vigorous treatment. As is evident from the clinical contributions of this volume, this has not always been recognized. Female patients have been diagnosed and treated by different clinical standards than male patients. Female patients, in particular those with angina pectoris, have been misunderstood, misinterpreted, and misdiagnosed. Even in the acute MI phase female patients have been judged differently and treated differently from male patients.

One important explanation, although not an excuse, for these gender differences is the difference in age span between male and female cardiac patients. Female patients, on average, are 10 to 15 years older than male patients. As is evident from this volume's section on psychophysiology, much of this age difference is due to the relative protection from early atherosclerosis that women obtain through their reproductive hormones. Before menopause, which occurs at a median age of 51 years in Sweden as in the United States, coronary heart disease is rare in women. Between ages 50 and 60, incidence rates increase rapidly in women. In men under age 65 coronary disease is still three to five times more common than in women, but after that age the rates in men and women become similar.

It is not surprising, then, that some physicians try to delay menopause and prolong the relative protection, by advocating female sex hormone replacement therapy to all women after age 50. It is even more understandable when we consider the evidence that this therapy may not only protect against heart disease, but also against osteoporotic fractures, perhaps help alleviate depressive symptoms, and possibly even counteract central nervous degenerative processes like Alzheimer's disease (Grady et al., 1992).

What these physicians and many others tend to forget is that almost all this evidence is based on observational studies. Experimentally designed studies, in the form of randomized clinical trials that test these effects in a scientifically sound manner, are ongoing, but they will not provide answers until after the year 2000.

It has been commonly argued, both at U.S. and international clinical consensus conferences, that before results from these large ongoing clinical trials are known, general recommendations about hormone replacement therapy cannot be made. We simply do not know enough about the risks and the benefits of the treatments (Expertgruppen, Konsensusuttalande, Östrogenbehandling efter menopause, 1996, Report of the World Health Organization Scientific Group). And furthermore, with the present, strong focus among the public and the professions on hormone replacement, it is easy to forget that other preventive and protective measures may be as important, or even more important than hormones. For example, it is well known that early menopause is more common among women who are heavy smokers. It has also been observed that early menopause is more common in women with low education. Smoking is more common in low educated women. Thus some of the effect of low education on menopausal age is mediated by smoking. Other effects are mediated through more direct, neuroendocrine, physiological mechanisms. Several authors of this volume demonstrate the close interrelation and interaction between behavioral factors and hormonal status. These associations are found in animals as well as in human studies. The common finding is that psychosocial stress leads to ovarian dysfunction with attenuation of naturally occurring female sex hormone cycles. Female monkeys under heavy stress may even completely lose their ovulatory capacity. Thus from the preventive viewpoint it becomes as important to alleviate the stress and decrease smoking as it is to replace the hormones (Kaplan et al., 1996). As some evidence suggests that women after menopause become less resistant to stress and more physiologically reactive to laboratory stressors, future therapeutic and preventive actions must use an interactive approach relying on both hormones and behavioral factors (Kaplan et al., 1996).

These underlying physiological variations become even more important in the view of the enormous social and psychological changes that women undergo today. Perhaps the most visible of these changes has to do with women's move into the labor markets. In the Sweden of today, as many women as men are employed outside the home. In the United States the same situation is quickly approaching. These changes have profound effects on family life, on women's social and psychological well-being, and probably also on women's general as well as cardiovascular health status. In general, women who have many roles seem to be healthier. The diversity of different roles and the possible gratification from different kinds of functions, such as family and work, seem to be able to counteract each other. Stress in one role can always be neutralized through positive experiences in another role. But there seems to be one point at which, in modern society, the burden on women, who fulfill many roles, becomes too high (Frankenhaeuser, 1996). The price that they have to pay may be a damage to their health. The sections on work and stress and multiple roles in this volume deal in great detail with the various conditions under which women's social and psychological experiences may affect their health in general and their cardiovascular health in particular. Implications for interventions and preventive actions are addressed.

ACKNOWLEDGMENTS

The editors would like to thank the Swedish Social Science Research Council and the Swedish Society of Medicine for excellent collaboration and generous support of the work on this volume. It was inspired and initiated at an international and interdisciplinary seminar, held in Stockholm in September of 1994, on the topic "Women, Stress, and Heart Disease."

We would also like to thank the contributing authors for their great efforts as well as their willingness to comply with the special standards and requirements needed in a volume that extends from biology and medicine to behavioral and social sciences.

REFERENCES

Expertgruppen, Konsensusuttalande, Östrogenbehandling efter menopause. (1996). Mediciniska forskningsrådet, Spris förlag, Stockholm.

Frankenhaeuser, M. (1996). Stress and gender. *European Review, 4*(4), 313–327.

Grady, D., Rubin, S. M., Petitti, D. B., Fox, C. S., Black, D., Ettinger, B., Ernster, V. L., & Cummings, S. R. (1992). Hormone therapy to prevent disease and prolong life in postmenopausal women. *Annals of Internal Medicine, 117*(12), 1016–1036.

Kaplan, J. R., Adams, M. R., Clarkson, T. B., Manuck, S. B., Shively, C. A., & Williams, J. K. (1996). Psychosocial factors, sex differences, and atherosclerosis: Lessons from animal models. *Psychosomatic Medicine, 58*(6), 598–611.

Orth-Gomér, K., Mittleman, M., Schenck-Gustafsson, K., Wamala, S. P., Eriksson, M., Belkic, K., Kirkeeide, R., Svane, B., & Rydén, L. (1997). Lipoprotein(a) as determinant of coronary heart disease in younger women. *Circulation, 95*, 329–334.

Report of World Health Organization Scientific Group. Research on menopause in the 1990s. World Health Organization, Geneva.

1

Coronary Heart Disease in Women: Evolution of Our Knowledge

Nanette K. Wenger
Emory University School of Medicine
and Grady Memorial Hospital, Atlanta, Georgia

This chapter addresses the medical components of coronary heart disease (CHD) in women, its presentation and clinical outcomes, and the coronary risk factors important for women. The information should buttress the need to identify the psychosocial components or contributors that relate to CHD because it will become evident that women have less favorable outcomes once CHD becomes clinically manifest than do their male counterparts.

The data presented here derive from information gathered in the United States. Although this information can, in part, be extrapolated to other countries, specific incidence and outcome variables require validation in different populations, particularly where CHD rates are low. Comparable reports to those for the United States have appeared in England and New Zealand. Coronary disease, the medical problem that results in myocardial infarction (MI), is the major cause of mortality among women in the United States, accounting for almost 250,000 deaths annually. However, when one examines the information used in regard to prevention, to clinical features, and to therapy and prognosis of CHD in women, it is based on studies in populations that involved predominantly or exclusively middle-aged men (Wenger, Speroff, & Packard, 1993a). It has yet to be ascertained how much of this middle-aged male model of CHD is applicable to the older women in whom CHD occurs.

Age is an important factor in women regarding CHD (Lerner & Kannel, 1986). Whereas one in eight or nine women in the 45–64-year age group has clinical evidence of CHD, this is present in one in three women older than

65 years of age. What must be addressed, therefore, is the combination of both a female incidence and prevalence of coronary disease and an elderly age incidence and prevalence of coronary disease; often the two may not be separable.

ANGINA PECTORIS

As with much of the epidemiologic information about coronary disease in the United States, the initial components were derived from the Framingham Heart Study; however, whereas Framingham provided enormously valuable information, it also engendered some misinformation that adversely affected the clinical care of women for a number of years. Perhaps one difficulty was the delineation of the benignity of angina pectoris (AP) in women. Angina, which probably should have been titled "chest pain" in the Framingham reports, because it was based solely on the clinical history without objective test documentation, was the major initial manifestation of CHD in women, occurring in 56% of Framingham women as compared with 43% of men. However, one in four men in Framingham who had AP developed MI within the ensuing 5 years, clearly a serious outcome, whereas 86% of women in the Framingham cohort described to have angina never incurred MI (Kannel & Feinleib, 1972; Lerner & Kannel, 1986). The conclusion, although erroneous, was that AP was not a serious problem for women; therefore, little research attention was paid to coronary disease in women and, indeed, little attention was addressed in clinical practice to evaluation of chest pain problems of women, because no serious consequence such as MI was considered to ensue. Of interest is that, even within this Framingham cohort, there was a small overlooked subset, the women aged 60–69 years, who had the same adverse prognosis as did the men; this constitutes further evidence for the important age dependency of CHD in women. It was only with publication of information from the Coronary Artery Surgery Study (CASS) Registry in the 1980s that the challenge was offered to the benignity of AP in women. The CASS Registry was a compilation of information regarding men and women referred for coronary arteriography to participating institutions by their treating physicians because their chest pain was judged of sufficient severity to warrant consideration for coronary artery bypass surgery; coronary arteriography provided objective confirmation as to whether the chest pain reflected myocardial ischemia due to coronary arterial obstruction. In the CASS Registry, 50% of the women had little or no objective documentation of coronary disease at coronary arteriography as contrasted with 17% of the men (Kennedy et al., 1982; The Principal Investigators of CASS, 1981). If this had been the case in Framingham as well, that may explain why 86% of Framingham women never developed MI; their chest pain was not due to coronary atherosclerotic heart disease. One message is that women may have chest pain syndromes that mimic AP, but are due to etiologies other than atherosclerotic obstructive coronary artery disease (CAD). Another message is that for women with chest pain who have CHD, the outlook is more ominous than suggested by the Framingham data.

This misinterpretation of the Framingham findings led to a number of missed opportunities. Inadequate attention was directed to preventive care, that is, coronary risk reduction in women; the research and clinical emphasis focused on preventive care for men. Further, inadequate attention, until very recent years, was devoted to procedures needed to identify whether chest pain syndromes in women were related to CHD and to stratify their risk for proximate coronary events; this diagnostic testing was predominantly studied in and applied to populations of men.

PREVENTION OF CHD IN WOMEN

Why is prevention of CHD important for women? First, in the United States, 40% of all coronary events in women are fatal. Second, 67% of all sudden deaths in women occur in those not previously known to have CHD (Kannel & Abbott, 1987). Certainly this mortality issue is extremely relevant, but morbidity concerns are also of major importance. Of women aged 55–64 years in the United States who have CHD, 36% are disabled by their disease, and this increases to 55% among women older than 75 years of age. High priority must be accorded to education of women about CHD; unless women worldwide consider coronary disease to be part of their illness experience, they are unlikely to heed preventive messages when young or to respond appropriately to chest pain symptoms when older. Coronary disease in the United States, until very recent years, was viewed as a problem of men, to whom informational and educational messages were addressed. Coronary disease was thus considered by women to be a problem for their spouse, their father, their male siblings, and their male children. Today, rather than, to paraphrase a Broadway musical, addressing "why can't a woman be more like a man?", we must examine those relevant gender differences that warrant specific attention.

The prevalence of coronary risk factors among United States women is alarming; in the cohort of women aged 20–74 years (National Center for Health Statistics [NCHS], 1991), over one third have hypertension, using as a definition a systolic blood pressure in excess of 140 mm Hg, a diastolic blood pressure in excess of 90 mm Hg, or both, or those using antihypertensive medications. Over one fourth have elevated cholesterol levels, using as a cut point 240 mg/dl. More than one fourth of U.S. women are cigarette smokers, more than one fourth are overweight and more than one fourth have a sedentary lifestyle. In the United States, as in many other nations, coronary risk factors predominate among subsets of the population with less favorable socioeconomic circumstances and with less favorable educational levels, and these two features commonly coexist.

The decreases in both cardiovascular and coronary mortality in recent years in the United States have been less pronounced for women than for men; concomitantly, the decreases in coronary risk factors have been less pronounced for women than for men during the past two to three decades (Eaker et al., 1993). In this period, the emphasis was on risk reduction for men; an important missing link is the exclusion of women and of elderly persons of both genders from research studies that limits reliable estimates both regarding coronary risk attributes and regarding the efficacy of risk interventions in these populations. In another publication (Wenger, 1994), I identified women and elderly persons as the "understudied majority"; the challenge is that coronary risk factors are highly prevalent in the elderly, and we must learn their clinical impact and the effects of their modification.

Gender comparisons of the relative risk of CHD imparted by major risk factors are derived from data amassed in the National Health and Nutritional Evaluation Survey in the United States (Centers for Disease Control, 1992). Hypertension imparts comparable risk by gender, the risk of hypercholesterolemia is somewhat greater for men, diabetes confers substantially greater coronary risk for women, the risk of being overweight is comparable for women and men, and smoking imparts a somewhat greater coronary risk for women than for their male counterparts.

Particular attention is warranted regarding the coronary risk of cigarette smoking for women; in the United States there is currently an equal prevalence of cigarette smoking in women than in men, because there has been greater smoking cessation among men. Unless this trend changes, the United States may be the first nation in the world to have more women than men who smoke cigarettes. From the 1950s to the 1990s, 30% of White women and 36% of Black women in the United States decreased or stopped cigarette smoking; despite these changes, 23% of U.S. women older than 18 years of age currently smoke cigarettes, and the data on younger women, although not reliably tabulated, suggest an even more serious problem. Additionally, women have increased their intensity of smoking (the number of cigarettes smoked daily) and have an earlier onset of smoking behavior. A number of reports document that smoking at least triples the risk of MI, even among premenopausal women. Smoking lowers the age at menopause, on average about 2 years, and this earlier menopause, in addition to the smoking behavior, may be an added feature that imparts coronary risk (Hansen, Andersen, & Von Eyben, 1993; NCHS, 1991). Based on data from the United States Nurses' Health Study (Willett et al., 1987), the number of cigarettes smoked correlated with the risk of fatal CHD, nonfatal MI, and AP—that is, all of the coronary manifestations. However, smoking imparted the greatest risk for women already at high risk because they were older, had a family history of coronary disease, and were overweight, hypertensive, hyper-lipidemic, and diabetic. The converse, that is, the potential benefits of smoking cessation, is that within 2 years of cessation former smokers decreased their cardiovascular mortality risk by almost one fourth. Why the emphasis on smoking cessation for women? Cigarette manufacturers target women with smoking advertisements, both in the United States and likely in others, emphasizing the reason for which many women smoke, namely weight control. Therefore the educational messages from health care professionals, governments, and other concerned health agencies must counteract this advertising targeted at populations at high risk, women and, in particular, young women. Further, smoking cessation programs for women must incor-porate dietary and exercise interventions for weight control if they are likely to be successful. In the Nurses' Health Study (Kawachi et al., 1993), cardio-vascular mortality risk declined 24% within 2 years of smoking cessation. Based on data from the CASS Registry (Hermanson, Omenn, Kronmal, Gersh, and Participants in CASS, 1988), the benefit of smoking cessation did not lessen with older age.

In the United States, more than 50% of White women and 79% of Black women older than 45 years of age have hypertension. This percentage increases to 71% among women older than 65 years of age. It is important that, after age 65, more women than men have hypertension, in contrast to the reversed prevalence at a younger age; also, women have more compli-cations of their hypertension at all ages than do men (Anastos et al., 1991; NCHS, 1991). Systolic blood pressure levels in men peak in middle age; systolic blood pressure levels in women continue to rise until beyond age 80, such that isolated systolic hypertension, which imparts comparable risk to combined systolic/diastolic hypertension, is more common in elderly women than in elderly men. Importantly, control of isolated systolic hyper-tension at an elderly age can decrease the risk of fatal and nonfatal cardio-vascular events (SHEP Cooperative Research Group, 1991).

Hypercholesterolemia is more prevalent in men at middle age and in older women, but hypercholesterolemia becomes particularly prominent in women after menopause. Women have higher concentrations of high density lipoprotein (HDL) cholesterol and lower levels of low-density lipoprotein (LDL) cholesterol than do men at young to middle age. Total cholesterol levels among women increase with age, at least to age 70; LDL cholesterol levels rise progressively after menopause to exceed levels in men at elderly age (Kannel, 1988). In 1980, one third of U.S. women had seriously high levels of total cholesterol, rising to over 50% after 55 years of age; this occurred despite the U.S. survey data showing continuing lowering of cholesterol concentrations in U.S. adults. Recommendations from the first report of the

Adult Treatment Panel of the National Cholesterol Educational Program (NCEP) cited only male gender as a risk attribute. Adult Treatment Panel II recommendations (Expert Panel on Detection, 1993) identify women older than 55 years of age or those who have premature menopause without estrogen replacement as being at increased risk. The recently reported Scandinavian Simvastatin Survival Study (4S; 4S Group, 1994) for the first time documented coronary benefit of cholesterol lowering by pharmacotherapy for women, even at elderly age, albeit in a secondary prevention study.

Glucose intolerance and diabetes mellitus are important contributors to coronary risk for women of all ages. Diabetes is a far more powerful risk factor for women than for men, negating the gender protection even for premenopausal women (Barrett-Connor, Wingard, & Edelstein, 1991). Maturity-onset diabetes mellitus in the Nurses' Health Study was associated with a three- to sevenfold increased risk of cardiovascular events (Manson, Colditz, et al., 1991), with the risk of diabetes compounded by the presence of associated coronary risk factors. It is uncertain which mechanisms confer risk: associated hypertension? associated lipid abnormalities? fibrinogen? upper body obesity? other? We now know the value of precise blood glucose control in limiting coronary risk, in addition to the benefit shown for this approach for microvascular complications of diabetes. In the Nurses' Health Study, a lowered incidence of diabetes mellitus was evident in women who exercised regularly (Manson, Rimm, et al., 1991), again likely an interaction of risk factors, but a potentially highly valuable intervention for women at risk for diabetes. Diabetes is associated with a less favorable hospital and long-term prognosis in women with MI, with the adverse impact of diabetes mellitus being greater for women than for men (Donahue, Goldberg, Chen, Gore, & Alpert, 1993; Greenland, Reicher-Reiss, Goldbourt, Behar, and the Israeli SPRINT Investigators, 1991; Liao et al., 1993). Diabetic women with MI had double the risk of recurrent MI and a fourfold increase in risk of heart failure compared with nondiabetic women. Importantly, among patients who undergo coronary artery bypass graft surgery (CABG) and percutaneous transluminal coronary angioplasty (PTCA), the prevalence of diabetes in women is greater than that for men, which may be a contributor to the increased mortality for women who have myocardial revascularization procedures.

Obesity has increased serially in the United States in recent years in both genders (NCHS, 1991), but the prevalence is greatest in Black, Hispanic, and Native American women; as with other coronary risk attributes, obesity is more common in populations with lower educational levels and lower socioeconomic status, defined by income levels. Based on 1988 data from the National Center for Health Statistics, half of U.S. Black women and one third of U.S. White women were 20% or more above their desirable weight. In the Framingham Heart Study, obesity significantly and independently predicted cardiovascular disease (CVD), but particularly so among women (Kannel, Garrison, & Wilson, 1986). There are multiple mechanisms whereby obesity imparts risk in that obesity is associated with raised levels of total cholesterol, triglycerides, and LDL cholesterol and lowered levels of high-density lipoprotein (HDL) cholesterol; obesity is also associated with insulin resistance, hyperuricemia, and hypertension (Manson et al., 1990).

Exercise and physical activity data for women in the United States, which may be more unfavorable than in some European populations, show that 6 out of 10 U.S. women are sedentary (Anda et al., 1990), with a tendency toward a sedentary lifestyle that has been progressive over recent years. Physical inactivity is more likely to be associated with lower educational levels and lower income levels. Improved physical fitness, objectively measured, has been associated in a number of studies with lessened cardiovascular and total mortality (Blair et al., 1989). Increased levels of physical fitness are associated with more favorable coronary risk profiles, with this association being more powerful for women than for men. Habitual exercise is associated with decreased coronary risk even in old age, although the mechanisms remain conjectural.

EVALUATION AND TREATMENT OF AP

Women in the United States who have angina are less likely to undergo invasive diagnostic testing and myocardial revascularization, both CABG and PTCA, than are men (Ayanian & Epstein, 1991; Steingart et al., 1991; Tobin et al., 1987), although gender differences have decreased substantially in recent years (Shaw et al., 1994). An enormous number of questions remain unanswered. Are these gender differences in procedure use appropriate or inappropriate, that is, do men undergo too many procedures, do women have too few, or is the gender distribution reasonable? Nor do we know whether differences in procedure use reflect physician decisions or patient decisions—and the basis for these decisions. Warranting consideration is the effect of societal perception of coronary risk in women in this decision making. Although procedure use is considered a medical model, the physician is only one component of this model; the patient is another and societal values may be the third. Typically, when I suggest to an older patient, woman or man, that an invasive procedure be undertaken for diagnosis or for therapy, that older patient will consult with family and with friends as to its advisability and desirability; if there is not a societal perception that coronary disease is an important component of the illness experience of older women, an older woman will be less likely to receive support from family or friends to undergo invasive procedures. This potentially important component has not been examined in an organized fashion across populations.

In regard to treatment strategies for AP, the performance of a coronary arteriogram appears to be a major determinant of access to myocardial revascularization procedures. Stated otherwise, once the presence of coronary disease is documented in women with chest pain and its severity and prognostic significance ascertained, interventions are comparable by gender. In several studies, comparable numbers of women and men considered to have high-risk lesions at coronary arteriography—that is, lesions considered to impart high risk for coronary mortality—underwent coronary artery bypass surgery. However, when coronary lesions were considered to impart a low or intermediate mortality risk, more men than women were referred for coronary artery bypass surgery. Although some researchers concluded that women received better care because they were referred for invasive therapies only when improvement in survival was likely (Bickell et al., 1992; Laskey, 1992), mortality provides only a partial assessment of efficacy. Particularly in older populations, in addition to concern with mortality, we must consider symptomatic and functional status; these are the outcomes valued by older patients. This aspect was highlighted in a gender-comparison report of the study of ventricular enlargement (SAVE). Patients enrolled in this study had to have an index MI of such severity that it decreased their ventricular ejection fraction below 40%, a sizeable infarction. Prior to this index infarction, coronary arteriography had been performed in 15% of the women as compared with 27% of the men, with a comparable proportion referred for coronary artery bypass surgery (Steingart et al., 1991). These percentages contrast with the far greater limitation of activities of daily living due to symptoms of angina in women than in men, occurring in half of the women as compared with one third of the men. Two important facets emerge from these data. First, one half of the women with angina did not have adequate control of their anginal symptoms with medical therapy; this warrants precise examination of the efficacy and application of medical therapies for women with angina to reduce symptoms and improve function. Second is that, for more severe symptoms and functional limitation, fewer invasive diagnostic interventions were undertaken in women than in men.

MYOCARDIAL INFARCTION

Based on Framingham data, although MI was less often the initial presentation of CHD for women than for men, 38% versus 50%, respectively (Kannel & Abbott, 1987), women had greater mortality with an initial MI than did their male counterparts. Women also had more unrecognized MI, much of which was characterized as silent infarction. These observations would not be considered surprising today, as silent or unrecognized infarction is more common in older age and when there is concomitant diabetes and hypertension; indeed, such were the characteristics of the women in the Framingham cohort. In the Framingham Heart Study, the one-year mortality for women was enormous—45%—as contrasted with 10% for men. Myocardial infarction mortality has decreased substantially with contemporary therapies, but although mortality has lessened, U.S. data from the 1990s from a community-wide Registry in Seattle report a hospital mortality in women with MI of 16% as contrasted with 11% for men (Maynard et al., 1992).

How have contemporary medical therapies helped? Coronary thrombolysis, use of drugs that dissolve clots in the acute phase of myocardial infarction, has provided equal gender benefit. Benefit for women occurs despite the documentation that women have more bleeding complications of this therapy, particularly serious intracerebral bleeding (GISSI, 1986, 1987). This raises further questions about drug therapies. Thrombolytic drugs are given in fixed dosage; in the early years of coronary thrombolysis, the higher drug dosage customarily used was associated with greater bleeding complications, but bleeding complications decreased with change to lower drug dosages. Do women who have a smaller body mass receive a relatively higher drug dosage using these fixed dosage regimens? Is this why women have excess bleeding? Clearly dose-ranging studies are needed, and they have only now begun to be undertaken. Also important, however, is the lesser eligibility of women for this lifesaving therapy, with a major contributor being the late presentation of women to hospital (Maynard, Althouse, Cerqueira, Olsufka, & Kennedy, 1991); thrombolytic drugs must be used in the initial 6 to 8 hours after the onset of pain of MI. Again we return to societal perceptions; does the older woman with chest pain receive the same urgency and reinforcement from friends or family to come immediately to hospital during the initial hours' window of opportunity for use of thrombolytic therapy? Or do many older women come to hospital after many hours to days, only when chest pain recurs or persists, such that they are not eligible for this lifesaving therapy?

Gender differences are equally prominent in use of exercise rehabilitation after MI and myocardial revascularization procedures. Fewer women than men are referred to structured exercise programs by their treating physicians (Ades, Waldmann, Polk, & Coflesky, 1992; Boogaard & Briody, 1985; Oldridge, LaSalle, & Jones, 1980), despite documentation of comparable improvements in functional capacity as a result of rehabilitative exercise training for women as for men. Even among referred women, their attendance at cardiac rehabilitation programs is lower and their dropout rate is higher. Are women bad patients? Do they not like to exercise? Or is it that, at least in the United States, most supervised cardiac rehabilitation programs are designed by time of day, by location, by type of exercise, to meet the needs of the predominant population—middle-aged and working men—with little relevance or applicability for elderly women with symptomatic coronary heart disease?

MYOCARDIAL REVASCULARIZATION: CORONARY BYPASS SURGERY AND CORONARY ANGIOPLASTY

For examination of gender differences in myocardial revascularization, CABG and PTCA, virtually no randomized trial data are available, and information must be derived from case series. As such, differences in baseline characteristics assume enormous importance. In all reported series, women are older, and have more angina, more diabetes, and more hypertension; using the male model of coronary disease, they would be expected to have less favorable outcomes. However, women have less multivessel coronary disease, less prior MI and less abnormal ventricular function; using the male model of coronary disease, they would be expected to do better. What actually happens?

In all reported series, female gender was associated with an increased risk of perioperative death and coronary artery bypass surgical complications (Kahn et al., 1990; Loop et al., 1983), entailing a more ominous prognosis than did ventricular dysfunction. In the only randomized clinical trial and the oldest of the studies, the Coronary Artery Surgery Study (CASS; Kennedy et al., 1981), perioperative mortality for women was substantially greater than that for men, 4.5% versus 1.9%. Contemporary data from the MITI Registry also defined a greater mortality with coronary artery bypass surgery for women than for men, 13% versus 6.5%; the higher contemporary CABG mortality rates for both genders reflect the older and sicker patients referred for surgery, but surgical mortality for women remains double that for men. Worthy of emphasis is that the high risk for women is solely a perioperative mortality risk, in that, among women who survive the postoperative hospital stay, there is comparable 5-, 10-, and 15-year survival to that for men.

Currently there are equal procedural success rates for PTCA in both genders, and no gender difference in procedural mortality (Bell et al., 1993). Despite this, in-hospital mortality remains higher, although long-term outcomes are comparable by gender (Weintraub et al., 1994). Registry data of the National Heart, Lung, and Blood Institute regarding gender differences in patients receiving coronary angioplasty identify that women who undergo PTCA are older, have had less prior MI, more heart failure, more hypertension, and substantially more diabetes. More procedures in women are done for unstable angina, hence are urgent or emergency procedures. Despite somewhat better ventricular function, more women sent to coronary angioplasty were considered either inoperable or at very high risk for CABG surgery. Four-year follow-up Registry data show that women were more likely to have died within the ensuing 4 years and survivors were more likely to have angina and more severe angina than their male counterparts; not surprisingly, they received more maintenance antianginal medications.

SUMMARY

To summarize the current status of CHD in women in the United States, there remains less aggressive diagnosis and management than for men, although gender differences have decreased substantially during the past decade (Krumholz, Douglas, Lauer, & Pasternak, 1992). Women have a greater hospital and one-year mortality than do men when they sustain MI and have less successful outcomes from myocardial revascularization procedures. Women have higher mortality rates with coronary bypass surgery, their graft patency rates are lower, and they have less symptomatic relief. Although comparable gender success rates are reported with coronary angioplasty, the newer atherectomy procedures have lower success rates and more complications in women, likely related to the larger size of these devices and smaller coronary artery size of women.

Today we know that the female heart is vulnerable to coronary disease (Wenger, Speroff, & Packard, 1993b) but that it becomes clinically manifest at older age than is the case for men. We also know that women have greater mortality both with MI and with myocardial revascularization procedures. What we do not yet know is whether this a gender-specific effect or reflects the host characteristics in that women are older and have greater comorbidity, particularly diabetes and hypertension. Is there suboptimal use of medical therapies for women in that the drugs used were tested in young or middle-aged men; are the same drugs and same dosages reasonable or unreasonable for women? Does the less favorable revascularization outcome derive from an excess of urgent or emergency myocardial revascularization procedures, which always carry higher risk than elective revascularization? Are women then not referred earlier because of this higher risk, completing the vicious circle of late referral, urgent or emergency interventions and resultant excess risk?

We must examine the coronary risk attributes unique to women, in particular the role of postmenopausal hormone replacement therapy (Grady et al., 1992; Manolio et al., 1993; Stampfer & Colditz, 1991; The Writing Group for the PEPI Trial, 1995) in primary and secondary coronary prevention. We must learn the impact both of medical and surgical coronary therapies for women not only on mortality but on morbidity—that is, symptomatic status, functional limitations, and quality of life. These aspects have not been well examined in either gender, but have been less well studied in women. Perhaps even more important than gender comparisons, related to the clinical care of women with CHD, is assessment of the impact of earlier diagnosis and therapy of CHD among populations of women; when women are at less advanced age, when they have less advanced coronary disease and myocardial dysfunction, when they have fewer and potentially less severe comorbid medical problems, and when there is less urgency or emergency of the myocardial revascularization procedures. These data are needed to guide clinical practice; these are data we do not yet have. We have learned over the last two decades that CHD in the United States is an equal opportunity killer for women and for men. Answers to the questions raised are likely to improve the outcomes of CHD for half of the patients seen in clinical practice—the women.

REFERENCES

Ades, P. A., Waldmann, M. L., Polk, D. M., & Coflesky, J. T. (1992). Referral patterns and exercise response in the rehabilitation of female coronary patients aged ≥ 62 years. *American Journal of Cardiology, 69*, 1422–1425.

Anastos, K., Charney, P., Charon, R. A., Cohen, E., Jones, C. Y., Marte, C., Swiderski, D. M., Wheat, M. E., & Williams, S. (1991). Hypertension in women: What is really known? The Women's Caucus, Working Group on Women's Health of the Society of General Internal Medicine. *Annals of Internal Medicine, 115*, 287–293.

Anda, R. F., Waller, M. N., Wooten, K. G., Mast, E. E., Escobedo, L. G., & Sanderson, L. M. (1990). Behavioral risk factor surveillance, 1988. In CDC Surveillance Summaries, June 1990. *Morbidity and Mortality Weekly Report, 39*(SS-2), 1–21.

Ayanian, J. Z., & Epstein, A. M. (1991). Differences in the use of procedures between women and men hospitalized for coronary heart disease. *New England Journal of Medicine, 325*, 221–225.

Barrett-Connor, E. L., Cohn, B. A., Wingard, D. L., & Edelstein, S. L. (1991). Why is diabetes mellitus a stronger risk factor for fatal ischemic heart disease in women than in men? The Rancho Bernardo Study. *Journal of the American Medical Association, 265*, 627–631.

Bell, M. R., Holmes, D. R., Jr., Berger, P. B., Garratt, K. N., Bailey, K. R., & Gersh, B. J. (1993). The changing in-hospital mortality of women undergoing percutaneous transluminal coronary angioplasty. *Journal of the American Medical Association, 269*, 2091–2095.

Bickell, N. A., Pieper, K. S., Lee, K. L., Mark, D. B., Glower, D. D., Pryor, D. B., & Califf, R. M. (1992). Referral patterns for coronary artery disease treatment: Gender bias or good clinical judgment? *Annals of Internal Medicine, 116*, 791–797.

Blair, S. N., Kohl, H. W., III, Paffenbarger, R. S., Jr., Clark, D. G., Cooper, K. H., & Gibbons, L. W. (1989). Physical fitness and all-cause mortality. A prospective study of healthy men and women. *Journal of the American Medical Association, 262*, 2395–2401.

Boogaard, M. A. K., & Briody, M. E. (1985). Comparison of the rehabilitation of men and women post-myocardial infarction. *Journal of Cardiopulmonary Rehabilitation, 5*, 379–384.

Centers for Disease Control. (1992). Coronary heart disease incidence, by sex—United States, 1971–1987. In CDC Surveillance Summaries, July 1992. *Morbidity and Mortality Weekly Report, 41*(SS-2), 526–529.

Donahue, R. P., Goldberg, R. J., Chen, Z., Gore, J. M., & Alpert, J. S. (1993). The influence of sex and diabetes mellitus on survival following acute myocardial infarction: A community-wide perspective. *Journal of Clinical Epidemiology, 46*, 245–252.

Eaker, E. D., Chesebro, J. H., Sacks, F. M., Wenger, N. K., Whisnant, J. P., & Winston, M. (1993). Cardiovascular disease in women. *Circulation, 88*, 1999–2009.

Expert Panel on Detection, Evaluation, and Treatment of High Blood Cholesterol in Adults. (1993). Summary of the Second Report of the National Cholesterol Education Program (NCEP) Expert Panel on Detection, Evaluation, and Treatment of High Blood Cholesterol in Adults (Adult Treatment Panel II). *Journal of the American Medical Association, 269*, 3015–3023.

Grady, D., Rubin, S. M., Petitti, D. B., Fox, C. S., Ettinger, B., Ernster, V. L., & Cummings, S. R. (1992). Hormone therapy to prevent disease and prolong life in postmenopausal women. *Annals of Internal Medicine, 117*, 1016–1037.

Greenland, P., Reicher-Reiss, H., Goldbourt, U., Behar, S., and the Israeli SPRINT Investigators. (1991). In-hospital and 1-year mortality in 1,524 women after myocardial infarction. Comparison with 4,315 men. *Circulation, 83*, 484–491.

Gruppo Italiano per lo Studio della Streptochinasi nell'Infarto Miocardioco (GISSI). (1986). Effectiveness of intravenous thrombolytic treatment in acute myocardial infarction. *Lancet, 1*, 397–402.

Gruppo Italiano per lo Studio della Streptochinasi nell'Infarto Miocardico (GISSI). (1987). Long-term effects of intravenous thrombolysis in acute myocardial infarction: Final report of the GISSI study. *Lancet, 2*, 871–874.

Hansen, E. F., Andersen, L. T., & Von Eyben, F. E. (1993). Cigarette smoking and age at first acute myocardial infarction, and influence of gender and extent of smoking. *American Journal of Cardiology, 71*, 1439–1442.

Hermanson, B., Omenn, G. S., Kronmal, R. A., Gersh, B. J., and Participants in the Coronary Artery Surgery Study. (1988). Beneficial six-year outcome of smoking cessation in older men and women with coronary artery disease. Results from the CASS Registry. *New England Journal of Medicine, 319*, 1365–1369.

Kahn, S. S., Nessim, S., Gray, R., Zcer, L. S., Chaux, A., & Matloff, J. (1990). Increased mortality of women in coronary artery bypass surgery: Evidence for referral bias. *Annals of Internal Medicine, 112*, 561–567.

Kannel, W. B. (1988). Nutrition and the occurrence and prevention of cardiovascular disease in the elderly. *Nutrition Reviews, 46*, 68–78.

Kannel, W. B., & Abbott, R. D. (1987). Incidence and prognosis of myocardial infarction in women: The Framingham Study. In E. D. Eaker, B. Packard, N. K. Wenger, T. B. Clarkson, & H. A. Tyroler (Eds.), *Coronary heart disease in women* (pp. 208–214). New York: Haymarket Doyma.

Kannel, W. B., & Feinleib, M. (1972). Natural history of angina pectoris in the Framingham study: Prognosis and survival. *American Journal of Cardiology, 29*, 154–163.

Kannel, W. B., Garrison, R. J., & Wilson, P. W. F. (1986). Obesity and nutrition in elderly diabetic patients. *American Journal of Medicine, 80*(suppl. 5A), 22–30.

Kawachi, I., Colditz, G. A., Stampfer, M. J., Willett, W. C., Manson, J. E., Rosner, B., Hunter, D. J., Hennekens, C. H., & Speizer, F. E. (1993). Smoking cessation in relation to total mortality rates in women. A prospective cohort study. *Annals of Internal Medicine, 119*, 992–1000.

Kennedy, J. W., Kaiser, G. C., Fisher, L. D., Fritz, J. K., Myers, W., Mudd, G., & Ryan, T. J. (1981). Clinical and angiographic predictors of operative mortality from the Collaborative Study in Coronary Artery Surgery (CASS). *Circulation, 63*, 793–802.

Kennedy, J. W., Killip, T., Fisher, L. D., Alderman, E. L., Gillespie, M. J., & Mock, M. B. (1982). The clinical spectrum of coronary artery disease and its surgical and medical management, 1974–1979. Coronary Artery Surgery Study. *Circulation, 66*(suppl III), III-16–III-23.

Krumholz, H. M., Douglas, P. S., Lauer, M. S., & Pasternak, P. C. (1992). Selection of patients for coronary angiography and coronary revascularization early after myocardial infarction: Is there evidence for a gender bias? *Annals of Internal Medicine, 116*, 785–790.

Laskey, W. K. (1992). Gender differences in the management of coronary artery disease: Bias or good clinical judgment? *Annals of Internal Medicine, 116*, 869–871.

Lerner, D. J., & Kannel, W. B. (1986). Patterns of coronary heart disease morbidity and mortality in the sexes: A 26-year follow-up of the Framingham population. *American Heart Journal, 111*, 383–390.

Liao, Y., Cooper, R. S., Ghali, J. K., Lansky, D., Cao, G., & Lee, J. (1993). Sex differences in the impact of coexistent diabetes on survival in patients with coronary heart disease. *Diabetes Care, 16*, 708–713.

Loop, F. D., Golding, L. R., MacMillan, J. P., Cosgrove, D. M., Lytle, B. W., & Sheldon, W. D. (1983). Coronary artery surgery in women compared with men: Analyses of risks and long-term results. *Journal of the American College of Cardiology, 1*, 383–390.

Manolio, T. A., Furberg, C. D., Shemanski, L., Psaty, B. M., O'Leary, D. H., Tracy, R. P., & Bush, T. L., for the CHS Collaborative Research Group. (1993). Association of postmenopausal estrogen use with cardiovascular disease and its risk factors in older women. *Circulation, 88*(1), 2163–2171.

Manson, J. E., Colditz, G. A., Stampfer, M. J., Willett, W. C., Krolewski, A. S., Rosner, B., Arky, R. A., Speizer, F. E., & Hennekens, C. H. (1991). A prospective study of maturity-onset diabetes mellitus and risk of coronary heart disease and stroke in women. *Archives of Internal Medicine, 151*, 1141–1147.

Manson, J. E., Colditz, G. A., Stampfer, M. J., Willett, W. C., Rosner, B., Monson, R. R., Speizer, F. E., & Hennekens, C. H. (1990). A prospective study of obesity and risk of coronary heart disease in women. *New England Journal of Medicine, 322*, 882–889.

Manson, J. E., Rimm, E. B., Stampfer, M. J., Colditz, G. A., Willett, W. C., Krolewski, A. S., Rosner, B., Hennekens, C. H., & Speizer, F. E. (1991). Physical activity and incidence of non-insulin-dependent diabetes mellitus in women. *Lancet, 338*, 774–778.

Maynard, C., Althouse, R., Cerqueira, M., Olsufka, M., & Kennedy, J. W. (1991). Underutilization of thrombolytic therapy in eligible women with acute myocardial infarction. *American Journal of Cardiology, 68*, 529–530.

Maynard, C., Litwin, P. E., Martin, J. S., & Weaver, W. D. (1992). Gender differences in the treatment and outcome of acute myocardial infarction: Results from the Myocardial Infarction Triage and Intervention Registry. *Archives of Internal Medicine, 152*, 972–976.

National Center for Health Statistics. (1991). *Health: United States, 1990.* Hyattsville, MD: U.S. Public Health Service, Centers for Disease Control.

Oldridge, N. B., LaSalle, D., & Jones, N. L. (1980). Exercise rehabilitation of female patients with coronary heart disease. *American Heart Journal, 100*, 755–757.

Scandinavian Simvastatin Survival Study Group. (1994). Randomised trial of cholesterol lowering in 4444 patients with coronary heart disease: The Scandinavian Simvastatin Survival Study (4S). *Lancet, 344*, 1383–1389.

Shaw, L. J., Miller, D. D., Romeis, J. C., Kargl, D., Younis, L. T., & Chaitman, B. R. (1994). Gender differences in the noninvasive evaluation and management of patients with suspected coronary artery disease. *Annals of Internal Medicine, 120*, 559–566.

SHEP Cooperative Research Group. (1991). Prevention of stroke by antihypertensive drug treatment in older persons with isolated systolic hypertension. Final results of the Systolic Hypertension in the Elderly Program (SHEP). *Journal of the American Medical Association, 265*, 3255–3264.

Stampfer, M. J., & Colditz, G. A. (1991). Estrogen replacement therapy and coronary heart disease: A quantitative assessment of the epidemiological evidence. *Preventive Medicine, 20*, 47–63.

Steingart, R. M., Packer, M., Hamm, P., Coglianese, M. E., Gersh, B., Geltman, E. M., Sollano, J., Katz, S., Moye, L., Basta, L. L., Lewis, S. J., Gottlieb, S. S., Bernstein, V., McEwan, P., Jacobson, K., Brown, E. J., Kukin, M. L., Kantrowitz, N. E., & Pfeffer, M. A., for the Survival and Ventricular Enlargement Investigators. (1991). Sex differences in the management of coronary artery disease. *New England Journal of Medicine, 325*, 226–230.

The Principal Investigators of CASS and Their Associates. (1981). The National Heart, Lung, and Blood Institute Coronary Artery Surgery Study (CASS). *Circulation, 63*(suppl 1), 1–81.

The Writing Group for the PEPI Trial. (1995). Effects of estrogen or estrogen/progestin regimens on heart disease risk factors in postmenopausal women. The Postmenopausal Estrogen/Progestin Interventions (PEPI) Trial. *Journal of the American Medical Association, 273*, 199–208.

Tobin, J. N., Wassertheil-Smoller, S., Wexler, J. P., Steingart, R. M., Budner, N., Lense, L., & Wachspress, J. (1987). Sex bias in considering coronary bypass surgery. *Annals of Internal Medicine, 107*, 19–25.

Weintraub, W. S., Wenger, N. K., Kosinski, A. S., Douglas, J. S., Jr., Liberman H. A., Morris, D. C., & King, S. B., III. (1994). Percutaneous transluminal coronary angioplasty in women compared with men. *Journal of the American College of Cardiology, 24,* 81–90.

Wenger, N. K. (1994). The understudied majority: Women and the elderly. In *From theory to practice: Intervention can be critical,* based on a roundtable program, Oslo, Norway, June 1993. Third International Conference on Preventive Cardiology (pp. 15–19). Whitehouse Station, NJ: Merck & Company.

Wenger, N. K., Speroff, L., & Packard, B. (1993a). Cardiovascular health and disease in women. *New England Journal of Medicine, 329,* 247–256.

Wenger, N. K., Speroff, L., & Packard, B. (Eds.). (1993b). *Cardiovascular health and disease in women.* In Proceedings of the National Heart, Lung, & Blood Institute Conference. Greenwich, CT: LeJacq Communications.

Willett, W. C., Green, A., Stampfer, M. J., Speizer, F. E., Colditz, G. A., Rosner, B., Monson, R. R., Stason, W., & Hennekens, C. H. (1987). Relative and absolute excess risks of coronary heart disease among women who smoke cigarettes. *New England Journal of Medicine, 317,* 1303–1309.

CLINICAL FINDINGS AND RISK FACTORS FOR CORONARY HEART DISEASE

2

Less Prominent Electrocardiographic Changes During Myocardial Ischemia in Women May Explain Differences in Treatment as Compared to Men

Mikael Dellborg
Östra University Hospital, Göteborg, Sweden

Although recent advances in the pharmacological treatment of myocardial infarction (MI) with agents such as intravenous beta-blockade, aspirin, and thrombolytic drugs have dramatically improved the short- and long-term prognosis in patients with acute MI (Dellborg, Eriksson, Riha, & Swedberg, 1994), women still have a significantly higher in-hospital mortality as compared to men (Wilkinson, Kooridhottumkal, Kulasegaram, Parsons, & Timmis, 1994). There are several explanations for the higher in-hospital mortality in women: higher age at the time of infarction, an increased prevalence of diabetes, longer delay before seeking medical attention, less distinctive symptoms of myocardial ischemia, and less coronary angiography and revascularization (Ayanian & Epstein, 1991). An additional explanation may be less aggressive pharmacological treatment in women, as recently shown by our group (Dellborg & Swedberg, 1993) as well as confirmed by others (Clarke, Gray, Keating, & Hampton, 1994). Several of the agents used for treating MI have potential severe side effects such as intracerebral bleeding after thrombolysis, and these treatments are therefore generally only given to patients who exhibit distinct signs on the electrocardiogram of an acute ongoing MI. Patients with at least 1–2 mm of ST-segment elevation are generally considered for thrombolytic treatment, whereas patients with similar symptoms but less electrocardiographic changes in most hospitals do not receive such treatment. The number of patients with acute chest pain presenting to any emergency department widely exceeds the capacity of the coronary-care unit. Thus, the electrocardiogram is also used for selecting patients with a moderate or high probability of infarction, whereas patients without electrocardiographic signs of ischemia will either be admitted to observation units or sent home.

Our group has a substantial experience in multilead computerized ECG monitoring and therefore investigated whether differences between men and women in electrocardiographic changes during myocardial ischemia could explain some of the differences found in pharmacological treatment and thus subsequently in prognosis. These results have recently been published (Dellborg, Herlitz, Emanuelsson, & Swedberg, 1994) and are reviewed and discussed here.

PATIENTS AND METHODS

Patients

We studied two patient groups. The first was a substudy of 178 patients (135 men and 43 women) of a total of 352 patients included in a randomized double-blind study of alteplase (rt-PA) or placebo. All patients included had chest pain strongly suggestive of acute MI. However, this study had one relatively unique feature: The protocol specifically stated that an electrocardiogram should *not* be obtained prior to randomization. Randomization was only possible during the very first hours of a suspected infarction, the time limit was set to less than 2 hr and 45 min of chest pain before randomization. After treatment with alteplase or placebo was begun patients were admitted to the coronary care unit. They were monitored with continuous computerized multilead electrocardiography (dynamic vectorcardiography).

The second group consisted of 81 patients with stable angina undergoing elective angioplasty and monitored with continuous multilead electrocardiography using the same method as the first patient group, described in more detail later. These patients were selected from a larger group of 114 patients and represent a subset that did develop chest pain when the angioplasty balloon was inflated, briefly occluding the coronary artery. There were 59 men and 22 women with a mean age of 56 for men and 61 for women. There were no significant differences between men and women regarding the vessel dilated, the number of inflations performed, or the presence of collaterals. The total inflation time, however, was significantly longer in men, 278 versus 180 seconds ($p < 0.05$).

Methods

Because myocardial ischemia is a highly variable phenomenon during the first hours of an acute MI (Hackett et al., 1987), obtaining a standard ECG every 1 or 2 hr is not sufficient if detailed studies of ischemic changes are to be done. We have participated in the development of continuous vector-cardiography and used it clinically since 1986. In brief, the system used (MIDA system, Ortivus Medical AB, Täby, Sweden) uses 8 electrodes placed according to Frank (1956) in a circle around the chest in the level of the fifth intercostal, including one in the back, one in the neck, and one in the left hip. With these electrodes a three-lead system is continuously monitoring the heart. These three leads are orthogonal and have the same weight, that is, 1 mm of ST-change in one lead is equivalent to 1 mm in any of the other leads. This continuous ECG is fed into a computer that will perform signal averaging to reduce noise and to omit beats with a different morphology, that is, ectopic beats. The computer will in real time calculate several parameters. The present results deal mainly with the ST-vector magnitude (ST-VM), which can be described as the summarized ST-changes in all three leads. The ST-VM is presented in real time on a computer screen as a trend graph with time on the x-axis. In Fig. 2.1 a schematic trend curve from a patient with an acute myocardial infarction is shown. The points of specific interest are marked and these are (a) the initial ST-vector magnitude, (b) the maximum ST-vector magnitude, and (c) the minimum ST-vector magnitude. A trend curve such as this can be translated into a patient coming in with a moderate degree of ST-elevation that after a sudden increase will rapidly decrease over the next couple of hours. In Fig. 2.2 a schematic trend curve is shown from a patient undergoing a coronary angioplasty. As the balloon is inflated, the summarized ST-changes (the ST-VM) increases rapidly and reaches a peak within 30–60 sec after inflating the balloon. As the balloon is deflated and flow is restored the ST-changes quickly go back down. A

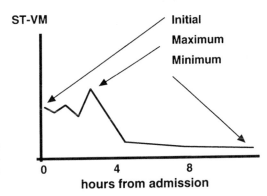

FIG. 2.1. Schematic trend curve from a patient with acute myocardial infarction. ST-VM: ST vector magnitude.

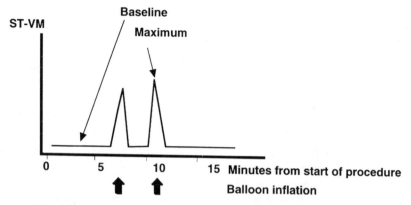

FIG. 2.2. Trend curve from a patient during PTCA. ST-VM: ST vector magnitude. PTCA: percutaneous transluminal coronary angioplasty.

patient with a spontaneous episode of severe rest angina will, of course, look very similar although the time frame may be somewhat different.

RESULTS

In patients with suspected acute MI, men had significantly higher initial ST-VM, higher maximum ST-VM, and also higher minimum ST-VM as compared to women (see Fig. 2.3). The results on all three points were statistically significant. When we restricted the analysis to patients with a confirmed MI, the differences remained but, due to the reduced number of patients, they were borderline statistically significant. In patients monitored during

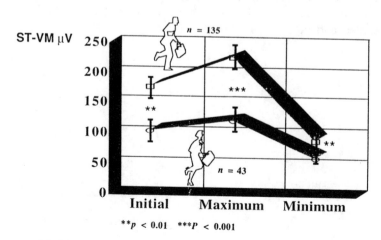

FIG. 2.3. Results—patients with suspected acute myocardial infarction.

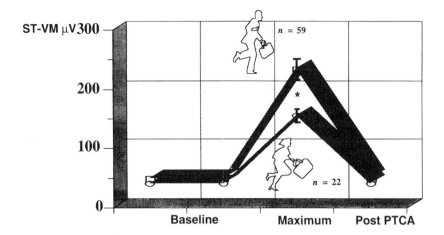

FIG. 2.4. Results–patients during PTCA. ST-VM: ST vector magnitude. μV: microVolts.

angioplasty there were no differences in the baseline or postangioplasty ST-VM between men and women, but men had significantly higher ST-VM during balloon inflation (see Fig. 2.4).

DISCUSSION

Our data indicate that women with myocardial ischemia, either during the early hours of an acute MI or provoked by an angioplasty balloon, have less prominent electrocardiographic changes as compared to men. There are virtually no other studies that have examined this issue. There are several reports on the magnitude of ST-changes on the standard ECG in men and women receiving thrombolytic treatment. However, these reports are difficult to interpret because most studies have required a minimum amount of ST-change for inclusion in the study or have inadvertently, by obtaining a prerandomization ECG, been biased against patients with less prominent ECG changes. Thus, our results are from a small patient population but are unique in that our patients were selected only on the basis of clinical suspicion of an acute MI.

Several reports have described the electrocardiographic changes during balloon angioplasty, but many have not included women or have not reported the results separately for each gender. Although the difference in electrocardiographic ST-changes is significant between men and women during angioplasty, it may not be easily translated into clinically meaningful differences for physicians not familiar with continuous vectorcardiography. The standard limit for initiating thrombolytic therapy of 1–2 mm ST-elevation in at least two leads will approximately translate into 150 μV of ST-VM. Thus, the results in Fig. 2.2 may also be expressed as follows: When a balloon is used to occlude a coronary artery briefly, 36% of all women will develop ST-changes that, if they persisted, would make them eligible for thrombolytic treatment. In contrast, 61% of the men will develop such changes. If a fixed limit of ST-change is used for selecting patients for thrombolytic treatment, this will favor treatment of men. It therefore seems justified to suggest a somewhat lower requirement for ST-change in women for administrating thrombolytic drugs. Our data indicate that 1.5 mm of ST-elevation in at least two anterior leads in women will correspond to 2 mm of ST-elevation in at least two leads in men. Accordingly, if 1 mm of ST-elevation in at least two is used for men, then 0.7 mm should be used for women.

CONCLUSION

Women with acute MI have higher mortality during the hospital stay than men. One reason may be underuse of infarct-size-limiting pharmacologic therapy in women, which may be explained by less prominent electrocardiographic signs of ischemia in women. It is suggested that a gender-adjusted limit is used for administrating thrombolytic drugs to patients with acute MI.

REFERENCES

Ayanian, J., & Epstein, A. (1991). Differences in the use of procedures between women and men hospitalized for coronary heart disease. *New England Journal of Medicine, 325*, 221–225.

Clarke, K., Gray, D., Keating, N., & Hampton, J. (1994). Do women with acute myocardial infarction receive the same treatment as men? *British Medical Journal, 309*, 563–566.

Dellborg, M., & Swedberg, K. (1993). Acute myocardial infarction: Difference in the treatment between men and women. *Quality Assurance in Health Care, 5*, 261–265.

Dellborg, M., Eriksson, P., Riha, M., & Swedberg, K. (1994). Declining hospital mortality in acute myocardial infarction. *European Heart Journal, 15*, 5–9.

Dellborg, M., Herlitz, J., Emanuelsson, H., & Swedberg, K. (1994). Electrocardiographic changes during myocardial ischemia: Differences between men and women. *Journal of Electrocardiology, 27*(suppl), 42–45.

Frank, E. (1956). An accurate, clinically practical system for spatial vectorcardiography. *Circulation, 13*, 737–744.

Hackett, D., Davies, G., Chierchia, S., & Maseri, A. (1987). Intermittent coronary occlusion in acute myocardial infarction. *New England Journal of Medicine, 317*, 1055–1059.

Wilkinson, P., Kooridhottumkal, L., Kulasegaram, R., Parsons, L., & Timmis, A. (1994). Acute myocardial infarction in women: Survival analysis in first six months. *British Medical Journal, 309*, 566–569.

3

Psychosocial Risk Factor Profile in Women With Coronary Heart Disease

Kristina Orth-Gomér
Karolinska Institute, Stockholm, Sweden

As most research on risk factors and prediction of cardiovascular disease (CVD) has been carried out in men, especially in men below age 65, our knowledge about the female risk factor profile is unsatisfactory (Eaker, Chesebro, Sacks, Wenger, & Whisnant, 1993; Higgins, 1990; Wenger, Chapter 1, this volume; Wenger, Speroff, & Packard, 1993). Our knowledge about traditional risk factors in women mainly stems from studies like the Framingham Study, the Gothenburg Study, the MONICA study and other population-based longitudinal studies (Eaker, Pinsky, & Castelli, 1992; Johansson, 1983; Tunstall-Pedoe et al., 1994).

In these studies, smoking, hypertension, and dyslipidemia account for part of the cardiovascular risk in women, as it does in men. For example, the Framingham risk equation for women includes age, SBP, cholesterol, HDL, glucose intolerance, smoking, and ECG evidence of myocardial hypertrophy. Framingham women, who were 60–64 years old and who were in the upper 10% of the risk factor distribution, had a 12% probability of acquiring coronary heart disease (CHD) during a 6-year follow-up as compared to a 20% risk for men (Andersson, Wilson, Odell, & Kannel, 1991). It is evident that there is a lack of specificity in the prediction of CHD risk for men, but even more so for women. It is also clear that these risk factors explain but a proportion of the risk, and that other less established risk factors must contribute as well. Other factors include social, psychological, and behavioral factors, the role of which has been extensively investigated in men, but not in women (LaCroix, 1994). In men such factors as psychosocial work strain, lack of social support, and hostile behaviors have been shown to contribute to CHD risk. In women these aspects have been rarely studied and the relevance of the concepts from male studies has not been confirmed. The relative importance of psychosocial as compared to traditional factors in women is the main issue to be addressed in this chapter.

PSYCHOSOCIAL WORK STRAIN AND CVD
IN WOMEN

In men, stressors in work and social life have been widely investigated as important contributors to psychosocial risk (Karasek & Theorell, 1990; Orth-Gomér & Schneiderman, 1996). Karasek and coworkers originally defined job strain according to a model combining psychological demands with decision latitude at work. According to his hypotheses, the worst possible combination for adverse health effects was high job demand with low job decision latitude, whereas the best combination was low demand with high decision latitude. The other two combinations were intermediate in terms of hypothesized risk. A large number of cross-sectional, case-control, and cohort studies have examined the validity of this hypothesis on CHD outcome variables. A majority of these studies have shown definite effects of job strain on both all cause mortality—mortality from CHD as well as incidence of myocardial infarction (MI). Schnall and Landsbergis (1994) summarized the consistency of results across populations: "Where comparisons could be made, effects of similar magnitude have been found in male and in female working populations" (p. 381). They also found consistency across outcome variables.

As a conclusion of this review, the cardiovascular effects of psychosocial work strain in women seems to equal that in men. It has to be pointed out, however, that the studies which were under review have not evaluated the effects of work strain in relation to other domains in life. This seems to be particularly important in women, as women's lives and social roles in modern society are characterized by multiple functions and multiple roles, which go far beyond employment and gainful occupational activities.

It is interesting to note therefore, that when evaluating the relative importance of overtime work at the workplace, the outcome and conclusions differed substantially between genders.

In a population-based survey of 100,000 working Swedish men and women, Alfredsson, Spetz, and Theorell (1985) compared the effects of psychosocial work strain and overtime work on the risk of MI in men and women. MI risks of work-related strain factors were increased in both genders, except for one factor, overtime work. In men working overtime was beneficial, that is, associated with a decreased cardiovascular risk as compared to the general population risk. In women, long work hours—that is, overtime of 10 hr or more per week—increased the cardiovascular risk by 30% in comparison to the general population risk. There are several possible interpretations of this finding. However, the one that seems most plausible in view of other research on work load and gender differences is that in women, overtime work will impinge on other functions and other duties, namely the ones outside those of gainful employment, and that it is the addition of workload, regardless of its nature, which constitutes the main risk.

In the recent study of Female Coronary Risk Factors in Stockholm (Fem-CorRisk), several psychosocial risk factors for CHD were investigated, including questions about work strain. The job strain assessments were combined into the demand-control model proposed by Karasek and Theorell (1990). In this model, those reporting jobs with high demand and low control are considered to experience the highest strain, with those reporting low demand and high control experiencing the lowest strain. The odds ratio of CHD in the Female Coronary Risk Factors Study for the highest versus the lowest quartile of job strain was highly significant. After adjustment for multivariate traditional risk factors, the odds ratio still remained significant (OR = 2.49, 95% c.l. 1.18; 5.27, $p = 0.02$).

SOCIAL SUPPORT AND CVD IN WOMEN

In men it has been shown that several aspects of socially supportive functions protect against premature mortality and also, more specifically, against CHD incidence and mortality (Berkman & Orth-Gomér, 1996). Furthermore, studies from the United States and from Scandinavia point to the risk associated with social isolation in men. Social isolation is mostly defined as lack of or relatively few social contacts among both family, friends, coworkers and neighbors. Using quantitative measures, these studies have invariably shown that men who have a small number of contacts are prone to die earlier than men with an extended network. Some of these studies have also used CHD mortality as an end point, and have found equally strong predictions as for all cause mortality (House, Landis, & Umberson, 1988).

In a survey of a representative sample obtained from the adult Swedish population, 17,400 men and women were interviewed about quantitative aspects of their social networks and then followed for a 6-year period. In both men and women there was an excess cardiovascular mortality risk in those with few contacts. In the lower third of the social network index distribution, the odds ratio for CVD mortality was 1.5 (95% c.l. 1.3; 1.7) signifying an excess CVD mortality of 50%. This risk was obtained after controlling for age, smoking, lack of exercise, low education, unemployment, and presence of hypertension or cardiovascular disease at entry into the study. Thus it seems that both men and women benefit from having a certain crucial number of social contacts (Orth-Gomér & Johnsson, 1987). However, there was no health advantage or increased survival in those who had *many* social contacts. In contrast, they had a slightly higher mortality than people with a medium-sized network. This was particularly true for older women, in whom those with a great number of contacts had the highest mortality.

In our attempt to understand these relationships, we asked whether the function of the contacts could be more important than just the number of available persons in the network and the frequency of interaction with network members. We wanted to know whether these contacts were really supportive, or whether they were perhaps more demanding and stressful.

The different and separate functional dimensions, which are assessed by many instruments of social support, such as the Interpersonal Support Evaluation List (ISEL) and the Interview Schedule for Social Interaction (ISSI; Cohen & Syme, 1985; Henderson, Duncan-Jones, & Byrne, 1980), include:

1. Emotional support or attachment, usually provided by close friends or family members.
2. Tangible support, meaning practical help.
3. Appraisal support, meaning good advice, and help to properly recognize and cope with problems and difficulties.
4. Belongingness, meaning the need to belong to groups of people with whom one shares interests and values.

The latter three functions are usually provided by the extended social network, whereas emotional support is typically found within family and close friends. The strongest effects on CHD are often seen when there is lack of social integration, that is, the functions provided by the extended network which give guidance, advice, practical help, and belongingness.

The second important aspect of social support, the very close emotional relationships that provide comfort, trust, and love, and enhance self-esteem, are usually less predictive of MI. However, in a study of 50-year-old men from Gothenburg, Sweden, a smaller group of men (23%) really lacked this kind of support. They also had an increase in MI risk, both with lack of attachment and lack of social integration (Orth-Gomér, Rosengren, & Wilhelmsen, 1993) (Figs. 3.1 and 3.2).

SOCIAL SUPPORT IN RELATION TO SOCIAL STRAIN IN WOMEN

In large-scale, population-based studies of social support in both men and women, results for men are often clear-cut and obvious, whereas for women they are confusing rather than conclusive (House et al., 1988; Shumaker & Hill, 1991).

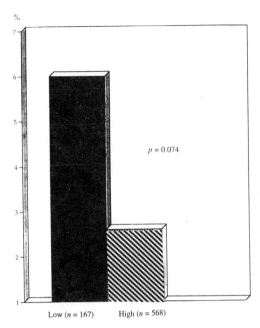

FIG. 3.1. Six-year incidence of myocardial infarction in men with low vs. high "attachment" (749 men, 50 years of age).

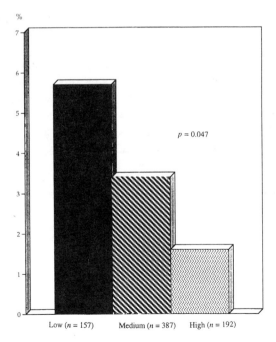

FIG. 3.2. Six-year incidence of myocardial infarction by "social integration" (749 men, 50 years of age).

29

In the aforementioned Survey of Living Conditions of the Swedish population, women were as much in need as men of a basic number of contacts for
their survival (Orth-Gomér & Johnsson, 1987). The same was found in a study
in Alameda County, CA, where women who lacked social ties had an excess
mortality risk that was even slightly higher than that of men (Berkman & Syme,
1979). Both of these studies obtained the majority of their participants from
urbanized, highly developed societies and civilizations. In contrast, women of
the North Karelia study, from Eastern rural Finland, and women from Evans
County, GA, did not seem to be endangered if they had smaller networks and
fewer contacts. Both of these populations are characterized by stable living
conditions and well-defined female roles and positions in their respective
societies (Kaplan et al., 1988; Schoenbach, Kaplan, Fredman, & Kleinbaum,
1986). Possibly, women who lead a more unstable life and who are subjected
to more changes and contradictory demands from multiple roles are in
greater need of their social networks. However, it would also seem that the
functions which network members fill are more important than the number
of contacts. Therefore, in the FemCorRisk study the effort was made to try to
disentangle the role of strain and the role of support from women's social
networks and their significance for cardiovascular health.

From the Framingham and other studies it is known that low socioeconomic status and relative social deprivation are risk factors in women as
well as in men, as seen in the women of the Framingham study, who had
so few of their own resources that in a 6-year period they could not take a
vacation, and thus had an eightfold increased risk of MI (Eaker et al., 1992).

It has also been observed, in Framingham as in Sweden (Vågerö & Lahelma, Chapter 6, this volume), that employed women seem to be in better
health than homemakers. In employed Framingham women, MI risk was
increased only when economic difficulties were present (Eaker et al., 1992).
Homemakers had more psychological risk factors and a higher overall risk.
This finding may be explained both by a social gradient and by a healthy
worker effect. Women who were able to work outside the home in the
Framingham society may have been socially and economically better
equipped from the beginning. Many women also benefited from increased
economic resources as a consequence of their employment.

In recent years, practically all Swedish women have become employed
outside the home. There is even formal legislation requiring every citizen,
male or female, to work and to provide an income for him- or herself.
Consequently, investigating whether the multiple roles and double burden of
employment and homemaking could be detrimental to women's cardiovascular health is a priority for Swedish women.

As documented by Frankenhaeuser, Lundberg, and Chesney (1991), employment outside the home means an additional workload for Swedish
women. In their studies of male and female employees in large companies,
they estimated the total number of hours per week spent on paid work and

on work at home for the service of the family. Full-time employed men and women without children both worked a total average of 60 hours per week; women with children increased their total workload to 90 hours per week—if they had three children. Men in the same situation increased their total work load to 70 hours per week.

THE STOCKHOLM FEMALE CORONARY RISK STUDY

All female residents of the greater Stockholm area who were hospitalized for an acute CHD event between February 1991 and February 1994 were asked to participate in the study. Control subjects were randomly obtained from the census register of greater Stockholm, using a population-based case-control design.

When women characterized their social supports using the aforementioned Interview Schedule for Social Interaction (ISSI), the effects were generally weaker than they have been found to be in men. Only the scale describing social integration, which was also the best predictor for men, showed a significant, but small difference between cases and controls (OR = 1.7; 95% c.l. 1.2; 2.4 for women—OR = 3.8 95% c.l. 1.1; 13.9 for men, see Fig. 3.3).

The scale describing lack of attachment, which predicted CHD in Gothenburg men, showed absolutely no difference between women with or without heart disease (see Fig. 3.4). Furthermore, when the results in women were adjusted for standard risk factors, the net effect of lack of social integration was no longer significant (OR = 1.46; 95% c.l. 0.98; 2.19).

To further scrutinize the role of social integration in women, its different subcomponents were studied, using the Interpersonal Support Evaluation List (ISEL). Subscales for appraisal support, tangible support, and belongingness were analyzed (Cohen & Syme, 1985). The scales for appraisal support ($p = 0.004$) and for tangible support ($p = 0.03$) were significantly associated with CHD in univariate analyses; the scale describing belongingness was not. Multivariate adjustment for standard risk factors for CHD modified the effects, with the strongest remaining effect found for appraisal support. Thus the only supportive function that was clearly protective against CHD in women was appraisal support. This is often provided by coworkers and friends. It offers help, guidance, and good advice on a cognitive level and is a strong prerequisite for successful coping with adverse life events.

COMPREHENSIVE MEASURE OF SOCIAL STRAIN

Because of the contradictory patterns that became apparent when examining the social network in women, we decided to design an interview procedure that would explore not just the concept of support, but also the concept of strain from the social sphere. The general goal of the interview was to

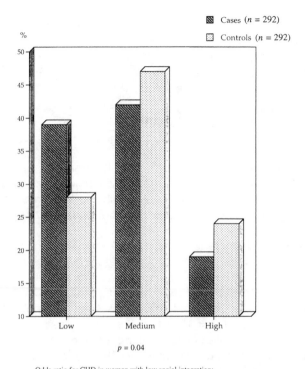

Odds ratio for CHD in women with low social integration:
1.65 (95% C.L; 1.16, 2.35).

FIG. 3.3. Social integration and CHD in women.

describe all possible sources of strain in sick and healthy women. The concept and methodology of family strain were similar to those used by Karasek et al, for work strain, that is, both demand and control dimensions were considered (Karasek & Theorell, 1990).

The interview was structured to describe both the work and family life career of women, specifically addressing employment, marriages, divorces and separations, childbirths, and the rearing of children as well as caring responsibilities for elderly and other relatives. The general methodology of the interview procedure and overall results are described elsewhere (Moser et al., 1996). Here it is sufficient to point out that, in order to minimize recall bias, interview questions were aimed at concrete and "objective" issues that could not be submitted to too much change and reinterpretation in the light of disease and ill health.

In Fig. 3.5, the sources of strain have been quantified and compared between women with CHD and healthy women. Most pronounced are the excess strain scores for women with CHD as concerns strain from the present job and strain from having too little time for relaxation, leisure, and personal growth and development. This is in accordance with the results from the

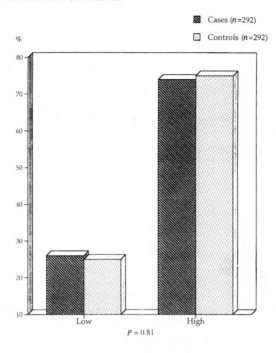

Odds ratio for CHD in women with low attachment:
1.06 (95% C.L; 0.72, 1.55).

FIG. 3.4. Attachment and CHD in women.

standardized measures of work demand and decision latitude at work. Above all, the latter factor differed between women with CHD and healthy women. Thus in women with CHD there was lack of opportunity for growth and development *both at work and in leisure time*. This finding is congruent with the 20-year follow-up of the Framingham Study, in which women who were deprived of financial and recreational resources had a substantially increased MI risk (Eaker et al., 1992).

FAMILY STRAIN AND CHD

Women with CHD both had more children (2.0 vs. 1.8 on average, $p = 0.10$) and had experienced more separations (0.6 vs. 0.4 on average, $p < 0.001$) than healthy controls. Women with CHD also reported more strain from problems with children, but above all more problems associated with spousal relationships. In particular, the separations caused these women to report stress and strain (see Fig. 3.5). As these assessments were made in women who were already diseased, it is of course possible that their perception of family strain was compromised by the knowledge of their heart

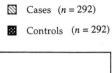

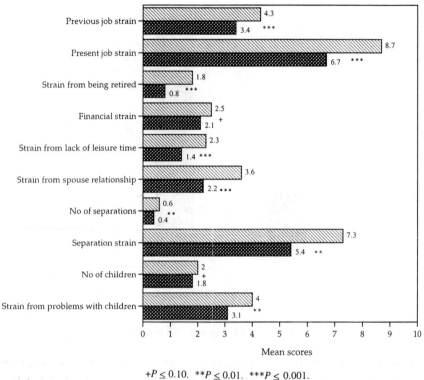

$+P \le 0.10.$ $**P \le 0.01.$ $***P \le 0.001.$

FIG. 3.5. Psychosocial strain and CHD in women.

disease. It is unlikely however, that the sick women would consciously blame their heart disease on family problems. When asked this question directly, most of them blamed it on family history of heart disease and on their own unhealthy lifestyle, such as smoking and lack of exercise. It is also unlikely that the heart disease could have caused the family problems. Most of the women had their first clinical signs within a few years before examination. Their mean age at interview was 56 years, which meant most of them had already left reproductive age, and childrearing was behind them.

PERSONALITY AND INDIVIDUAL CHARACTERISTICS IN RELATION TO CVD

In this review of psychosocial factors in women, the emphasis on stress and strain originating from the social environment has been strong. This is congruent with the findings in the more recent literature, which in particular for women, underscore the importance of the "coronary-prone situations" rather than "coronary-prone personalities" (Weidner, in press).

The Coronary Prone Behavior Pattern, referred to as Type A Behavior, has been frequently examined in men. The typical characteristics include aggressive and hostile behavior, time urgency, competitiveness, and strong work involvement. Empirical findings of Type A in relation to CHD in men are mixed, with studies supporting the hypothesis of Type A as a risk factor for future MI, like the Western Collaborative Group Study (WCGS; Brand, Rosenman, Sholtz, & Friedman, 1976), and studies that refute Type A as a primary risk factor for CHD. An example of the latter is the Multiple Risk Factor Intervention Trial (MRFIT), which examined men who were at high risk for future CHD as assessed by their lipid, blood pressure, and smoking status. Type A Behavior was unrelated to incidence of CHD in these men (Shekelle et al., 1985).

In women the picture is less controversial. None of the prospective population-based studies has found Type A to predict CHD in women. In the Framingham Study, both the 10- and 20-year follow-up evaluations of Type A Behavior failed to predict hard CHD endpoints.

In contrast, the Framingham Type A scale was predictive of self-reported angina pectoris (AP) both at 10- and 20-year follow-up. In women, however, the self-reported diagnosis of anginal pain is not specific for CHD, because many other diagnostic categories (GI-disorders, musculoskeletal disease, etc.) may explain the chest pain. As often pointed out by clinical cardiologists, the diagnosis of AP in women is particularly difficult and questionable.

In the Stockholm Female Coronary Risk Study the Framingham Type A scale did not discriminate between CHD patients and healthy women. Among patients with AP only, the prevalence of Type A Behavior was higher than among women who had suffered an MI (54% vs. 41%, $p < 0.05$).

The second major prospective population-based study of female CHD examined a group of middle-aged women born in Gothenburg, Sweden. Type A measures were derived from the Eysenck Personality Inventory and described achievement, aggression, and dominance. In the 12-year follow-up examination, none of these measures was predictive of any CHD outcome. In contrast, several other psychological characteristics were predictors of CHD. The most consistent results were found for "subjective feelings of stress and strain" and for depressive symptoms (Hällström, Lapidus, Bengtsson, & Edström, 1986). In this context it is interesting to note that in the FemCorRisk Study Stockholm women with heart disease had significantly more depressive symptoms than healthy women. Women with CHD had an average of four symptoms, as compared to a mean of two symptoms in healthy women ($p < 0.001$). Although some of this difference is most likely caused by the disease itself, other factors, such as lack of social support and social strain, were also associated with depressive symptoms. When adjusting for standard risk factors, the OR in the high versus low quartile of depression was 4.0 (95% c.l. 2.2; 7.2), suggesting a fourfold increase in risk of CHD with depression. Because of the retrospective assessments, great caution is needed in the interpretation of these results. The increased rate of depressive symptoms in women with CHD could have been due to their knowledge of having a potentially life threatening, chronic illness.

However, two recent studies, which have included both men and women, indicate that depressive symptoms may be an important prognostic marker for CHD. In the Glostrup Study from Denmark, depression was a predictor of all cause and cardiovascular mortality in a population sample of elderly men and women, who were followed for 12 years (Barefoot & Schroll, 1996).

In a Canadian study of post-MI patients, the mortality risk 1½ years after the event increased sevenfold in depressed patients (Frasure-Smith, Lespérance, & Talajic, 1995). Both of these studies were careful in controlling for prognostic risk factors of cardiological origin, which might explain the depression–mortality association. These factors included symptoms of congestive heart failure, left ventricular ejection fraction, presence of anginal pain, size of the myocardial infarction, and so forth. Taken together, these studies suggest that in women, depressive symptoms are far more important as risk factors and as prognostic factors than, for example, the Type A Behavior Pattern.

SUMMARY AND CONCLUSIONS

In this chapter the role of the psychosocial work environment, the role of social support, and the role of strain in the social sphere have been discussed in relation to female CVD. It has been emphasized that employment in general seems to be beneficial for women's health. However, when the job is characterized by high strain and low support from coworkers, it means an additional cardiovascular health risk.

Likewise, good social and emotional support from the family and from extended social networks are necessary and beneficial for women's health. However, these effects are often contaminated by the sources of strain inherent in women's social networks. Often, networks are more demanding than supportive; this is a trend which seems to differ from that in men, where both quantitative and qualitative measures of social support have shown beneficial effects on health.

Furthermore, coronary-prone behavior patterns are less evident in women than in men. The Type A Behavior pattern does not predict CHD in women. Instead, depression and depressive symptoms seem to play an important role, both as indicators of a poor prognosis and even as possible primary risk factors for CHD in women.

Future investigations need to examine the interactive role of work strain, family strain, and depressive feelings. Furthermore, their role in affecting health behaviors and health attitudes need to be further examined. Finally, biological mechanisms are crucial in our understanding of how these factors contribute to the increased CHD risk.

As our knowledge about psychosocial risk factors in women is growing, and the general picture becomes increasingly clear, there is an imperative demand to use this knowledge in preventive efforts. The introductory review in the first chapter of this volume has made it clear that women's prognosis after an acute MI, after cardiovascular surgery, and after PTCA is poorer and that preventive efforts are less intensive and less successful in women than in men. These facts call for action. They provide a strong imperative to implicate and integrate the knowledge about psychosocial risk factors in clinical practice and clinical care of women with heart disease.

REFERENCES

Alfredsson, L., Spetz, C.-L., & Theorell, T. (1985). Type of occupation and near-future hospitalization for myocardial infarction and some other diagnoses. *International Journal of Epidemiology, 4*, 378–388.

Andersson, K. M., Wilson, P. W. F., Odell, P. M., & Kannel, W. B. (1991). An updated coronary risk profile. A statement for health professionals. *Circulation, 83*(1), 356–362.

Barefoot, J. C., & Schroll, M. (1996). Symptoms of depression, acute myocardial infarction and total mortality in a community sample. *Circulation, 93*(11), 1976–1980.

Berkman, L. F., & Orth-Gomér, K. (1996). Prevention of cardiovascular morbidity and mortality: Role of social relations. In K. Orth-Gomér & N. Schneiderman (Eds.), *Behavioral medicine approaches to cardiovascular disease prevention* (pp. 51–67). Hillsdale, NJ: Lawrence Erlbaum Associates.

Berkman, L. F., & Syme, S. L. (1979). Social networks, host resistance, and mortality: A nine-year follow-up study of Alameda County residents. *American Journal of Epidemiology, 109*(2), 186–204.

Brand, R. J., Rosenman, R. H., Sholtz, R. I., & Friedman, M. (1976). Multivariate prediction of coronary heart disease in the Western Collaborative Group Study compared to the findings of the Framingham Study. *Circulation, 53*, 348–355.

Cohen, S., & Syme, S. L. (Eds.). (1985). *Social support and health.* New York: Academic Press.

Eaker, E. D., Chesebro, J. H., Sacks, F. M., Wenger, N. K., & Whisnant, J. P. (1993). Cardiovascular disease in women. *Circulation, 88*(4), 1999–2009.

Eaker, E. D., Pinsky, J., & Castelli, W. P. (1992). Myocardial infarction and coronary death among women: Psychosocial predictors from a 20-year follow-up of women in the Framingham Study. *American Journal of Epidemiology, 135*(8), 854–864.

Frankenhaeuser, M., Lundberg, U., & Chesney, M. (Eds.). (1991). *Women, work and health: Stress and opportunities.* New York: Plenum.

Frasure-Smith, N., Lespérance, F., & Talajic, M. (1995). Depression and 18-month prognosis after myocardial infarction. *Circulation, 91*(4), 999–1005.

Hällström, T., Lapidus, L., Bengtsson, C., & Edström, K. (1986). Psychosocial factors and risk of ischemic heart disease and death in women: A twelve-year follow-up of participants in the population study of women in Gothenburg, Sweden. *Journal of Psychosomatic Research, 30*, 451–459.

Henderson, S., Duncan-Jones, P., & Byrne, D. (1980). Measuring social relationships. The interview schedule for social interaction. *Journal of Psychological Medicine, 10*, 723–734.

Higgins, M. (1990). Women and coronary heart disease: Then and now. *Women's Health Issues, 1*, 5–11.

House, J. S., Landis, K. R., & Umberson, D. (1988). Social relationships and health. *Science, 241*, 540–545.

Johansson, S. (1983). *Female myocardial infarction in Göteborg.* Academic thesis, Department of Medicine, University of Göteborg, Sweden.

Kaplan, G. A., Salonen, J. T., Cohen, R. D., Brand, R. J., Syme, S. L., & Puska, P. (1988). Social connections and mortality from all causes and from cardiovascular disease: Prospective evidence from Eastern Finland. *American Journal of Epidemiology, 128*(2), 370–380.

Karasek, R. A. (1979). Job demands, job decision latitude and mental strain: Implications for job redesign. *Administrative Science Quarterly, 24*, 285–307.

Karasek, R., & Theorell, T. (1990). *Healthy work: Stress, productivity, and the reconstruction of working life.* New York: Basic Books.

LaCroix, A. Z. (1994). Psychosocial factors and risk of coronary heart disease in women: An epidemiologic perspective. *Fertility and Sterility, 62*(suppl. 2, 6), 133S–139S.

Moser, V., Blom, M., Eriksson, I., Hogbom, M., Wamala, S., Schenck-Gustafsson, K., & Orth-Gomér, K. (1996). Psykosocial Stress hos Kvinnor med Hjärtsjukdom [Psychosocial stress in women with heart disease]. *Stress Research Reports*, No. 68, pp. 1–37, National Institute for Psychosocial Factors and Health, Stockholm.

Orth-Gomér, K., & Johnsson, J. V. (1987). Social network interaction and mortality. A six year follow-up study of a random sample of the Swedish population. *Journal of Chronic Disease, 40*(10), 949–957.

Orth-Gomér, K., Rosengren, A., & Wilhelmsen, L. (1993). Lack of social support and incidence of coronary heart disease in middle-aged Swedish men. *Psychosomatic Medicine, 55*, 37–43.

Orth-Gomér, K., & Schneiderman, N. (Eds.). (1996). *Behavioral medicine approaches to cardiovascular disease prevention.* Hillsdale, NJ: Lawrence Erlbaum Associates.

Schoenbach, V. R., Kaplan, B. H., Fredman, L., & Kleinbaum, D. G. (1986). Social ties and mortality in Evans County, Georgia. *American Journal of Epidemiology, 123*(4), 577–591.

Schnall, P. L., & Landsbergis, P. A. (1994). Job strain and cardiovascular disease. *Annual Review of Public Health, 15*, 381–411.

Shekelle, R. B., Hulley, S. B., Neaton, J. D., Billings, J. H., Borhani, N. O., Gerace, T. A., Jacobs, D. R., Lasser, N. L., Mittlemark, M. B., & Stamler, J. (1985). The MRFiT Behavior Pattern Study. II. Type A behavior and incidence of coronary heart disease. *American Journal of Epidemiology, 4*(122), 559–570.

Shumaker, S. A., & Hill, D. R. (1991). Gender differences in social support and physical health. *Health Psychology, 10*(2), 102–111.

Tunstall-Pedoe, H., Kuulasmaa, K., Amouyel, P., Arveiler, D., Rajakangas, A.-M., & Pajak, A. (1994). Myocardial infarction and coronary deaths in the World Health Organization MONICA Project. *Circulation, 90*(1), 583–612.

Weidner, G. (in press). Personality and coronary heart disease in women: Past research and future directions. *Zeitschrift für Psychologie.*

Wenger, N. K., Speroff, L., & Packard, B. (1993). Cardiovascular health and disease in women. *New England Journal of Medicine, 329*(4), 247–256.

World Health Statistics 1992. (1993). Geneva: World Health Organization.

WORK, STRESS, AND SOCIAL CHANGE IN WOMEN

4

Work and Stress in Women

Ulf Lundberg

Stockholm University

BACKGROUND

As in many other research areas, investigators of human stress have generally chosen to study males rather than females. Traditions, convenience, and women's biological rhythms are likely expectations for the preference of males as subjects. Consequently, systematic investigations of, for instance, the influence of the menstrual cycle on physiological stress responses, are scarce (Tersman, Collins, & Eneroth, 1991).

Once the study of a particular population has become widespread, investigators are likely to continue to examine the same population for reasons of comparison and it was generally assumed that men and women would respond similarly to stressful conditions. However, comparisons between men and women during the 1970s showed that this was not always the case (e.g., Frankenhaeuser, Dunne, & Lundberg, 1976). With regard to the bodily reactions to stress, two neuroendocrine systems have been of particular interest (Henry, 1992); the sympathetic adrenal medullary system with the secretion of the catecholamines epinephrine and norepinephrine, and the pituitary adrenal cortical system with the secretion of corticosteroids, particularly cortisol.

GENDER AND PHYSIOLOGICAL STRESS RESPONSES

In the early 1970s, investigators in Frankenhaeuser's group in Stockholm started to compare stress responses of males and females. Johansson, Frankenhaeuser, and Magnusson (1973) measured urinary catecholamines in schoolchildren during active and passive conditions. Despite the fact that boys and girls performed equally well, it was found that only the boys increased their epinephrine responses significantly during the tests. Provided that body weight was taken into account, there were no gender differences in epinephrine levels at rest.

These findings were confirmed in a series of subsequent studies (see the review by Frankenhaeuser, 1983). Women were found to be less reactive than men in terms of epinephrine output during experimental stress (e.g., Frankenhaeuser et al., 1976), although their performance level on the various stress tests was as high or even higher than that of the males. It was also found that school achievement (grades, peer ratings) was significantly positively correlated with epinephrine output in male but not in female students (Rauste-von Wright, von Wright, & Frankenhaeuser, 1981). Thus, women's performance level seems to be unrelated to their epinephrine output, whereas good performance or "overachievement" (cf. Bergman & Magnusson, 1979) in men is associated with elevated catecholamine excretion. In addition, men are generally more confident than women in their ability to perform well. However, during more intense stress, such as a stressful examination (Frankenhaeuser et al., 1978), female students did increase their epinephrine output significantly, but still to a lesser extent than the male students did. With regard to norepinephrine responses, no consistent gender differences were found.

In the studies comparing men and women, experimental stress has generally been induced by exposing the subjects to a performance task under time pressure ("work as fast and correct as possible"). It is possible that men are more challenged or threatened than women by such tasks and that this could have contributed to the gender difference in epinephrine output.

Indirect support for this assumption was obtained in a natural stress situation, where parents followed their 3-year-old child to the hospital for a routine checkup (Lundberg, de Château, Winberg, & Frankenhaeuser, 1981). In this more emotional stress situation, the mothers' urinary epinephrine level was as high or even slightly higher than that of the fathers (see Fig. 4.1). A possible explanation for this is that women perceive this kind of interpersonal or emotional stress as more of a challenge than a performance task.

With regard to cortisol, Kirschbaum, Wüst, and Hellhammer (1992) found gender differences in response to psychological stress induced by public speaking and mental arithmetic in front of an audience. Although there were

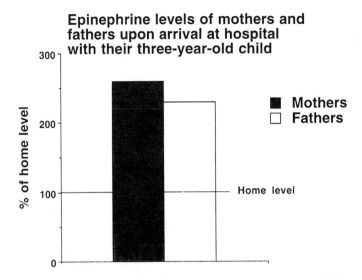

FIG. 4.1. Epinephrine levels of mothers and fathers arriving at hospital with their 3-year-old child for a routine checkup. Baseline levels were obtained another day at home. Based on Lundberg et al. (1981).

no significant baseline differences, males consistently responded with a more pronounced salivary cortisol output following this standardized stress situation. However, the salivary cortisol responses found after the injection of human corticotropin releasing hormone (CRH) and following bicycle ergometry until exhaustion, respectively, did not differ between men and women.

Again, this indicates that the qualitative aspect of the stress situation, for example, physical versus psychological stress, is of importance for the gender differences in physiological responses. Kirschbaum, Klauer, Filip, and Hellhammer (1995) also found gender-specific effects of social support on salivary cortisol responses to acute psychological stress. However, Forsman and Lundberg (1982) did not find any significant gender differences in urinary cortisol responses during different experimental conditions, but did find a more variable physiological stress response over conditions in the females.

The possible influence of personality characteristics, such as masculinity and femininity, on cardiovascular stress responses was investigated in an experimental study (Myrsten et al., 1984) of four groups of male and female students: (a) Subjects with high scores in both femininity and masculinity, that is, males and females having an androgynous sex-role profile; (b) subjects with low scores in both femininity and masculinity; (c) subjects with high scores in femininity and low scores in masculinity; and (d) subjects with low scores in femininity and high scores in masculinity. In addition to normal gender differences in blood pressure (higher in males) and heart rate (higher in females), a positive relationship was found between femininity scores and heart rate among the female students. No other cardiovascular stress responses were associated with masculinity or femininity. Androgynous females were found to be superior to all other groups on all performance tests.

The possible influence of sex roles on physiological stress responses was also examined by Collins and Frankenhaeuser (1978), who studied a group of females who had chosen a male-dominated line of education. Female engineering students were found to excrete as much epinephrine as their male colleagues during performance stress. Possible explanations for this "male-like" stress responses are (a) that the female students had been influenced by the masculine environmental demands and challenges, (b) that the female students who had chosen this line of education were atypical, or both. However, retrospective estimations by the female students of their behavior as children did not indicate that they had been more masculine or behaved as tomboys (Frankenhaeuser, 1983).

Another possible explanation for the gender differences in physiological stress responses is that steroid sex hormones play a role, that is, either that androgens increase or estrogens decrease the physiological responses to stress. In a study of the influence of estrogen replacement therapy on stress responses in postmenopausal women, Collins et al. (1982) failed to find any treatment effects on catecholamine or cortisol reactivity. Comparisons of women with elevated versus normal androgen levels (Lundberg et al., 1983), and the study of an antiandrogen treatment of hirsute women (Lundberg, Hansson, Eneroth, Frankenhaeuser, & Hagenfeldt, 1984), did not reveal any significant influence of androgen hormones on catecholamine levels or other physiological stress responses. However, in a recent, carefully controlled experimental study, Tersman et al. (1991) measured physiological stress responses during different phases of the menstrual cycle and found a small but significant increase in blood pressure reactivity and cortisol levels during the luteal phase. Another study (Lundberg, Wallin, Lindstedt, & Frankenhaeuser, 1990) indicated that individual differences in testosterone and estradiol levels of healthy women are positively correlated with blood pressure levels. Furthermore, Kirschbaum, Pirke, and Hellhammer (1995) found reduced cortisol responsivity to psychological stress in women using oral contraceptive medication.

In a recent study of preschool children, we did not find any significant gender differences in physiological activity at the mean age of 3.5 and 5.5 (Lundberg, Westermark, & Rasch, 1993), whereas an earlier study of 3–6-year-olds showed significantly higher catecholamine levels in boys than in girls during normal activities at a day-care center (Lundberg, 1983). It is possible that behavioral factors, such as gender differences in activities at the center, contributed to this difference.

Although the data are not conclusive, the studies of sex hormones indicate that there might be a moderate, but not always significant, influence of estrogen levels on the physiological stress responses of women, whereas no reliable influence of androgen levels has been seen. However, it is important to remember that even females with elevated plasma testosterone levels (e.g., 3–4 nmol/l) differ markedly from normal males (about 10–40 nmol/l). Hence, results based on women with different testosterone levels may not be relevant for making conclusions about the gender differences in psychophysiological stress responses. Nevertheless, it seems reasonable to conclude that psychological factors and sex-role patterns are more important than biological factors for the gender differences in physiological stress responses.

WORKLOAD AND STRESS IN EMPLOYED WOMEN AND MEN

In recent studies, groups of men and women matched for age, education, and occupation have been compared with regard to stress responses on their jobs well as in their homes. In the Volvo study (Frankenhaeuser, Lundberg, Fredrikson, et al., 1989), male and female managers and male and female clerical workers were compared with regard to personality characteristics and psychophysiological stress responses during (a) a normal day at their job, (b) work-free conditions at home, and (c) experimental conditions in the laboratory.

The female managers were found to be more competitive than the other groups according to a Type A interview (Lundberg, Hedman, Melin, & Frankenhaeuser, 1989) and to have a more androgynous sex-role profile; that is, they described themselves both as confident, independent, dominating, determined, and so forth, and as attached, warm, kind, shy, and so forth. The female and male clerical workers and the male managers had a more sex-typical personality profile. By exposing the participants to experimental stress, it was found that the female managers had the most pronounced epinephrine response of the four groups (see Fig. 4.2), indicating that they had adopted a "male" stress response.

During the normal day at work, all groups had about the same physiological stress levels but, after work and at home, the female managers were found to have higher catecholamine levels than the others (Frankenhaeuser, Lundberg, Fredrikson, et al., 1989). This indicates that the female managers had difficulties relaxing after work and during work-free conditions at home. Elevated epinephrine levels in female managers after work were also found in a recent study (Frankenhaeuser & Lundberg, 1997), which also showed that lack of unwinding was more common among female managers with children.

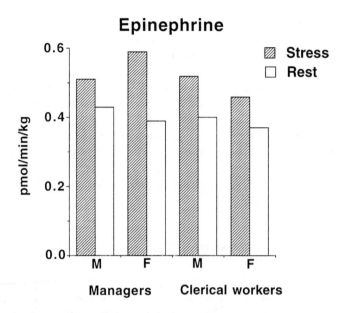

FIG. 4.2. Epinephrine reactivity during experimental stress in male (M) and female (F) managers and male (M) and female (F) clerical workers. Based on Frankenhaeuser, Lundberg, Fredrikson, et al. (1989).

Despite the fact that both male and female white-collar workers in the Volvo study were employed full time and had comparable occupational positions, women were carrying the main responsibility for all unpaid duties except maintenance of the car and the home and for managing finances (Frankenhaeuser, Lundberg, Augustson, et al., 1989). This gender difference is likely to explain the lack of unwinding among the females, particularly the female managers, who had to combine their responsibility for unpaid work at home with a qualified and demanding paid job.

THE INTERACTION BETWEEN STRESS AT WORK AND AT HOME

In the study of stress at work in men, a positive correlation is usually found between perceived stress and the physiological stress responses. For example, male assembly-line workers' catecholamine responses at the job were significantly correlated with their self-reports of demands and time pressure at work (Lundberg, Granqvist, Hansson, Magnusson, & Wallin, 1989). In keeping with this, self-reported stress among the male white-collar workers in the Volvo study (Frankenhaeuser, Lundberg, Augustson, et al., 1989) were positively correlated with increases in systolic and diastolic blood pressure

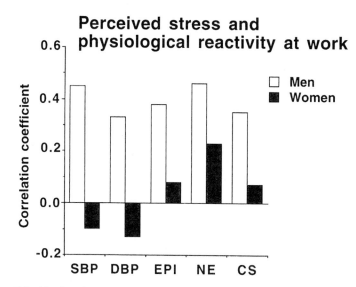

FIG. 4.3. Correlation between perceived stress and physiological stress responses at work in male and female white-collar workers. SBP = systolic blood pressure; DBP = diastolic blood pressure; EPI = epinephrine; NE = norepinephrine; CS = cortisol. Based on Frankenhaeuser, Lundberg, Augustson, et al. (1989).

and catecholamine and cortisol excretion at work (see Fig. 4.3). In the females, the corresponding correlations were close to zero, sometimes positive and sometimes negative. However, an interesting finding was that women's stress levels at work were correlated with corresponding measurements at home; that is, women with high stress levels at work had also high stress levels at home (see Fig. 4.4).

It seems as if employed women's stress is determined by a complex interaction between conditions at work and conditions at home, whereas men respond more selectively to the specific stress situations at work. Men also seem to be able to relax more rapidly after work and during work-free conditions at home.

Rissler (1977) examined female employees at an insurance company during a period of overtime and found that extra hours of work during the weekend were reflected in significantly elevated catecholamine levels in the evening after work in the middle of the week. The relationship between overtime and catecholamine excretion has also been examined in (full-time employed) parents of preschool children (Lundberg & Palm, 1989). Figure 4.5 shows that extra hours at work were associated with elevated epinephrine levels during the weekend at home in the mothers but not in the fathers, despite the fact that the fathers on average worked more overtime than the mothers.

Stress levels at work and at home

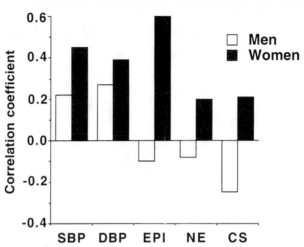

FIG. 4.4. Correlation between stress at work and at home in male and female white-collar workers. SBP = systolic blood pressure; DBP = diastolic blood pressure; EPI = epinephrine; NE = norepinephrine; CS = cortisol. Based on Frankenhaeuser, Lundberg, Augustson, et al. (1989).

It is interesting to compare these findings with data reported by Theorell (1991), based on large representative samples of male and female workers. He related various conditions at work to the risk of coronary heart disease (CHD) and found that overtime at work (10 hours or more per week) was associated with elevated risk of myocardial infarction in women, but not in men. Overtime at work in men was even associated with a significantly reduced risk of infarction.

A possible explanation for this gender difference is that women compared to men often are employed in low-status jobs, where high demands are combined with little influence over the pace and content of work. Such "high-strain" jobs, as described by the Karasek-Theorell model (Karasek, 1979), are related to significantly increased risk of CHD in men (Johnson, Hall, & Theorell, 1989) and women (Haynes, 1991). Workers in low-status job also have less possibilities to influence when and how much overtime they work.

Another possible explanation for the elevated CHD risk in women with overtime at work is that they have to face more pronounced role conflicts than men, in trying to combine the extra load in their paid job with responsibility for various unpaid duties. The stress from work overload and role conflicts, combined with low influence, may have contributed to the elevated risk of CHD (Haynes, 1991).

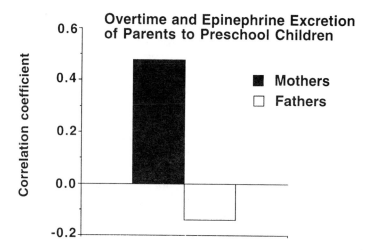

FIG. 4.5. Overtime at work and epinephrine levels at home in mothers and fathers of preschool children. Based on Lundberg and Palm (1989).

TOTAL WORK LOAD

In order to further investigate the stress from paid and unpaid work of employed men and women, a special questionnaire—the Total Workload Scale—has been developed (Mårdberg et al., 1991). "Total work load" or "productive activity" refers to the combined load from paid and unpaid duties, that is, paid employment, extra jobs, household chores, child care, care of sick or elderly relatives, and so forth.

The aim is to compare full-time employed men and women, at approximately the same educational and occupational level. Although employed women often work part time, a comparison of stress and workload among full-time employed men and women will provide important information on women's possibilities to make a professional career on the same terms as men.

In a recent study (Lundberg, Mårdberg, & Frankenhaeuser, 1994), matched groups of 1,300 men and 1,300 women between the ages of 32 and 58 were sampled from four occupational areas in the white-collar sector:

- Technology and natural science: architects, engineers, and technicians in chemistry, physics, and construction.
- Education: university professors and lecturers, school principals and other faculty members, schoolteachers.
- Heath care: physicians, nurses, dentists, psychologists.
- Administrative work: company and personnel administrators, computer programmers and system operators.

In order to include women in relatively high positions, priority was given to jobs where the proportion of women in managerial positions is known to be relatively high.

The response rate was 70% and, whereas men and women were found to be equal with regard to educational level, men were overrepresented at the higher occupational levels and women in jobs with no managerial responsibilities (Mårdberg, Lundberg, & Frankenhaeuser, 1991).

As in the Volvo study, a traditional gender-role pattern was found for the distribution of responsibilities for unpaid duties (see Fig. 4.6). A greater proportion of women than men reported having the main responsibility for all unpaid duties except car and household maintenance and managing of finances. In one case—gardening—the responsibility was about equally divided between men and women. Somewhat surprisingly, the pattern of responsibilities for unpaid work did not differ significantly between the different age groups and occupational levels.

With regard to the total work load in terms of hours per week, the conflict between demands, and the control over household work, the number of children at home was found to be of considerable importance (see Fig. 4.7). In families with no children at home, the total work load of full-time employed men and women was about the same, that is, a little more than 60 hours per week. Men did a few more hours in their paid job and women a few more hours at home. For women, the number of hours per week increased rapidly with the number of children at home, but for men this increase was much smaller. For example, in families with three or more children at home, women's total work load was almost 90 hours and men's about 70 hours a week—a mean gender difference of about 2½ hours a day. Furthermore, the conflict between demands increased and the control over home and household work decreased with the number of children at home (Lundberg, Mårdberg, & Frankenhaeuser, 1994).

Between the ages of 35 and 39, the total work load and the role conflicts for both sexes reached a peak, whereas the level of control over domestic work was low, that is, a high-strain situation (Karasek, 1979). It is likely that many people, and women in particular, experience a considerable amount of stress and work overload during this period of life, due to the combined load from taking care of relatively small children and from coping with a demanding occupational situation.

STRESS AND MUSCULOSKELETAL DISORDERS IN MEN AND WOMEN

The interaction between conditions at work and responsibilities for home and family may also help to explain the high rate of musculoskeletal disorders in women. On general grounds, one would expect that women's higher

MAIN RESPONSIBILITY

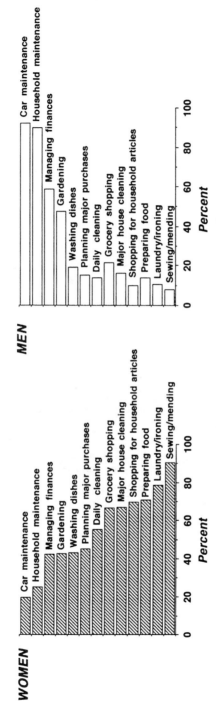

FIG. 4.6. Responsibility for unpaid duties among male and female white-collar workers. From Lundberg, Mårdberg, and Frankenhaeuser (1994). Reprinted with permission.

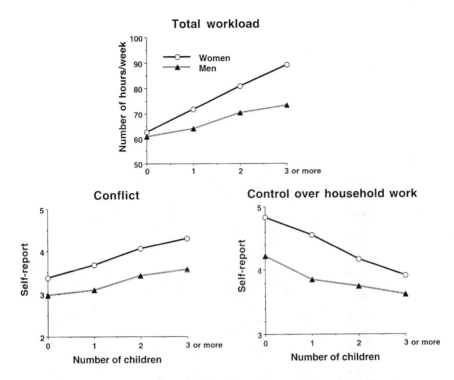

FIG. 4.7. Total work load, conflict, and control as related to the number of children. From Lundberg, Mårdberg, and Frankenhaeuser (1994). Reprinted with permission.

incidence of, for instance, neck and shoulder problems is due to their lower physical capacity. However, several recent studies show that physical characteristics of the individual, such as muscular strength, aerobic fitness, and flexibility, do not seem to predict future musculoskeletal disorders (e.g., Battié, 1989). It has also been found that low-load work situations, such as light assembly work, work at video-display terminals, and work as cashiers at banks, post offices, and supermarkets may cause muscular disorders (Veiersted, Westgaard, & Andersen, 1993). In addition, ergonomic improvements of the work environment during the last decades have not been followed by a corresponding reduction of neck, shoulder, and lower back pain problems. These data indicate that a high physical capacity in relation to the demands does not necessarily protect against muscular problems.

Alternative explanations for the higher incidence of muscular pain in women could be that stressful conditions at work and at home interact and that women have less possibilities than men to unwind and relax at home.

A recent experimental study (Lundberg, Kadefors, et al., 1994) shows that psychological stress induces elevated muscular tension in women and that the increase is enhanced if she is at the same time exposed to a physical load. This suggests the possibility that muscular disorders may occur also in low-load work situations, or even in the absence of physical load, due to the additional muscular tension induced by mental stress. In women more than in men, lack of relaxation and elevated stress levels off their paid job may further contribute to muscular tension. In a long-term perspective, injuries ("red ragged" fibers) and pain may be caused by too prolonged an activation without rest of muscle fibers belonging to the low-threshold motor units. This hypothesis is based on a new explanation model for the high incidence of muscular disorders in light industrial work suggested by Hägg (1991).

DISCUSSION

The interaction between demands at work and at home are likely to induce elevated psychophysiological stress levels in women and influence their efficiency, well-being, and long-term health. This interaction is also important for the interpretation of data collected at work, because stress induced by the paid job may not always be seen as elevated physiological stress levels at work, but may instead influence women's stress levels at home (Lundberg & Palm, 1989). Thus, to learn about women's stress, it is necessary not only to examine psychophysiological responses and conditions at work, but also to study the pattern of responsibilities and the workload outside the paid job. Men who try to change traditional gender roles by assuming the main responsibility for household chores and child care also have to face more stress and role conflicts. However, in general, men still have more of a choice than women due to less expectations from the environment. In addition, men who break the traditional roles also tend to get more appreciation for doing so than women who occupy the same multiple roles.

It may seem surprising that the age of the male and female white-collar workers did not matter very much for the gender differences in responsibility for home and family (Lundberg, Mårdberg, & Frankenhaeuser, 1994). Considering the changes in gender roles during the last decades, it would be expected that men and women in young couples share the responsibility for unpaid duties more equally than older couples. This trend toward greater equality between the sexes is also illustrated by the fact that men use almost as much time as full-time employed women in unpaid work, at least as long as there are no children in the family (cf. Fig. 4.7). Nevertheless, women still tend to carry the main responsibility for these duties and see to it that things get done, even if they do not have to do all the work themselves. Women tend to take the responsibility for planning, organizing, and remembering things at home.

Although it has consistently been found that women's employment per se does not seem to carry any negative health consequences (Waldron, 1991), the total work load, the role conflicts, and the responsibility for unpaid work may have adverse effects not only on women's possibilities to make a professional career, but also on their well-being and long-term health (Frankenhaeuser, Lundberg, & Chesney, 1991; Hall, 1990). In keeping with this, women in most industrialized countries tend to report more health problems than men, such as psychosomatic and musculoskeletal symptoms, absenteeism from work, use of medical drugs, visits to doctors, and so forth (Waldron, 1991).

It is important to emphasize that women's employment also contributes to several positive effects, which may balance the stress from role conflicts and work overload. A paid employment makes a woman socially and economically more independent and her occupational role contributes to higher self-esteem, learning and experience, social support and emotional stimulation from colleagues, and so on.

In conclusion, it seems as if adverse work conditions, such as high demands and little influence at work, have similar negative health effects on employed women as on men, whereas stress and work overload seems to be a greater problem for full-time employed women, particularly in families with small children. Although the long-term health consequences of employed women's stress and work overload are not yet known, large groups of women do report elevated distress, tiredness, and psychosomatic problems and show elevated psychophysiological arousal; however, multiple roles can also be an asset. The balance between negative and positive effects vary over time and between individuals depending on their age, marital status, family size, type of occupation, and so on.

ACKNOWLEDGMENTS

Research reported in this chapter has been supported by grants from the Swedish Council for Work Life Research, the Swedish Council for Research in the Humanities and Social Sciences, The Swedish Medical Research Council and the John D. and Catherine T. MacArthur Foundation Network on Health and Behavior.

REFERENCES

Battié, M. (1989). *The reliability of physical factors as predictors of the occurrence of back pain reports: A prospective study within industry.* Unpublished doctoral dissertation, Gothenburg University, Sweden.

Bergman, L. R., & Magnusson, D. (1979). Overachievement and catecholamine output in an achievement demanding situation. *Psychosomatic Medicine, 41,* 181–188.

Collins, A., Hansson, U., Eneroth, P., Hagenfeldt, K., Lundberg, U., & Frankenhaeuser, M. (1982). Psychophysiological stress response in postmenopausal women before and after hormonal replacement therapy. *Human Neurobiology, 1*, 153–159.

Collins, A., & Frankenhaeuser, M. (1978). Stress responses in male and female engineering students. *Journal of Human Stress, 4*, 43–48.

Forsman, L., & Lundberg, U. (1982). Consistency in catecholamine and cortisol excretion in males and females. *Pharmacology, Biochemistry & Behavior, 17*, 555–562.

Frankenhaeuser, M. (1983). The sympathetic-adrenal and pituitary-adrenal response to challenge: Comparison between the sexes. In T. M. Dembroski, T. H. Schmidt, & G. Blümchen (Eds.), *Biobehavioral bases of coronary heart disease* (pp. 91–105). Basel, Switzerland: Karger.

Frankenhaeuser, M., Lundberg, U., & Chesney, M. (1991). *Women, work and health. Stress and opportunities.* New York: Plenum.

Frankenhaeuser, M., Dunne, E., & Lundberg, U. (1976). Sex differences in sympathetic adrenal medullary reactions induced by different stressors. *Psychopharmacology, 47*, 1–5.

Frankenhaeuser, M., & Lundberg, U. (1997). *Stress and workload of single and dual career couples in high-grade positions.* (Manuscript under revision for publication)

Frankenhaeuser, M., Lundberg, U., Augustson, H., Nilsson, S., Hedman, M., & Wahlström, K. (1989). *Stress, health, job satisfaction. A summary of research projects on stress and the psychosocial work environment.* Stockholm: The Swedish Work Environment Fund.

Frankenhaeuser, M., Lundberg, U., Fredrikson, M., Melin, B., Tuomisto, M., Myrsten, A.-L., Hedman, M., Bergman-Losman, B., & Wallin, L. (1989). Stress on and off the job as related to sex and occupational status in white-collar workers. *Journal of Organizational Behavior, 10*, 321–346.

Frankenhaeuser, M., Rauste-von Wright, M., Collins, A., von Wright, J., Sedvall, G., & Swahn, C.-G. (1978). Sex differences in psychoneuroendocrine reactions to examination stress. *Psychosomatic Medicine, 40*, 334–343.

Hägg, G. (1991). Statis work loads and occupational myalgia—a new explanation model. In P. A. Anderson, D. J. Hobart, & J. V. Danhoff (Eds.), *Electromyographical kinesiology* (pp. 141–144). New York: Elsevier.

Hall, E. M. (1990). *Women's work: An inquiry into the health effects of invisible and visible labour.* Unpublished doctoral dissertation, Karolinska Institute, Stockholm.

Haynes, S. G. (1991). The effect of job demands, job control, and new technologies on the health of employed women: A review. In M. Frankenhaeuser, U. Lundberg, & M. Chesney (Eds.), *Women, work and health. Stress and opportunities* (pp. 157–170). New York: Plenum.

Henry, J. P. (1992). Biological basis of the stress response. *Integrative Physiological and Behavioral Science, 1*, 66–83.

Johansson, G., Frankenhaeuser, M., & Magnusson, D. (1973). Catecholamine output in school children as related to performance and adjustment. *Scandinavian Journal of Psychology, 14*, 20–28.

Johnson, J. V., Hall, E., & Theorell, T. (1989). The combined effects of job strain and social isolation on the prevalence of cardiovascular disease and death in a random sample of the Swedish working male. *Scandinavian Journal of Work, Environment, and Health, 15*, 271–279.

Karasek, R. A. (1979). Job demands, job decision latitude and mental strain: Implications for job redesign. *Administrative Science Quarterly, 24*, 285–307.

Kirschbaum, C., Klauer, T., Filip, S.-H., & Hellhammer, D. H. (1995). Sex specific effects of social support on cortisol and subjective responses to acute psychophysiological stress. *Psychosomatic Medicine, 57*, 23–31.

Kirschbaum, C., Pirke, K.-M., & Hellhammer, D. H. (1995). Preliminary evidence for reduced cortisol responsivity to psychological stress in women using oral contraceptive medication. *Psychoneuroendocrinology, 20*, 509–514.

Kirschbaum, C., Wüst, S., & Hellhammer, D. (1992). Consistent sex differences in cortisol responses to psychological stress. *Psychosomatic Medicine, 54*, 648–657.

Lundberg, U. (1983). Sex differences in behavior patterns and catecholamine and cortisol excretion in 3–6 year old day-care children. *Biological Psychology, 16*, 109–117.

Lundberg, U., Westermark, O., & Rasch, B. (1993). Cardiovascular and neuroendocrine activity in preschool children: Comparison between day-care and home levels. *Scandinavian Journal of Psychology, 34*, 371–378.

Lundberg, U., de Château, P., Winberg, J., & Frankenhaeuser, M. (1981). Catecholamine and cortisol excretion patterns in three year old children and their parents. *Journal of Human Stress, 7*, 3–11.

Lundberg, U., Hansson, U., Andersson, K., Eneroth, P., Frankenhaeuser, M., & Hagenfeldt, K. (1983). Hirsute women with elevated androgen levels: Psychological characteristics, steroid hormones and catecholamine. *Journal of Psychosomatic Obstetrics and Gynaecology, 2*, 86–93.

Lundberg, U., Granqvist, M., Hansson, T., Magnusson, M., & Wallin, L. (1989). Psychological and physiological stress responses during repetitive work at an assembly line. *Work & Stress, 3*, 143–153.

Lundberg, U., Hansson, U., Eneroth, P., Frankenhaeuser, M., & Hagenfeldt, K. (1984). Anti-androgen treatment of hirsute women: A study on stress responses. *Journal of Psychosomatic Obstetrics and Gynaecology, 3*, 79–92.

Lundberg, U., Hedman, M., Melin, B., & Frankenhaeuser, M. (1989). Type A behavior in healthy males and females as related to physiological reactivity and blood lipids. *Psychosomatic Medicine, 51*, 113–122.

Lundberg, U., Kadefors, R., Melin, B., Palmerud, G., Hassmén, P., Engström, M., & Elfsberg Dohns, I. (1994). Psychophysiological stress and EMG activity of the trapezius muscle. *International Journal of Behavioral Medicine, 1*, 354–370.

Lundberg, U., Mårdberg, B., & Frankenhaeuser, M. (1994). The total workload of male and female white collar workers as related to age, occupational level, and number of children. *Scandinavian Journal of Psychology, 35*, 315–327.

Lundberg, U., & Palm, K. (1989). Workload and cathecolamine excretion in parents of preschool children. *Work & Stress, 3*, 255–260.

Lundberg, U., Wallin, L., Lindstedt, G., & Frankenhaeuser, M. (1990). Steroid sex hormones and cardiovascular function in healthy males and females: A correlational study. *Pharmacology Biochemistry & Behavior, 37*, 325–327.

Mårdberg, B., Lundberg, U., & Frankenhaeuser, M. (1991). The total workload of parents employed in white-collar jobs: Construction of a questionnaire and a scoring system. *Scandinavian Journal of Psychology, 32*, 233–239.

Myrsten, A.-L., Lundberg, U., Frankenhaeuser, M., Ryan, G., Dolphin, C., & Cullen, J. (1984). Sex-role orientation as related to psychological and physiological responses during achievement and orthostatic stress. *Motivation and Emotion, 8*, 243–258.

Rauste-von Wright, M., von Wright, J., & Frankenhaeuser, M. (1981). Relationships between sex-related psychological characteristics during adolescence and catecolamine excretion during achievement stress. *Psychophysiology, 18*, 362–370.

Rissler, A. (1977). Stress reactions at work and after work during a period of quantitative overload. *Ergonomics, 20*, 577–580.

Tersman, Z., Collins, A., & Eneroth, P. (1991). Cardiovascular responses to psychological and physiological stressors during the menstrual cycle. *Psychosomatic Medicine, 53*, 185–197.

Theorell, T. (1991). On cardiovascular health in women. In M. Frankenhaeuser, U. Lundberg, & M. Chesney (Eds.), *Women, work and health. Stress and opportunities* (pp. 187–204). New York: Plenum.

Veiersted, K. B., Westgaard, R. H., & Andersen, P. (1993). Electromyographic evaluation of muscular work pattern as a predictor of trapezius myalgia. *Scandinavian Journal of Work and Environmental Health, 19*, 284–290.

Waldron, I. (1991). Effects of labour force participation on sex differences in mortality and morbidity. In M. Frankenhaeuser, U. Lundberg, & M. Chesney (Eds.), *Women, work and health. Stress and opportunities* (pp. 17–38). New York: Plenum.

5

Trends in Women's Psychosocial Work Environment and Health, and Structural Changes on the Labor Market

Olle Lundberg
Stockholm University
and
University of Helsinki

Lena Gonäs
Swedish Institute for Work Life Research
and
London School of Economics

During the past three decades, women's lives have changed dramatically in many Western countries, not least in Sweden. Most noticeable, women's labor force participation has increased rapidly. This increase has paralleled a transformation of the labor market into a postindustrial one, characterized by a shrinking number of those employed in manufacturing and an increased proportion of people working in the service sector (health care, schooling, child care, etc.). These jobs have, in large part, been taken by women. The organization of reproductive work has thus been shifted over to the labor market and become both a condition for women's waged labor and the most important labor market for women in Sweden.

At the beginning of the 1990s, the Swedish economy was hit by a severe recession. Initially, this resulted in a higher unemployment rate for men than for women, due to heavy restructuring in the male-dominated manufacturing and construction sectors. With a large budget deficit and a huge state debt, however, cuts in the public sector has affected also female employment rates. This development is likely to have an impact on many women's lives in general, and in the longer term also affect stress and heart disease among women, employed as well as unemployed. It is yet too early

58

to analyze these trends in any detail, but here we attempt to discuss the present labor-market development, and to analyze the effects of structural changes that begun already during the second half of the 1980s.

WOMEN AND WORK

Women's Labor-Market Participation

In 1963, 53% of Swedish women were in the labor force, compared with 93% of men. Thirty years later, 77% of women and 81% of men 16–64 years were in the labor force either employed or unemployed (Statistiska Centralbyrån [SCB], 1993; see also Vågerö & Lahelma, Chapter 6, this volume).

During the first years of the 1990s, a drastic decrease in the overall employment intensity took place. It fell from 83.5% in 1990 to 72.6% in 1993, corresponding to an employment decrease of 544,000 individuals. It is also interesting to note that the sharpest decreases are reflected in the young age groups, causing a reshaping of the curve toward a higher proportion of middle-aged workers. 1993 saw an almost equal employment-intensity pattern for men and women, where the changes during the first years of the 1990s have also hit the oldest age groups among men, but not among women (see Fig. 5.1).

It is possible to say that, quantitatively, the employment pattern for women and men has become more equal. If we examine the number of hours

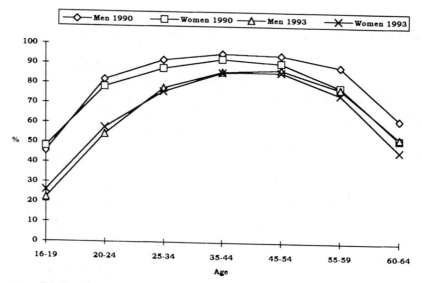

FIG. 5.1. Employment intensity in Sweden for women and men in different age groups for the years 1990 and 1993. From Statistika Centralbyrån (1990, 1993). Reprinted with permission.

TABLE 5.1
Changes in Women's Working Hours in Household Work and Gainful Employment

	1974	1981	1991
Average time spent on household work among women (h/w)	31.9	26.6	18.7
Average time spent in gainful employment among women (h/w)	17.1	21.0	26.4
Women's total working time on average (h/w)	49.0	47.6	45.1

Note. The figures are based on unmarried/cohabiting, employed/home working 18–60-year-olds. From Nermo (1994). Adapted with permission.

in gainful employment per week, however, the picture changes. Clearly noticeable are the differences in reproductive responsibilities and the employer's desire to offer women only part-time work instead of full-time work. Almost 60% of all employed women between 16 and 64 years of age worked full-time (35 hr or more a week) in 1993. Another 35% worked extended part-time (20–34 hr a week), and 6% worked less than 20 hr a week. Nevertheless, women increased their working hours during the 1980s while reducing the time spent on domestic work (not including child care; see Table 5.1). This development led to men and women spending roughly the same amount of time on work, defined as paid work and household work (other than child care) taken together, in the early 1990s.

One important development is the changed labor-market behavior for women with small children (under 7 years). The participation rate for this group of women increased from 38% in 1963 to 81% in 1993. This is caused by the fact that more women now stay in the labor market as they form a family and have children. They no longer leave their positions, but instead take parental leave or a leave of absence with a right to return to their former job. When they return, they most often reduce their working hours per week, and as the children grow older they increase their working hours up to full time.

Taking the actual number of hours worked per week into account, differences between women in Sweden and those in other European countries have decreased (Jonung & Persson, 1990). An important difference still exists in that Swedish women are on leave of absence with paid wages, whereas many European women do not have that opportunity. Instead, they are either counted as unemployed or out of the workforce.

A Gender-Divided Labor Market

Although women in Sweden today are gainfully employed to almost the same degree as men, women and men still belong to different parts of the labor market. This is obvious on national as well as regional levels. Table 5.2 shows the sectorial distribution of men's and women's employment in 1990.

TABLE 5.2
Female and Male Employment by Economic Sectors in 1990

	Women		Men	
	Number	%	Number	%
Agriculture, forestry	38,000	2	111,000	5
Industry	302,000	14	1,011,000	43
Education, health care	1,003,000	46	221,000	9
Other services	819,000	38	1,002,000	43
Total	2,162,000	100	2,346,000	100

Note. From Statistiska Centralbyran (1991). Adapted with permission.

The majority of women work in service sectors. Eighty-four percent of all employed women were in public or private service areas in 1990, and even in the most heavily industrialized regions 70% to 80% of the employed women worked in public and private services (Gonäs, 1991). For men the picture was quite different. Almost 50% were employed in industry, agriculture, and forestry. However, women and men do not only participate in different segments of the labor market, but these segments also tend to function in quite different ways. More specifically, the wage-setting systems differ, the possibilities for part-time work differ, and the social norms of female participation in decision making are different.

Not only are men and women found in different sectors of the labor market, they also hold quite different occupations, in Sweden as well as in other countries (Charles, 1992). If separate lists are made with the 10 most common occupations for women and men, no one occupation appears on both lists. Women work as cashiers in stores, and as nurses, cleaners, and office workers. Men have technical work, are salesmen, or truck drivers. About one third of the women work in occupations where 9 out of 10 are women and 40% of the men are in occupations where 9 out of 10 are men (SCB, 1991).

Even though women in younger cohorts are now slightly more educated than men, they still hold the less qualified jobs. This means that they are concentrated in occupations in the lower nonmanual and unskilled manual social classes (see Table 5.3), whereas men to a larger extent are found among higher nonmanual and skilled workers positions.

These differences cannot be accounted for by the fact that women and men work in different sectors of the labor market. Looking at like occupations, 53% of men and 22% of women have tasks that require more than 2 months of training (SCB, 1991). Although the physical work environment on the whole tend to be worse in male-dominated occupations, improvements

TABLE 5.3
The Distribution Over Social Classes Among Men and Women in Sweden 1991, Percent

Class Category	Men	Women
Higher nonmanual	15.3	7.6
Intermediate nonmanual	15.5	16.4
Lower nonmanual	9.4	21.0
Skilled workers	24.0	11.0
Unskilled workers	22.5	36.3
Self-employed	9.4	4.0
Farmers	3.9	3.7
Total	100.0	100.0
n	3079	3072

in physical working conditions for men during the 1980s were not found for women (Fritzell & Lundberg, 1993). Influence over the job showed the same picture, as well as monotonous jobs, work injuries, and bad working conditions (SCB, 1991).

Women's Economic Position

Not only are women generally working in other occupations and other sectors than men, their wages are also generally lower. This can partly be explained by women having (on the average) less education and shorter occupational experience, that is, less human capital, which normally is counted as a legitimate basis for wage differences. However, even after adjustment for differences in human capital, a substantial difference in wage between men and women is still found in Sweden. Although gross differences in wages between men and women have decreased in the period from the late 1960s to the early 1980s, no further reduction of this wage gap have taken place thereafter (le Grand, 1994). Until 1981, about one fifth of this gap could be understood in terms of gender differences in the length of education and the number of years in the labor force. In 1991, however, much less of the gross difference was due to these factors, and hence the reduction in the wage difference obtained when controlling for human capital factors is minimal (from 21% to 19% male excess wage).

In fact, even when including class and labor-market sector in the regression analysis it is not possible to wholly account for gender difference in wages. When comparing men and women with equal length of education, equal number of years on the labor market, in the same social class, and in the same labor-market sector, men still earn more than women. Although this difference decreased until 1981, it has remained stable since then, and in 1991 the extra "male wage supplement" amounted to 13% (le Grand, 1994).

On a family basis, this means that many women are economically dependent on their spouses, albeit they are gainfully employed. However, the percentage of families where the spouses contributes with roughly the same amount of money to the family income did increase somewhat during the 1980s, from 8.7 in 1981 to 12.5 in 1991 (Nermo, 1994).

Women's Work and Stress

Women's increasing labor-force participation may have both positive and negative implications for their health. From the discussion so far, we might infer that labor-market changes, both in general terms such as employment chances and in terms of job characteristics, will be influential on stress and health among women. In addition, a number of factors related to the interaction between working life and family life are likely to be linked to health outcome, especially for women (Arber & Lahelma, 1993). Such factors include the economic remuneration from employment, working hours, working conditions, and the division of unpaid work within the family, but also include welfare state arrangements, such as rules for parental leave. Three important factors that are of special importance for women's health in this respect also changed during the 1980s in Sweden. These factors were (a) the total amount of time spent on work; (b) the economic returns from gainful employment, and more specifically the economic balance between the spouses in a family; and (c) job characteristics such as physical and psychosocial work environment. The first two of these have been touched on earlier. In the following we undertake a more detailed analysis of recent changes in women's psychosocial work environment, and the effects of this trend on women's health.

When analyzing psychosocial working conditions, the combined effects of job demands and job decision latitude are in focus (see, i.e., Karasek, 1979; Karasek & Theorell, 1990). A job where the demands are high might be interesting, stimulating, and personally rewarding as long as the employee decides him- or herself when and how the job should be done. If this is not the case, the demands will transfer into a negative element. The combinations of job demands and job decision latitude are shown in Fig. 5.2. The worst possible combination according to this theory, both per se and in terms of subsequent health, is high demands *and* low control, which create a *high-strain job* and is the key variable in the following analyses.

DATA AND METHODS

Data

The empirical analyses are based on panel data from the Swedish Level of Living Surveys undertaken in 1981 and 1991. These surveys are following a random sample of $\frac{1}{1000}$ in the Swedish population aged 15–75 in 1968. Samples

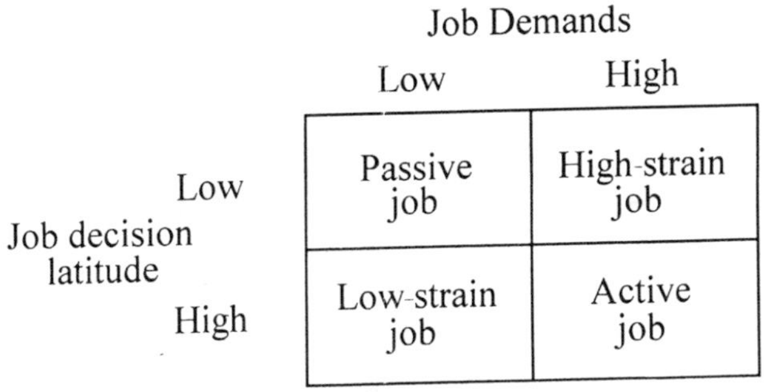

Job Demands

Low   High

	Low	High
Low Job decision latitude	Passive job	High-strain job
High	Low-strain job	Active job

FIG. 5.2. The Karasek Demand/Control model.

of young people and immigrants are added at each panel wave in order to assure cross-sectional representativeness as well. Personal interviews are carried out in the respondent's home, and cover topics like health, family situation, working conditions, economic resources, housing conditions, leisure-time activities, education, political resources, and personal security (Erikson & Åberg, 1987). In addition, information on income and mortality, among other things, have been linked from registers.

The panel data design enables us to study social change and causal processes, because we are able to follow individuals over time. In our main analyses we use panel data from the 1981 and 1991 surveys. In total, 5,531 persons were in the sample of both surveys, and 3,987 of these responded (72.1%). Two inclusion criteria have been used in this chapter (in addition to the obvious requirement that respondents must have participated at both occasions), namely (a) respondents should be 25–65 years old in 1991, and (b) they should have been employed at both occasions. These criteria applied to 1,017 women and 1,067 men.

Variable Definitions

As discussed earlier, high-strain jobs combine high job demands with a low job decision latitude. Four variables have been used in order to measure this combination. The measure of job demands is based on two questions, namely, "Is your work mentally taxing?" and "Is your work stressful?" If the answer to both of these questions is "Yes," the job is classified as demanding, otherwise not. Job decision latitude is also based on two dichotomous questions, namely, "Can you yourself determine your pace of work?" and "Is your work monotonous?" If the answer to the first of those questions is "No" or the answer to both questions is "Yes," then the decision latitude is low.

Using the same variables from the 1981 and 1991 surveys respectively, we are also able to construct a measure of change in high-strain job status, which then take the values No/No (constantly not in the high strain combination), Yes/No (improvement), No/Yes (deterioration) and Yes/Yes (Constantly in high strain).

Health outcome is measured by an index of circulatory illness.[1] This index is based on the general question, "Have you during the last 12 months had any of the following illnesses or ailments?" Following this question is a list of 50 different illnesses and symptoms, covering all kinds of health problems. Five items covering circulatory problems are included in the index, namely, "Aches or pains in the chest," "Weak heart," "High blood pressure," "Giddiness," and "Coronary thrombosis, heart attack." The four first of these are summed, using the weights 0, 1, and 3 for the three response alternatives "No," "Yes, mild," and "Yes, severe," respectively. Those with 3 points or more on this scale, or who have reported at least mild problems of coronary thrombosis, are coded as having circulatory illness, others not. Also this measure have been constructed identically for 1981 and 1991 in order to analyze change in circulatory illness. In addition, variables measuring age, smoking behavior, and job content have been used as control variables in the multivariate modeling. Multivariate analyses are undertaken by means of logit regression, performed with the CATMOD procedure in the SAS® statistical package.

RESULTS

Between 1981 and 1991, the prevalence of high-strain jobs increased in Sweden, from 13% to 17%. This increase almost solely took place among women (from 15% to 21%), thereby causing a further deterioration of women's situation as compared to men's in this respect. When following individual men and women over time, it appears even more clearly that a number of women have had a change of their working conditions to the worse in 1991 as compared to 10 years earlier (see Table 5.4).

In their work on changes in working conditions in general, Szulkin and Tåhlin (1994) also analyzed the divergent pattern in the exposure for high-strain jobs found for men and women. First, they showed that the negative trend among women is caused by an increase in the psychological demands, whereas decision latitude, or autonomy, have remained stable. Second, they tried to disentangle the reasons behind this increase in job demands. Two main possible explanations are put forward, namely that the job content have changed or that women have changed their perception of their job

---

[1]Note that circulatory illness defined in this way is not synonymous with clinical coronary heart disease. Although the measure used here predicts mortality over a 10-year follow-up period (odds ratios are 2.48 and 2.15 for overall mortality and CHD mortality, respectively), some of the symptoms referred to may be explained by other disorders. Conversely, some cases of CHD may go subjectively unrecognized, not least among women.

TABLE 5.4
Changes and Stability in Exposure to High-Strain Work ("Yes") Between 1981 and 1991,
Percent

High Strain Work 1981/1991	Men	Women
No/No	80.9	69.4
Yes/No	8.4	8.8
No/Yes	7.7	15.5
Yes/Yes	3.0	6.3
Number	1,067	1,017

content due to other changes in their lives. It might, for example, be the case that the increase in working hours among women during the 1980s led to increased difficulties in combining work and family obligations, which in turn might affect the way in which psychological job demands are perceived and reported. However, they found no support for this explanation. Instead, their analyses clearly show that the gender difference in exposure to high-strain jobs is caused by a negative development in female-dominated occupations.

More specifically, there are a number of female-dominated occupations at the lower and intermediate levels, predominantly found in the public sector, where an increase in psychological demands, not accompanied by an increase in autonomy, have occurred (Fritzell & Lundberg, 1994a). Occupations where the largest increases in high-strain jobs have taken place are, for example, nurses, nursing assistants, elementary school teachers, and child-care providers (see Table 5.5).

What then, more precisely, has occurred in many caring and teaching occupations within the public sector? In order to shed some light on this issue, the relationships between deteriorating psychosocial working condi-

TABLE 5.5
Examples of Occupational Groups Where Women Have Experienced Large Increases in the
Prevalence of High-Strain Jobs, Percent

	High-Strain Work	
Occupational Group	No 1981/ Yes 1991	Yes 1981/ Yes/1991
Nursing assistants	27	13
Nurses	18	15
Elementary school teachers	20	6
Child-care providers	19	2

tions (the No/Yes category) and a range of specific questions on job content were explored. Of the 14 questions studied, however, a significant relationship with deteriorating psychosocial work environment was found for only 2, namely the degree to which the employees have influence over how work tasks are carried out, and the extent to which the work pace must be adapted to external persons, such as customers, patients, and pupils (see Table 5.6).

Women who have experienced a deterioration of their psychosocial work environment are also found to have little or no influence over how their tasks should be carried out, and are to a large extent compelled to adapt their work pace to other people. The latter finding is not surprising, considering that women in health care and schooling occupations to a larger extent than others have experienced a worsening of their psychosocial working conditions. That such changes are also linked to little influence over how the work should be undertaken is of interest, because it points to a possible way to restore working conditions for women holding these types of occupations. To be able to decide over how work tasks should be performed is clearly an aspect of job autonomy, and because the increase in high-strain jobs is caused by an increase in job demands not being matched by a similar increase in decision latitude, it seems possible to improve working conditions by allowing more autonomy in this sense.

It is, of course, of importance whether the changes in psychosocial working conditions experienced more than 15% of employed women have had any consequences in terms of health or not. In order to analyze that, changes in the prevalence of circulatory illness are related to changes in exposure to high-strain jobs (see Table 5.7).

The overall percentage reporting circulatory problems is rather low among employed women, but have increased somewhat from 3.5% to 5%. In

TABLE 5.6
Relationship Between Job Characteristics and Mobility Into High-Strain Working Conditions Between 1981 and 1991 Among Women, Odds Ratios, and 95% Confidence Intervals, $n = 1017$

Job Characteristics	Level[a]	OR	95% CI
Influence over *how* tasks are carried out	1	1	(Ref.)
	2	1.19	(0.74-1.90)
	3	2.04	(1.29-3.22)
	4	3.23	(1.67-6.25)
	5	3.62	(1.66-7.86)
Pace of work adapted to customers, patients, pupils, etc.	1	1	(Ref.)
	2	0.63	(0.41-0.97)
	3	0.32	(0.18-0.57)
	4	0.14	(0.03-0.58)
	5	0.25	(0.13-0.49)

[a]Levels are: 1. To a very large extent; 2. To a large extent; 3. To a certain extent; 4. To a small extent; 5. Not at all.

TABLE 5.7
Percentage With Circulatory Illness by High-Strain Work in 1981/1991 Among Women

High Strain 1981/1991	Circulatory Illness 1981	Circulatory Illness 1991	Number
No/No	2.4	3.0	706
Yes/No	7.9	5.6	89
No/Yes	2.5	11.4	158
Yes/Yes	12.5	10.9	64
Total	3.5	5.0	1,017

the general population (men and women aged 18–75), 6.4% were classified as having circulatory illness in 1991, which represents a slight decrease from 8.1% in 1981 (Fritzell & Lundberg, 1994b). Employed women have thereby experienced a quite different development than other parts of the population. Those women who were not in high-strain jobs at any of the two times have remained at a low level of circulatory illness, whereas those who had such a job both times have had a constantly large proportion with such health problems. The large change in circulatory illness is found among those women who also had a negative change of their psychosocial work environment (the No/Yes category), where the percentage with circulatory illness rose from 2.5% to 11.4%. It appears, therefore, that the negative development in psychosocial working conditions have been paralleled by an equally negative change in these women's health.

At least two questions arise from the results presented earlier, namely (a) are these changes produced by changes in job characteristics or by confounding due to differences in, for instance, age; and (b) have changes in job characteristic had a direct (psychosocial) effect on circulatory illness, or is it mediated through, for example, smoking (see Table 5.8)?

In Model 1, differences in circulatory illness in 1991 between the four categories of change and stability in high strain, controlling for age, is presented. The same pattern as in Table 5.7 appears again, which means that the finding of a strong relationship between deteriorating psychosocial work environment and poor circulatory health is not an effect of differences in age structure. This holds true also when analyzing change in circulatory illness by including circulatory illness in 1981 as a control variable (Model 2). Finally, it can be seen from Model 3 that the different patterns of change in circulatory illness for the four categories are not related to different smoking habits in 1981 and 1991 (although smoking is strongly related to circulatory illness). If anything, differences between the No/No category and the others become larger when controlling for smoking. This could be due

TABLE 5.8
Logistic Regression Analysis of Circulatory Illness in 1991 by High-strain Work in 1981/1991
Among Women Controlling for Age Only (Model 1); Age and Circulatory Illness 1981 (Model 2);
and Age, Circulatory Illness 1981, Smoking 1981, and Smoking 1991 (Model 3).
Odds Ratios and 95% Confidence Intervals. *n* = 1017

	Model 1		Model 2		Model 3	
High Strain 1981/1991	OR	95% CI	OR	95% CI	OR	95% CI
No/No	1	(Ref.)	1	(Ref.)	1	(Ref.)
Yes/No	2.03	(0.74-5.56)	1.90	(0.69-5.27)	2.26	(0.77-6.01)
No/Yes	4.38	(2.25-8.49)	4.39	(2.26-8.53)	4.72	(2.40-9.26)
Yes/Yes	4.10	(1.66-10.13)	3.78	(1.51-9.49)	3.93	(1.53-10.08)

to the fact that smoking, although more common in the Yes/Yes category, have decreased in all groups except among those with improving psychosocial work environment (Yes/No). That means that among the women studied here, the overall percentage smoking have decreased from 23.7 to 19.9% during the studied period. In summary, then, it appears that changes in job demands not matched by increased job decision latitude have increased exposure to high-strain jobs for certain groups of women, and that this deterioration of their psychosocial work environment have had an impact on their circulatory health not mediated by smoking.

DISCUSSION: WOMEN'S WORK AND HEALTH AND THE FUTURE OF THE SCANDINAVIAN WELFARE STATE

In the analyses presented in this chapter we have tried to demonstrate that women in Sweden have experienced both structural changes on the labor market and in many cases increasing demands in their jobs. These changes are closely related to changes in the public sector, called for by the economic crisis following the recent recession. In order to have a better understanding of these changes, the way reproductive work is organized in Sweden must be put in a broader context. It is, in a way, possible to talk about the existence of at least three welfare models in Europe, the Scandinavian, the Continental-Conservative and the Liberal model (Esping-Andersen, 1990).

In the Scandinavian welfare regimes, education, health and care, and different social insurance forms are financed by taxes and distributed via individual rights. The general welfare policy implies that women, irrespective of the husband's income, have the right to unemployment benefits if they lose their job, pensions when they reach retirement age, and sickness insurance when they are sick, all of which are related to their income (Borchorst, 1992). Women are regarded as single individuals in terms of social policy. Nevertheless, a large part of the reproductive work is unpaid and done within families, mostly by women.

Women in countries belonging to the so-called continental welfare regime are conversely dependent on their husbands' work and income to a large extent. Here the family is the basic unit for social policy rather than the single individual. This also leads to the fact that the societal organization of health and care is on another level. The conditions for women's waged labor is not given by the state but should be organized by the family or the single individual (Esping-Andersen, 1990; Schmid, 1991).

A third regime is the liberal and unregulated market regime. British feminists point to the fact that the British government welcomes an increased labor-market participation of women, but at the same time they declare that the state is not responsible for organizing child care or anything else to support women's market participation (Lewis, 1993). This leads to women leaving the labor market when they have small children, which in turn often leads to occupational downgrading as they usually have to take low-status, part-time jobs when they return (Lahelma & Arber, 1994). Also here we find that the preconditions for women's waged labor is set on family basis or by the single individual.

There is a strong relationship between the public sector's share of total employment and women's participation rate in the labor market (Furåker, 1993). In countries belonging to the Scandinavian model where the public sector covers over 25% of the total employment, women have a labor-force participation rate between 70% and 80%. Countries belonging to the liberal regimes are at a middle level, with a participation rate of 60% to 70%, and the lowest level for female participation rate are in continental regime countries. In these countries the female participation rates are between 40% and 60% and the number publicly employed compared to the total number employed is less than 18% (Furåker, 1993).

In his study of women in the public sector in selected European countries, Schmid (1991) showed that the developments are very complex. Women's work in publicly organized services has been more secure and better paid during the stage of expansion. Later developments include an increased share of short-term contracts and increased wage differentials between women's work in private and public employment. At the same time, sex segregation between different professional areas is stronger in the public than in the private sector. The differences between local, regional, and national levels are also considerable (Organization for Economic Cooperation and Development, 1994; Schmid, 1991).

Deregulation, decentralization, and flexibility are all concepts that have had a practical application in the restructuring of the public sector. Cutting public expenditure by decreasing the number of employees has just started in Sweden. The employment in the public sector was stable in terms of number up to and including 1991. About 55% of all employed women in Sweden were in public employment in 1991, 44% were in the "welfare segment," that is, education, health, and care (Furåker, 1993). The following year saw changes begin that are very difficult to analyze. Employment in the public sector decreased by about 30,000 persons in 1992 (Arbetsmarknadsstyrelsen [AMS], 1993). During 1993 and the first half of 1994 some additional 70–75,000 jobs were expected to disappear.

A rough estimate is that the public sector will shrink by a couple of hundred thousand job opportunities during a 5-year period. This equals a decrease of employment in the sector of 15%—and most of the positions that will be cut away are now held by women (Gonäs, Johansson, & Svärd, 1995). In the beginning, restructuring was carried out through the exclusion of temporary staff. In the second stage, permanent employees have been fired. This means that young female workers have lost their jobs; for them a temporary job often has been their entrance to the labor market.

According to a survey by the National Labor Market Board (AMS), two out of three local governments will reduce their child-care staff during the years to come. A study of the cutbacks in Uppsala municipality shows that half of the permanent staff that the city fired 6 months later became re-employed on a temporary basis. At the same time, some 2,000 temporary employees had to leave at the end of their contracts (Svärd, 1993). In effect this means a centrifugal movement from the center to the periphery for the workers. Temporary employees lost their jobs, permanent employees got temporary jobs.

However, not only the employment status per se is important. As shown in our analyses of women's psychosocial working conditions, changing demands from work itself can have an immediate impact on women's health. Although changes in the public sector have been greater after 1991, the restructuring of, for example, health care had already started during the 1980s. This led to a heavier workload due to fewer "easy" patients, and many patients in need of more care due to extensive functional limitations, often in wards where equipment and facilities are not designed for such patients (Thorslund, 1988; Thorslund & Parker, 1994). When such changes in job demands have not been paralleled by an increase in the possibilities for lower and medium-level employees to decide how to perform their work, it appears that increasing demands have induced negative stress, which in turn have increased circulatory illness.

It is obvious today that the double dependence between women and the state in the Scandinavian regime increases women's vulnerability in times when the state is cutting back on services. It also means that the labor market for women is reduced. Therefore, women will have to meet cutbacks on both sides, both as worker and consumer. With accelerating restructuring of the organization of public service, an increasing number of old people that to a larger extent have to be cared for by their family, and a constantly high level of unemployment, women's health is likely to be threatened in more ways than one.

REFERENCES

Arbetsmarknadsstyrelsen. (1993). *Rapport från utredningsenheten 93:2.* Stockholm: Author.

Arber, S., & Lahelma, E. (1993). Inequalities in women's and men's ill-health: Britain and Finland compared. *Social Science & Medicine, 37,* 1055–1068.

Borchorst, A. (1992). Europeisk integration, könsarbejdsdeling og ligestillingspolitik. In B. Eneroth & I. Michaeli (Eds.), *Kvinnornas välfärdsstat? Nordiska kvinnoforskare diskuterar.* Gävle, Sweden: Statens institut för byggnadsforskning.

Charles, M. (1992). Cross-national variation in occupational sex segregation. *American Sociological Review, 57,* 483–502.

Erikson, R., & Åberg, R. (1987). *Welfare in transition. A survey of living conditions in Sweden 1968–1981.* Oxford, England: Clarendon.

Esping-Andersen, G. (1990). *The three worlds of welfare capitalism.* Cambridge, England: Polity Press.

Fritzell, J., & Lundberg, O. (1993). *Ett förlorat eller förlovat årtionde? Välfärdsutvecklingen mellan 1981 och 1991.* Stockholm: Institutet för social forskning.

Fritzell, J., & Lundberg, O. (1994a). Kvinnor, män och välfärdens utveckling. In *Har vi råd att avvara välfärden? Försäkringskasseförbundets FAKTA* (pp. 17–35). Stockholm: Försäkringskasseförbundet.

Fritzell, J., & Lundberg, O. (1994b). Välfärdsförändringar 1968–1991. In J. Fritzell & O. Lundberg (Eds.), *Vardagens villkor. Levnadsförhållanden i Sverige under tre decennier* (pp. 235–259). Stockholm: Brombergs.

Furåker, B. (1993). Vad händer med kvinnornas arbete när den offentliga sektorn bantas? In *Kvinnors arbetsmarknad. 1990-talet- återtågets årtionde?* Ds 1993:8. Stockholm: Arbetsmarknadsdepartementet.

Gonäs, L. (1991). *Industriomvandling i välfärdsstaten.* Stockholm: Arbetslivscentrum.

Gonäs, L., Johansson, S., & Svärd, I. (1995). *Vad händer med kvinnors arbete när den offentliga sektorn skär ner?* (Working paper). Stockholm: Arbetslivscentrum.

Jonung, C., & Persson, I. (1990). Hushållsproduktion, marknadsproduktion och jämställdhet. In *Kvinnors roll i ekonomin. Bilaga 23 till LU90.* Stockholm: Allmänna förlaget.

Karasek, R. (1979). Job demands, job decision latitude, and mental strain: Implications for job redesign. *Administrative Science Quarterly, 24,* 285–308.

Karasek, R., & Theorell, T. (1990). *Healthy work. Stress, productivity and the reconstruction of working life.* New York: Basic Books.

le Grand, C. (1994). Löneskillnaderna i Sverige: Förändring och nuvarande struktur. In J. Fritzell & O. Lundberg (Eds.), *Vardagens villkor. Levnadsförhållanden i Sverige under tre decennier* (pp. 117–160). Stockholm: Brombergs.

Lahelma, E., & Arber, S. (1994). Health inequalities among men and women in contrasting welfare states. Britain and three Nordic countries compared. *European Journal of Public Health, 4,* 213–226.

Lewis, J. (Ed.). (1993). *Women and social policies in Europe. Work, family and the state.* Aldershot, England: E E Publishing.

Nermo, M. (1994). Den ofullbordade jämställdheten. In J. Fritzell & O. Lundberg (Eds.), *Vardagens villkor. Levnadsförhållanden i Sverige under tre decennier* (pp. 161–183). Stockholm: Brombergs.

Organization for Economic Cooperation and Development. (1994). *Women and structural change.* Paris: Author.

Statistiska Centralbyrån. (1990). *Arbetskraftsundersökningarna.* Stockholm: Author.

Statistiska Centralbyrån. (1991). *Kvinnors och mäns arbetsmiljö.* IAM 1991:1. Stockholm: Author.

Statistiska Centralbyrån. (1993). *Arbetskraftsundersökningarna.* Stockholm: Author.

Schmid, G. (1991). *Women in the public sector.* Paris: Organization for Economic Cooperation and Development.

Svärd, I. (1993). *Omstrukturering i offentlig sektor. Uppsala kommun—ett lokalt exempel* (working paper). Uppsala, Sweden: Kulturgeografiska Institutionen.

Szulkin, R., & Tåhlin, M. (1994). Arbetets utveckling. In J. Fritzell & O. Lundberg (Eds.), *Vardagens villkor. Levnadsförhållanden i Sverige under tre decennier* (pp. 87–116). Stockholm: Brombergs.

Thorslund, M. (1988). The de-institutionalization of care of the elderly: Some notes about the implementation and outcome of a Swedish case-study. *Health Policy, 10,* 44–56.

Thorslund, M., & Parker, M. G. (1994). Care of the elderly in the changing Swedish welfare state. In D. Challis, B. Davis, & K. Traske (Eds.), *Community care: New agendas and challenges from the UK and overseas* (pp. 249–263). Kent: University of Kent, British Society of Gerontology.

6

Women, Work, and Mortality: An Analysis of Female Labor Participation

Denny Vågerö
Stockholm University

Eero Lahelma
University of Helsinki

The employment rate of Scandinavian women is about twice the average rate of that in the European Union (EU). Among Swedish women aged 55 to 64, two thirds are still working, as compared to one fourth in the non-Scandinavian EU countries. The present chapter asks, What are the health consequences for women of their labor-market participation? New data and interpretations of the relation between female work and health are presented in this study of 350,000 Swedish women who were housewives in 1970, the effects on mortality of entering the labor market are analyzed. It is suggested that entering the labor market is linked to improved survival chances and reduced mortality in general. In particular, ischaemic heart disease mortality was low among women taking up employment compared to those who remained housewives. The possibility that this is due to selection into the workforce of the most healthy women is discussed. It is suggested that health selection contributes to the better survival chances of women in the labor force, but at the same time that most of the excess mortality of housewives is not due to such selection. The high labor-market participation of Swedish women is therefore likely to have contributed to their falling mortality rates.

WOMEN'S LABOR-MARKET PARTICIPATION

Welfare states are not only characterized by extensive social-security systems, but also by a high degree of labor-market participation (Esping-Andersen, 1990). The "Scandinavian Model" (Esping-Andersen & Korpi, 1987)

73

of the welfare state has contributed to women's economic independence through tax-financed institutional support for their labor-market participation, such as publicly run day care for children and relatively generous parental leave systems. Social policies in the Nordic countries have enabled women to combine motherhood and paid employment, and have influenced men's views on female employment. Being a housewife is much more common in Britain, for example, than in the Nordic countries (Arber & Gilbert, 1992; Esping-Andersen, 1990; Joshi & Davies, 1992).

However, there are also differences between the Nordic countries, with women in Sweden having the highest labor-market participation. A substantial number of employed women in Sweden hold part-time jobs (normally 20 hours or more per week) or work flextime. Part-time jobs are comparable to full-time jobs in that they offer employment security and qualify for employment-related social rights, such as pensions (Esping-Andersen, 1990). This is not necessarily the case outside the Nordic countries. A high proportion of Nordic women are employed in the public sector.

In Finland, women's labor-market participation level is similar to that in Sweden. The main difference is that almost all Finnish women hold full-time jobs and only very few women take part-time employment. There are no substantial differences in the proportion of women working part time by age or stage of the life course. Thus Finnish women's labor-market participation pattern is broadly similar to that of Finnish men.

In Norway, women's employment pattern differs from that of Sweden and Finland in that full-time employment is more strongly age related: The proportion of women employed full-time in Norway is low except for those under the age of 25. Therefore, Norway has a large proportion of part-time employed women.

Despite the differences between Finland, Norway, and Sweden with regard to women's labor-market participation there are many common features. The "Scandinavian Model" differs from that of most other countries: Women's total labor-market participation is high (see Table 6.1), and even part-time jobs offer comparable status to full-time jobs. Additionally, it has been observed that small children in the family do not prevent women from returning to their jobs after childbearing and do not radically disrupt their work careers. For example, in Finland whether there are small children in the family makes little difference in regard to women's full-time employment (Lahelma & Arber, 1994). The "Scandinavian Model" has offered women opportunities for employment outside the family and thus economic independence; at the same time the Nordic welfare states have been highly dependent on women's employment in the public sector. It was clear to us that the unique experience of a very high female labor participation, and the context of a women-friendly welfare state, ought also to be evaluated from a public health point of view. How, then, has it affected women's health?

TABLE 6.1
Proportion of All Women (%) Who Were Economically Active* By Age Groups, in Scandinavia
and in Non-Scandinavian EU Countries

Age	25–49	50–54	55–59	60–64
Australia[b]	67	55	24	5
Belgium[a]	57	27	16	4
France[a]	65	56	38	13
Germany[a] **	59	49	35	10
Greece[a]	49	38	30	13
Ireland[a]	38	24	19	12
Italy[a]	49	31	19	12
Luxembourg[a]	50	25	17	8
Netherlands[a]	51	35	21	8
Portugal[a]	66	47	38	23
Spain[a]	37	25	17	8
United Kingdom[a]	68	64	51	22
12 EU countries	**55**	**40**	**27**	**12**
Denmark[a]	81	72	54	24
Finland[c]	84	83	58	19
Norway[b]		74	63	46
Sweden[d]	91	89	80	51

*The definition of economic activity varies somewhat between countries and sources. Hence
comparisons of figures in the table should be done with care.
**Former BRD
Sources:
[a]Eurostat Labour Force Survey (1989), Eurostat, Brussels (1991).
[b]Year book of Labour Statistics (1993), International Labour Organisation (ILO), Geneva (1993).
[c]Labour Force Survey, Statistics (Finnish Statistical Bureau), Helsinki, Finland (1991).
[d]Swedish AKU-Survey (1988). Annual averages, Swedish Labour Ministry and Swedish Statistical
Bureau, Stockholm (1990).

HEALTH EFFECTS

The present study was inspired by two strands of new research. First, there
was the study by Axelsson (1992), which examined the generations of Swedish women who took up paid work on a massive scale during the 1970s. Part
of her study examined the health changes associated with taking up employment as opposed to remaining a housewife. Axelsson reported that
psychological health and sense of well-being was improved and general
fatigue was reduced among women who took up paid work compared to
those who remained housewives.

Second, there was the thorough survey of health risks associated with
work that was undertaken by the Swedish Commission on Working Conditions (1990), which directed attention, in particular, to health hazards suffered by women workers. Although the main finding of the first study was
that female labor participation was associated with better health, the second
highlighted the occupational health risks associated with different types of
female employment.

A large body of literature on unemployment and health suggests that employment is in fact beneficial for health (see, for instance, Lahelma & Arber, 1994) or is beneficial for survival because most studies are based on mortality (see Stefansson, 1991; Valkonen & Martikainen, 1995). They are also normally studies of men. An exception is the study by Reviere and Eberstein (1992), who reported increased risk of heart disease among women who lost their job. The main problem in the interpretation of studies on unemployment and health is whether or not the better health of those employed is a result of selection of the most unhealthy workers out of the workforce. However, although the relative contribution of health selection out of the workforce and the detrimental effects of unemployment are not satisfactorily understood, there is a certain consensus that unemployment (among men) is associated with impaired psychological health, and perhaps with mortality. Valkonen and Martikainen (1995), for instance, estimated that in a Finnish male cohort aged 30 to 54 something like 8% of all deaths, and 5% of circulatory deaths, could be attributable to the experience of unemployment.

The related problem of whether or not, for women and for men, taking up employment is associated with health benefits is much less studied (but see Weatherhall, Joshi, & Macran, 1994). Pampel and Zimmer (1989), from their comparison of mortality rates and female labor-participation rates in 18 developed countries from 1950 to 1980, concluded that increased female labor participation was indeed linked to increased female survival advantage. Studies based on data on mortality and employment status for the same individual women are rare. Martikainen's (1995) recent study is one of those; it reports survival advantage for employed women as compared to housewives, controlling for a number of potentially confounding factors.

A massive influx of women to the Swedish labor market took place during the 1960s and 1970s. In the mid 1960s, among married women, the proportion of housewives was approximately the same as the proportion of gainfully employed women. Axelsson (1992), who studied the flow of married women in and out of the labor market, found that among married women born between 1917 and 1948, 47% were housewives in 1968. In 1974, the proportion was 29% and in 1981, 18%. Nearly every second woman changed employment status in this 13-year period. It seems, therefore, that Sweden provides a "natural experiment," in that, earlier than in most other developed countries, Swedish women took up paid employment on a massive scale.

During this same period Swedish female life expectancy improved; much more so than did male life expectancy. In comparing mortality in the 1961 to 1965 period and the 1981 to 1985 period, it was shown that female mortality levels fell with about one third, whereas male mortality levels fell less, only about one fifth (Vågerö & Lundberg, 1995). Over the 25-year period starting in the years 1951 to 1955, improvements in life expectancy due to improved survival at working ages (20 to 64 years) amounted to 1.4 years for women and a mere 0.2 years for men. In many other countries during the postwar period, female mortality, unlike male mortality, fell steadily with rising female labor-participation rates.

The period of increased female labor participation in Sweden, and elsewhere, thus coincides with a period of increased female survival advantage. One could therefore formulate the hypothesis that female labor participation is associated with survival advantages for women, through benefits for female health. Here, we would like to test the hypothesis that Swedish women's labor participation as such is, on average, beneficial for their survival.

POPULATION UNDER STUDY, METHODS OF ANALYSIS

This study was based on the Swedish Multiple Census-Linked Deaths Registry (MCDR), a database that contains individual information from several succesive censuses linked to cause-of-death registrations. Linking was possible on the basis of the national 10-digit personal identity number, used compulsorily in both cause-of-death registrations and censuses. The MCDR is considered to be virtually complete. (A more detailed description of this database is to be found in Vågerö & Lundberg, 1995).

All women enumerated in the 1970 and 1980 censuses, who were born between 1921 and 1950, and were married and classified as nonemployed at the first census, were included in a first step. This population consisted of 450,500 women. The 1980, but not the 1970, census allowed a classification of nonemployed women as "homeworkers" and "other nonemployed." Only the first category was included, as the second group was likely to include disabled and institutionalized women. By excluding the second group, the larger part of those women who were disabled or institutionalized already at the 1970 census would have been excluded.

At the 1980 census, women who worked at least 35 hours a week (full time) or at least 20 hours a week (long part time) were classified as employed. Women working shorter hours, or who were students or for whom no information was available on their 1980 employment status, were not included, as they would obscure the comparison of housewives and employed women. Therefore the study population consisted of a total of 352,900 women (see Table 6.2).

This population was followed up from the census date, October 1980, to the end of 1986, with regard to mortality. There were 4,919 deaths during the period, 1,062 of which were cardiovascular deaths. Deaths were classified according to the international classification of diseases, eighth revision

TABLE 6.2
Swedish Women Born 1921–1950 Who Were Housewives in 1970 by Employment Status in 1980.
Mortality Follow-up 1981–1986

	N	Deaths
Housewives	106,100	2,267
Part time	135,775	1,509
Full time	111,025	1,143
All	352,900	4,919

(ICD-8). Age-standardized death rates were calculated for ischaemic heart disease (ICD 410-414), and cardiovascular disease in general (ICD 390-458), for lung (ICD 162-163) and breast (ICD-174) cancer, and for cancer in general (ICD 140-209), as well as for total mortality disregarding the cause of death.

Age standardization was direct, so that death rates could be compared directly across classes and between tables. Weights corresponding to the Swedish population age structure in 1983 were applied. Death rates reported in Table 6.3 (in the three columns to the right) are based on the cumulative proportion of deaths occurring during the 1980 to 1986 period. In Fig. 6.1 *relative death rates* (RR) are reported; that is, the death rate is expressed as an index, which is set to 1.00 for the reference group (which here means full-time employed women). A relative death rate of 1.46 for housewives (as in Fig. 6.1, first column) thus means that the mortality in this group would be 46% higher than in the reference group, if the age distribution in both groups were identical.

Table 6.4 reports the proportion of women reporting psychological health problems, circulatory problems, and smoking in 1970 by their employment status in 1980. These proportions are estimated from the Swedish Level of Living Survey, in effect replicating Axelsson's study using the same data source, but this time including circulatory problems and smoking as well as psychological problems. The data source constitutes a random sample of

TABLE 6.3
Housewives 1970. Cumulative Mortality 1981-1986 by Type of Employment 1980

	Population n	Deaths n	All Causes	Cardio-vascular	Cancer
Higher/intermed. nonmanual	30,825	230	0.93	0.19	0.57
Lower nonmanual	56,650	558	1.08	0.19	0.64
Skilled manual	15,775	125	0.94	0.14	0.57
Nonskilled manual	116,875	1,377	1.19	0.27	0.67
Self-employed	25,050	331	1.22	0.24	0.73
Housewives	106,100	2,267	1.62	0.36	0.85

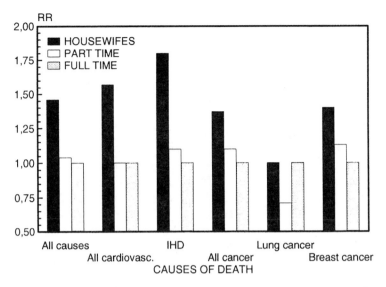

REFERENCE GROUP = FULL TIME EMPLOYED (RR = 1)

FIG. 6.1. Mortality 1981–1986 of Swedish women born 1921–1950 who were housewives in 1970 by employment status 1980.

Swedes, interviewed in 1968 and 1981 (Axelsson, 1992; Erikson & Åberg, 1987). Axelsson analyzed the health status of the housewife generation (in 1968) before they entered the labor market by their employment status in 1981. The group of women classified as housewives in 1970 and born between 1921 and 1950 in our study is nearly identical to the group of women classified as housewives in 1968 and born between 1917 and 1948 in Axelsson's study. The sampling frame of the Level of Living Survey of 1968 corresponds closely to the 1970 census, the birth cohorts included in each study overlaps almost completely and, importantly, the age distribution is virtually identical. In other words, Axelsson's sample is close to a sample

TABLE 6.4
Psychologial Health, Circulatory Problems, and Smoking. Estimated proportions prior to Labor-Market Entry by Employment Status 1970/1980

	Psych %	Psych+Circ %	Smoke %
Housewife/1970 Housewife/1980	39	26	24
Housewife/1970 Employed,1980	33	18	43

of the 1970 census population analyzed here. The classification into "permanent" housewives and women who became employed, and the time period over which labor-market entry took place, are also very nearly identical. It seems therefore justified to apply the proportions reporting psychological health problems, circulatory problems, and smoking from the Level of Living Survey of 1968 as the best available estimates for the corresponding groups in the 1970 census population.

Psychological health problems were defined from the answers to questions on whether or not one suffered from "general fatigue," sleeping disturbances, nervousness, and depression. Each item was dichotomized and the answers constitute an index, in the form of a scale. Johansson (1971) found this to approximate a scale obtained by the Guttman technique (Stouffer, 1950). The index is so dichotomized that those reporting no problems form one class and the others another class. The index of circulatory problems was in a similar fashion based on questions—whether or not one suffered from such problems as chest pain or high blood pressure—with those reporting at least one problem forming one class. Those who reported to be a smoker at the time of the interview were classified as smokers.

RESULTS

Table 6.3 demonstrates that those women who remained housewives between 1970 and 1980 had a higher mortality than those who took up work during this period. This was the case with regard to all cause mortality, as well as for cancer and cardiovascular disease. It seems to be the case that whatever type of employment (occupational class) the women moved into, they were always at an advantage compared to the housewife group. Figure 6.1 shows in more detail how housewifes, part-time employed women, and full-time employed women differ in mortality. Unexpectedly, the greatest difference (in relative terms) was found for cardiovascular disease. Housewives suffer a more than 50% excess mortality in cardiovascular disease, compared to employed women. For ischaemic heart disease there is an 80% excess mortality for housewives. There is no excess risk of lung cancer, but breast cancer mortality is elevated among housewives.

Table 6.4 gives the best estimate for the index of self-reported psychological health, for circulatory problems and for smoking prevalence as described earlier. It suggests, clearly, that women entering the labor force in the 1970s were a selected group of healthy women before this entry; this is in spite of their higher smoking rate. For instance, 26% of those who remained housewives, as opposed to 18% of the others, reported symtoms of both psychological and circulatory health problems. Thus the process of labor-market entry seems to select healthy women, but it also selects smok-

TABLE 6.5
Mortality of Housewives Compared to Employed Women. Estimated Excess Mortality Under
Modest, Strong, and Extreme Health Selection, Taking Psychological Problems, Circulatory
Problems, and Smoking Into Account

	Taking Into Account		
If Health Selection is	Psych	Psych+Circ	Psych + Circ + Smoking
Modest[a]	1.06	1.13	0.96
Strong[b]	1.09	1.21	0.92
Extreme[c]	1.15	1.37	0.79

Note. Observed excess mortality for housewives is 1.46; index for employed women (part or full time) equals 1.00.
[a]Death risk for those reporting each problem assumed to be twofold.
[b]Death risk for those reporting each problem assumed to be threefold.
[c]Death risk for those reporting each problem assumed to be tenfold.

ing women more often than nonsmoking women. Both these (contradictory) aspects are important in assessing the effect on health of labor-market participation.

In Table 6.5 we try to assess the potential contribution of selection when explaining the observed excess mortality of housewives. Selection is assumed to be modest, strong, or extreme, corresponding to assumptions of modest, strong, or extreme excess risks for those who report psychological problems, circulatory problems, or smoking. The table gives the expected mortality for the group of women who were housewives both 1970 and 1980 under each of these three assumptions. First (modest selection), it was assumed that women reporting symptoms of psychological ill health carried a twofold mortality risk compared to those not reporting such symptoms. Identical assumptions were made for those reporting circulatory problems and smoking. Carrying all three problems then corresponded to an 2 × 2 × 2-fold mortality risk. Second (strong selection), it was assumed that this mortality risk was threefold for each reported problem. Third (extreme selection), that it was tenfold. Under the extreme selection hypothesis someone who reported both circulatory and psychological health problems thus carried a hundredfold excess risk. If this person also reported to be a smoker, he was assumed to carry a thousandfold excess risk. It is enough, here, to point out that the latter estimates are indeed very extreme. The justification for the more moderate estimates is discussed later.

Taking only psychological and circulatory problems into account (disregarding smoking information), the expected excess mortality for housewives under these three assumptions were calculated to be 1.13, 1.21, or 1.37,

respectively. In other words, even with very extreme assumptions and ig-
noring the smoking information, health selection seems unable to explain
the observed excess mortality of housewifes with regard to total mortality
(RR = 1.46) and certainly with regard to ischaemic heart disease (RR = 1.80).
The latter is reinforced by the observation (Table 6.5, column 3) that when
we do take smoking habits before labor-market entry into account, we do
not expect any excess risk at all among housewives.

DISCUSSION

The cardinal issue in interpreting these results is whether or not they merely
reflect selection into the workforce of those women who had the best health
already before labor-market entry. There can be no doubt that such a
selection effect exists. The "healthy-worker effect" is well known in studies
of occupational cohorts (Vågerö & Olin, 1985). Is the issue of selection
adequately addressed by the "thought experiment" reported in Table 6.5?

     This is dependent, first, on how realistic the assumptions outlined earlier
are. For instance: Are self-reported psychological health problems associated with a twofold, a threefold, a tenfold, or an even greater mortality risk?
Welin et al. (1985) reported from a 9-year follow-up of 989 men. Self-perceived
health problems at the start of the study was a significant predictor for
mortality during the following 9 years. The excess risk associated with those
reporting the highest scores (5 to 7) on perceived health problems is not
given in the text but can be calculated from one of the graphs to be about
twofold. In another study including 12,774 women followed up for 9 years,
Östlin (1990) found that women reporting long-term illness at the beginning
of the follow-up had a 2.1-fold excess mortality compared to those not
reporting such illness. On the basis of these two studies it would be prudent
to suggest that self-reported health problems could be linked to something
like a twofold, or perhaps even a threefold, excess mortality, but hardly to
a tenfold excess mortality. If psychological and circulatory problems represented independent risks, which is unlikely, their combined effect could be
estimated to be 2×2, or perhaps even 3×3, giving rise to an excess mortality
of housewifes of the magnitude 1.1 to 1.2, in our study population (Table
6.5, column 2). Smoking patterns, on the other hand, would counteract this
particular selection effect, because they represent an influence in the opposite direction, leading us to expect a higher mortality among employed
women.

     Second, we could also ask if those differences in health status reported
before labor-market entry are sufficently detailed to exhaust the possibility
of selection effects. In particular, does the group of "permanent" housewives
include a number of severely ill, perhaps institutionalized women? There is

no way of giving a definitive answer to this question, because the 1970 census does not allow such detailed information. We could, however, look at the group of women classifed as other (than "homeworking") nonemployed women by the 1980 census. It constitutes about 30,000 women, that is, 6% to 7% of the total cohort of nonemployed women in 1970. This group may consist of an unusually large proportion of women with health problems. Its mortality in the follow-up period was about five times higher than that of employed women. Because this group was in fact excluded from the group defined as permanent housewives, it is unlikely that the mortality estimates of the latter group are severely biased. Nevertheless, we cannot exclude the possibility that some unobserved health-selection effect exists, but it is likely to be small.

The inevitable conclusion, therefore, is this: Health selection is unlikely to explain the observed excess mortality among housewives. It is also unlikely to explain the pattern of mortality by cause of death, which indicated that in particular ischaemic heart disease mortality is linked to the role of housewife.

The focus in this chapter has been an effort to exclude the possibility that our results are due to selection. The possible causal mechanisms that differentiate mortality of employed women from that of housewives will be the object of a further study. The literature on roles suggest that increasing the number of roles may be linked to ill health, through "role strain," or to good health through "role enhancement." Moen, Dempster-McClain, and Williams (1992) in their work supported the latter position, arguing that multiple roles and social integration are linked to health improvement. One could argue that employment is not just another role, on a par with churchgoing or membership in an association, but of a more fundamental nature. Nevertheless, it would represent both social integration and role enhancement, and thus these aspects could be mediating mechanisms. Martikainen (1995), who studied mortality among Finnish women, concluded that both motherhood and employment were associated with reduced mortality, but at the same time dismissed the role-accumulation hypothesis, because the combination of motherhood and employment had little significance.

There is a variety of suggestions in the literature for a causal relation between female employment and survival—for instance, the identification of salutogenic or protective factors, such as social networks (Orth-Gomér & Johnson, 1987), falling fertility rates (Beral, 1985) and behavioral factors (Hart, 1989). An important question may be what it is that distinguishes women who stayed housewives from those taking up employment, in a more fundamental sense—in particular, whether or not staying at home represents a choice, and hence a different orientation of life goals, or was seen by those women as a constraint imposed on them. Axelsson (1992) concluded that female labor participation was indeed beneficial for those aspects of health that she looked at, that is, psychological health and well-being. All aspects of health were not, however, improved. There was a tendency to increased consumption of painkillers among those women who took up paid work. A possible explanation for this latter finding is suggested by the increased number of women that during this period reported locomotor problems, such as pains in the extremities, back, and neck. The underlying causes are not totally known, but it would be quite logical that women taking up work in physically demanding jobs or jobs characterized by repetitive movements would be more at risk than other women. The previously mentioned survey of health risks associated with work, concluded that musculoskeletal problems were indeed closely linked to certain types of work common among women, such as low-level manufacturing work of a routine type (Swedish Commission on Working Conditions, 1990). If female labor participation has had negative effects on women's health, it is likely to be in this area. As the relation between such problems and mortality is modest, they are unlikely to influence average female survival chances strongly, and seem to be offset by improved cardiovascular function, in particular. Therefore, the best answer to the question of whether female labor participation has contributed to their improved survival is affirmative.

Finally, we considered whether the particular features of female labor participation in Sweden make generalizations to other populations problematic. Hoem (1993) has discussed how Swedish public policy and legislation, by enabling for mothers to participate in the labor market, may have contributed to the recent baby boom in Sweden, an atypical phenomenon in the Western world. If working life and parenthood were differently related in Sweden compared to other countries, the results reported here may not be generally true. However, because our finding is supported by other studies on longitudinal data, such as that of Weatherhall, Joshi, and Macran (1994), it is unlikely that any beneficial effect of employment is restricted to any particular group of countries.

REFERENCES

Arber, S., & Gilbert, N. (1992). Re-assessing women's working lives. In S. Arber & N. Gilbert (Eds.), *Women and working lives: Divisions and change* (pp. 1–13). London: Basingstoke.

Axelsson, C. (1992). *Hemmafrun som försvann* [The disappearing housewife]. Unpublished doctoral thesis, Stockholm University.

Beral, V. (1985). Long term effects of childbearing on health. *Journal of Epidemiology and Community Health, 39,* 343–346.

Erikson, R., & Åberg, R. (Eds.). (1987). *Welfare in transition. A survey of living conditions in Sweden 1968–1981.* Oxford, England: Clarendon.

Esping-Andersen, G. (1990). *Three worlds of welfare capitalism.* Oxford, England: Polity Press.

Esping-Andersen, G., & Korpi, W. (1987). From poor relief to institutional welfare states: The development of Scandinavian social policy. In R. Erikson, E. Hansen, S. Ringen, & H. Usitalo

(Eds.), *The Scandinavian model. Welfare states and welfare research* (pp. 39–74). Armonk, NY: M E Sharpe.

Hart, N. (1989). Sex, gender and survival: Inequalites of life chances between European men and women. In J. Fox (Ed.), *Health inequalities in European countries* (pp. 109–141). Aldershot, England: Gower.

Hoem, J. (1993). Public policy as the fuel of fertility rise. *Acta Sociologica, 36,* 19–31.

Johansson, S. (1971). *Den Vuxna Befolkningens Hälsotillstånd* [Health of the Adult Population in Sweden]. Stockholm: Allmänna Förlaget.

Joshi, H., & Davies, H. (1992). *Child care and mothers' lifetime earnings: Some European comparisons* (Discussion Paper No. 600). London: Centre for Economic Policy Research.

Lahelma, E., & Arber, S. (1994). Health inequalities among men and women in contrasting welfare states: Britain and three Nordic countries compared. *European Journal of Public Health, 4,* 213–226.

Martikainen, P. (1995). Women's employment, marriage, motherhood and mortality: A test of the multiple role and role accumulation hypotheses. *Social Science and Medicine, 40,* 199–212.

Moen, P., Dempster-McClain, D., & Williams, R. (1992). Successful aging: A life course perspective on womens multiple roles. *American Journal of Sociology, 97,* 1612–1638.

Orth-Gomér, K., & Johnson, J. (1987). Social network interaction and mortality: A six-year follow-up of a random sample of the Swedish population. *Journal of Chronic Disease, 40,* 947–957.

Östlin, P. (1990). Occupational history, self reported chronic illness and mortality: A follow up of 25,586 Swedish men and women. *Journal of Epidemiology and Community Health, 44,* 12–16.

Pampel, F., & Zimmer, C. (1989). Female labour force activity and the sex differential in mortality: Comparison across developed nations, 1950–80. *European Journal of Population, 5,* 281–304.

Reviere, R., & Eberstein, J. W. (1992). Work, marital status and heart disease. *Health Care for Women International, 13,* 393–399.

Stefansson, C.-G. (1991). Long term unemployment and mortality in Sweden 1980–86. *Social Science and Medicine, 32,* 419–424.

Stouffer, S. A. (1950). *Measurement and prediction. Studies in social psychology in World War II* (Vol. 4). Princeton, NJ: Princeton University Press.

Swedish Commisssion on Working Conditions. (1990). *A survey of jobs posing special risks to health. The report of the Health Risks Study Group.* Stockholm: Swedish Parliament, Gotab.

Vågerö, D., & Lundberg, O. (1995). Socio-economic mortality differentials among adults in Sweden. In A. Lopez, G. Caselli, & T. Valkonen (Eds.), *Adult mortality in developed countries. From description to explanation* (pp. 223–242). Oxford, England: Oxford University Press.

Vågerö, D., & Olin, R. (1985). How do we analyse a cohort of healthy workers? *Scandinavian Journal of Social Medicine, 13,* 165–167.

Valkonen, T., & Martikainen, P. (1995). Unemployment and mortality. Causation or selection? In A. Lopez, G. Caselli, & T. Valkonen (Eds.), *Adult mortality in developed countries. From description to explanation* (pp. 201–222). Oxford, England: Oxford University Press.

Weatherhall, R., Joshi, H., & Macran, S. (1994). Double burden or double blessing? Employment, motherhood, and mortality in the longitudinal study of England and Wales. *Social Science and Medicine, 38,* 285–297.

Welin, L., Tibblin, G., Svärdsudd, K., Tibblin, B., Ander-Peciva, S., Larsson, B., & Wilhelmsen, L. (1985). Prospective study of social influences on mortality. *The Lancet, 1*(8434), 915–918.

7

Men's Work, Women's Work? Occupational Sex Ratios and Health

Kate Hunt
Carol Emslie
MRC Medical Sociology Unit, Glasgow

In this chapter we review the growing literature from organizational theorists that considers the interrelationships between gender, sexuality, and power in the workplace (and specifically that which focuses on vertical and horizontal segregation by gender). This body of literature has remained largely separate from the literature on gender and *health* to date. We wish to argue that the interrelationship between gender, sexuality, and power may provide useful insights to mechanisms that link men's and women's differential experiences of paid work as at least part of the explanation for gendered patterns of health, including heart disease.

THEORETICAL BACKGROUND

Gender Differences in Health

Over the last 20 years an increasing amount of research has focused on gender differences in health (see Arber, 1989; Bartley, Popay, & Plewis, 1992; Verbrugge, 1989, for recent reviews); here we summarize the main arguments. Although reports of increased susceptibility to various aspects of ill health among women (in the face of higher mortality for men) have been quite consistent, there is less consensus about underlying mechanisms. Although some have suggested that women may appear to be in poorer health because they are more ready to recognize and report symptoms

(Nathanson, 1977), discussion of women's increased susceptibility to ill health (and notably their higher rates of symptom reports and poorer mental health) has often centered on the gendered allocation of social roles. Participation in paid work is one such role that has received a lot of attention in recent years (Arber, 1991; Arber, Gilbert, & Dale, 1985; Bartley et al., 1992; Elliot & Huppert, 1991; Hibbard & Pope, 1985, 1991; Hunt & Annandale, 1993).

As we have argued elsewhere (Hunt & Annandale, 1993), much of the literature on the health correlates and consequences of work has been imbued with a number of gender biases, from the definition of "real" work to assumptions about men's and women's prioritization of roles. There has been a tendency to assume that the content, experience, and conditions of paid work are important for men, whereas the number of roles occupied is important for women (and thus most of the literature on multiple role occupancy, for example, has used only female samples, work by Arber, 1991, Hibbard & Pope, 1991, and Hunt & Annandale, 1993, representing notable exceptions). Such assumptions follow on from the entrenched sexual division of labor, including the sexual division of domestic work that not only underlies and reinforces normative gender-role expectations, but has direct consequences for the structure of paid work in relation to gender.

Gender Segregation of Work

A key characteristic of the labor market is horizontal sex segregation, where jobs are stereotyped as either "male" or "female" (Arber & Gilbert, 1992). Employed women are concentrated within a limited number of occupations, notably service jobs, clerical work, and, among professional jobs, nursing, librarianship, teaching, and social work. These "female" jobs are characterized by relatively low wages and status with limited promotion opportunities; the fact that female-dominated professional jobs are often referred to as the "semiprofessions" (Bradley, 1993) is just one reflection of their devaluation. Women's occupational disadvantage is further compounded by *vertical* sex segregation; even where women have entered "male" jobs, they generally remain at the bottom of the ladder, and within "female" occupations are underrepresented in senior jobs (Arber & Gilbert, 1992). Conversely, although men less often work within "female" jobs (Jacobs, 1993; Kauppinen-Torpainen & Lammi, 1993), where they do they are overrepresented in more senior positions, ascending relatively rapidly on the "glass escalator" (Williams, 1992).

Thus, despite dramatic changes in women's participation in paid work in recent decades, occupational sex segregation remains an enduring feature of the labor market (see, for example, Reskin & Roos, 1990). This is the focus of a growing body of literature (Acker, 1991; Cockburn, 1990; Mills & Tancred, 1992; Reskin, 1991; Savage, 1992; Witz, 1990; Witz, Halford, & Savage, 1994;

Zimmer, 1988) which has sought to problematize and extend conventional organizational theory; in particular, the supposed gender "neutrality" of organizational theory has been criticized. Much of this has followed the influential work of Kanter, although the work of Acker and van Houten (1974) "initiated the process of gendering organisational analysis . . . [but] . . . was buried under the avalanche of masculinist organisational work of the period . . . [for] nearly a decade" (Mills & Tancred, 1992, p. 6).

Kanter's Theories of Tokenism

Kanter (1977b) argued that the "relative numbers of socially and culturally different people in a group . . . [are] . . . critical in shaping interaction dynamics" (p. 965). Following observation of male and female salespersons working for an American company, she developed a framework for conceptualizing the processes that occur between numerical "dominants" and rare "tokens." Theories of tokenism thus explicitly recognize structured imbalances (in this case, gender-based) in the occupational hierarchy and attempt to offer explanations that are situated within the structure of organizations, rather than based solely on individual attributes and experience.

Popularization of the term "token" has been credited to Judith Long Laws (Zimmer, 1988), who pointed out that the marginal position of women academics, although permitting them entrance to academic life, did not confer full participation. However, Kanter (1977a, 1977b) first expanded and formalized the concept. Since her study of a large multinational company (Indsco), the concept has been used to explain how women who work in nontraditional jobs often fail to achieve equality with male colleagues. Kanter noted that the company's attempts to integrate men and women in management ranks met with little success; large numbers of women remained in typically "female" jobs, while those in management did not seem to progress as well as expected. She argued that this was not related to their "femaleness," per se, but to the structural constraints of the positions they occupied. First, their positions lacked power, so women were unable to mobilize resources; second, they lacked opportunity for advancement; finally, and most importantly, women who reached management ranks were surrounded by men, so held token status.

In her analysis of the effect on group interactions of differing proportions of constituent social groups she identified four main group types. Among "uniform" groups (which she described as having a "typological ratio" of 100:0), cultural understandings are taken for granted and implicit among group members. In "skewed" groups (a ratio of up to 85:15) the "dominant" group is able to control the culture of the "token" group, the members of which often being treated as representatives of their category rather than as individuals. In "tilted" groups, characterized by a less extreme distribu-

tion of majority and minority groups (65:35), the minority group is sufficiently large for its members to be treated as individuals rather than as a
social type. Finally, "balanced" groups (60:40 or 50:50) comprise two potential subgroups (Kanter, 1977a, 1977b).

Kanter (1977b) was particularly interested in skewed or token groups
(which she operationalized as those with 15% or fewer of the minority
group). She identified "three perceptual phenomena ... associated with
tokens" (p. 965)—visibility, polarization, and assimilation. Tokens, she argued, are never "just another member," but are a symbol of their ascribed
category (e.g., "woman engineer" or "male nurse") and as such are subject
to greater scrutiny by members of the dominant group (visibility). The
presence of token group members fosters an increased self-consciousness
in the dominant group, who draw boundaries (to preserve their common
culture) that exaggerate the similarities of the dominant group and their
difference from the token group (polarization). Finally, the members of the
token group are attributed stereotypical qualities (assimilation); women
working in Indsco, for example, were ascribed to four gender-specific stereotypes—"mother," "pet," "seductress," and "iron maiden" (Kanter, 1977a,
1977b). Each of these processes operates to the disadvantage of members
of the token group: "Visibility generates performance pressures; polarisation
leads dominants to heighten their group boundaries [and thus to exclude
'tokens']; and assimilation leads to the tokens' role entrapment" (Kanter,
1977b, p. 965).

Kanter's research has been used as a starting point by many theorists
examining women (and, to a lesser extent, men; Williams, 1993) in nontraditional jobs, particularly those entering the professions. Studies of female
tokens have typically shown that women are underrepresented in high-pres-
tige areas, are paid less, and have fewer promotion opportunities than men
(see Bradley, 1989; Game & Pringle, 1983; Patterson & Engelberg, 1978; Savage, 1992). Spencer and Podmore (1987), for example, drew on their studies
of the legal profession and identified a number of factors (including stereotypes about women, the lack of role models and peers, and the fear that
women will lower the prestige of the profession) that they believe create
"discriminatory environments" for women in male-dominated professions;
Alban-Metcalfe and West (1991) described very similar processes for women
managers. Most studies of tokenism have focused more on career paths,
and potential gender-role conflicts than on well-being or health. Yet the
processes that Kanter described of increased visibility, polarization, and
assimilation, as well as the professional isolation and constant frustrations
of being a woman in a "man's" job (see, for example, Alban-Metcalfe & West,
1991) suggest obvious potential links with both mental well-being, the area
of health where gender differences are at their greatest amongst people of
working age (Macintyre, Hunt, & Sweeting, 1996), and with stress in the

workplace. Before looking at limited empirical evidence that compares the magnitude of gender differences between occupational "gender ratio" groups, we first highlight some criticisms that have been made regarding Kanter's theoretical perspective.

Critiques of Kanter's Work

Although Kanter's work was an important starting point, the debate has moved on, and her theories of tokenism have been criticized on a number of counts. First, not all theorists agree with Kanter's (1977b) assertion that increasing the size of a token group will automatically diminish the obstacles they face. Wharton and Baron (1987) found, in contrast to Kanter's assumptions, that men in mixed work settings (which they define as being 20–70% female with low segregation within and between establishments) had lower job-related satisfaction and self-esteem and more job-related depression than either token men or men who worked in male-dominated settings. Second, several critics (Cockburn, 1990; Reskin, 1991; Zimmer, 1988) have claimed that Kanter did not give sufficient recognition to inequalities of power, privilege, and prestige between dominant and token groups. Savage (1992), for example, suggested that the breakthrough of women into high-status occupational positions is little more than cosmetic. He argued that although women have moved into professional and skilled jobs, they have rarely been able to secure positions of managerial authority. The apparently dramatic changes in the gendered division of labor in banking, for example, cannot simply be taken at face value:

> The increasing number of "expert" women in the labour market should not be seen as evidence that women are moving into positions of organisational authority but rather that, as organisations restructure, there is increased room for women to be employed in specialist niches, subordinate to senior management although enjoying a degree of autonomy from direct control. (pp. 146–147)

Perhaps the most important criticism of Kanter's theory is that it is gender-blind (Acker, 1991; Zimmer, 1988). Although her research deals with the situation of female tokens surrounded by a male-dominant group, Kanter (1977b) asserted that her theory can be generalized; any token group faced with blocked opportunities and a lack of power will respond in a similar manner. She stated that, "The concepts identified . . . are also applicable to other kinds of tokens who face similar interaction contexts" (p. 985), although she commented that, "If the token's master status is higher than that of the situational dominants, some of the content of the interaction may change while the dynamics remain the same" (p. 986). In recent years, however, much has been written about how gender and sexuality structure organizations (see, for example, Cockburn, 1990; D. Collinson & Collinson, 1990; Davies, 1992; Feldberg & Glenn, 1979; Hearn & Parkin, 1987; Witz et al., 1994; Witz & Savage, 1992). Witz (1990) has argued that the very notion of a "profession" is in fact a gendered concept, involving class-privileged male actors. Acker (1991) also argued that although jobs and hierarchies as abstract categories are presented as if they have no gender in organizational logic, in fact the concept of "a job" is implicitly a gender concept because it "assumes a particular gendered organisation of domestic life and social production" (p. 170).

Of Kanter's work Acker (1991) stated:

> In posing the argument as structure *or* gender, Kanter also implicitly posits gender as standing outside of structure, and she fails to follow up her own observations about masculinity and organisations.... In contrast to the token woman, White men in woman-dominated workplaces are likely to be positively evaluated and to be rapidly promoted to positions of greater authority. The specificity of male dominance is absent. (p. 164)

Other feminists echo these criticisms: "Curiously absent is any sense that men and women are locked, indeed formed, in an unequal gender order.... In truth ... the societal gender order and society-wide systems of racial domination penetrate the workplace" (Cockburn, 1990, p. 86).

Such arguments suggest differential consequences of being a male token in a female environment. Fewer studies have looked at men in "female" jobs (Bradley, 1993, although see Williams, 1993), and the majority have focused on nursing, perhaps because of the contrast between the markedly female construction of nursing and the dominant construction of masculinity (Morgan, 1992). Segal (1962) found, in line with what Kanter might have expected, that the prestige and self-esteem of male nurses suffered because of the conflict between their high status as males and the low, female, status of nursing. In contrast, most studies have found that being a token in a highly skewed occupation has very different outcomes for men and women (Floge & Merrill, 1986; Grimm & Stern, 1974; Williams, 1992). Williams studied men in the four professional jobs where women predominate—nursing, teaching, librarianship, and social work—and found that many male tokens saw their gender as an advantage. They described being "tracked" into areas in the profession that were considered more "legitimate" for men, and that were often more prestigious. Williams suggested that rather than the invisible "glass ceiling," which constrains female tokens, a "glass escalator" operates for male tokens, moving them upward in their professions. She concluded that the effects of sexism outweigh the effects of tokenism. However, the work that has been done on men in "female" jobs suggests penalties for men as well (and, given the lower social and financial value placed on "women's" work, the gains are less obvious). First, the wage differential between "men's" and "women's" work is sufficiently great that even the tendency to rise to the "top" of female jobs may not offset the financial penalty for men of working in a female profession (England & Herbert, 1993). Second, although a number of different masculinities are associated with (and happily tolerated for) men working in gender-typical manual, professional, or managerial jobs (Morgan, 1992), for men in gender-atypical jobs masculinity becomes overtly problematic (see, for example, Allan, 1993; Pringle, 1993). It is perhaps easier (in this way at least) for women to push into men's jobs than vice versa: "Compromised femininity is still a possible female identity. . . . The threat to masculinity in entering a women's area is much greater because of the greater visibility and stigmatisation of male homosexuality" (Bradley, 1993, p. 14).

Hence contemporary work in the sociology of organizations has exposed the fallacy of organizations as being gender-neutral. As Witz et al. (1994) have recently stated:

> We are now rapidly moving beyond a situation where "organisation theorists were not particularly interested in gender, and feminist writers had little interest in organisations . . ." (Witz & Savage, 1992) to one where the internal dynamics of workplace organisations are being scrutinised far more closely as sites where male power is institutionalised. (p. 1)

"TOKENISM" AND GENDER DIFFERENCES IN HEALTH

What we wish to suggest here is that this literature could be more actively drawn into theorizations of the role of paid work in the generation and maintenance of gender differences in various aspects of health; it may be of particular relevance in relation to work stress and health. Although much work has focused on gender as a barrier to access to different occupations, it is relatively recently that the consequences of the proportion of men and women at different levels of the occupational structure have been studied, and even more recently that the gendered nature of jobs and organizations per se has been made so explicit (Acker, 1991; Cockburn, 1990; Witz et al., 1994; Witz & Savage, 1992). The fundamental role of gender and sexuality within the workplace has been highlighted, particularly in the work of Acker (1991), Cockburn (1990), and Witz and Savage (Savage, 1992; Witz, 1990; Witz et al., 1994; Witz & Savage, 1992), challenging "received wisdoms of organisations as gender-neutral" (Witz et al., 1994, p. 1). As Acker (1991) has said:

> The abstract, bodiless worker, who occupies the abstract, gender-neutral job has no sexuality, emotions, and does not procreate. . . . The abstract worker

is actually a man, and it is the man's body, its sexuality, minimal responsibility in procreation, and conventional control of emotions that pervades work and organisational processes. Women's bodies ... are suspect, stigmatised, and used as grounds for control and exclusion. (pp. 172–173)

The ways in which these processes of stigmatization, control, and exclusion are enacted are many and various, including occupational closure (Witz, 1990), the restriction of knowledge and opportunities through differential mentoring by gender (see, for example, Carter, 1994a, 1994b), and sexual harassment (see, for example, M. Collinson & Collinson, 1994). That these could combine to provide a uniquely stressing work environment is obvious. These recent developments have yet to be drawn into much of the literature on the relationship between *health* and gender and work. Although psychosocial mechanisms are often (more or less explicitly) invoked, to our knowledge, systematic comparisons of aspects of health that could plausibly result from these particular stresses have not been made. Attention has focused on self-esteem and work-related variables.

Taking mental health and general current health as examples, extrapolating from Kanter's original speculations, one might expect to see the lowest gender differences in mental health and current minor symptomatology among the occupations with the more equal proportions of men and women. All other things being equal, men in male token and women in female token environments should fare worst, as it is here that they are most "exposed." However, as indicated earlier, it is unlikely, in a society that places higher value on activities, values, and attitudes which are deemed to be "male" (both within and outside of the realm of paid work), that being a man in a "woman's" world should be the mirror image of being a woman in a "man's" world. Consequently, we might hypothesize that occupational gender ratios might not show the same relationship to the mental or other well-being of women and men. In the following we present an analysis that is in no way intended to be definitive, but rather aims to justify our contention that these hypotheses and current work in organizational theory warrant further attention in the health-related social sciences and public health.

Some Empirical Evidence

Here we present some data that derive from interviews with a random community sample of 40-year-olds, who represent the middle cohort of the Twenty-07 Study, a longitudinal study of social patterning of health that began in 1987 (Macintyre et al., 1989). The study is based in the Central Clydeside Conurbation, a predominantly urban area centered on Glasgow in Strathclyde Region in the West of Scotland. Sampling was conducted using a two-stage stratified random cluster sample design (see Ecob, 1987, for more details). This analysis uses data from the 1991 interviews (which were completed by 852 respondents) and is confined to those in paid work for at least 10 hours per week at the time of the interview ($n = 670$). Each job was allocated to an occupational "gender ratio" group in the following manner. Each occupation was first allocated an Office of Population Censuses and Surveys (OPCS) Key Occupations for Statistical Purposes (KOS) code; these were then grouped into the 17 occupational group "Orders" outlined in Britain's Registrar General's (RG) 1980 Classification of Occupations (OPCS, 1980). Following Kanter (1977b), these Orders were then assigned to an occupational "gender ratio" group according to the gender distribution within each Order using data from the 1991 Census for Strathclyde Region in West Scotland (General Register Office for Scotland, 1993, table 98). Those with 20% or fewer women were classified as *female token* occupations; 21–40% women as *female minority*; 41–60% women as *balanced*; 61–80% women as *male minority*; and 81% or more women as *male token*.

Occupational Orders represented by fewer than 15 respondents were excluded from further analysis. This excluded the small minority of the sample who were working in "balanced" occupations. No jobs were classified as "male token." Of the respondents, 96% ($n = 645$) were working in occupations that were classed as "female token," "female minority," or "male minority" and subsequent tables are limited to these three "gender ratio" groups.

Thus, as expected, most occupational Orders were clearly gendered. The majority of women (79%) were working in the "male minority" occupations, whereas most men were working in "female token" (47%) or "female minority" (30%) occupations. Just 7% of women were working in very male-dominated ("female token") occupations and the remaining 15% were in "female minority" occupations. One fourth (24%) of men worked in "male minority" occupations.

Each of the three gender ratio groups comprise both professional and managerial jobs and less skilled and nonmanual jobs (see Table 7.1). The female token group is the most differentiated (unsurprisingly, given that the OPCS occupational coding scheme has been criticized for its strong male bias); this comprises professional and related jobs in science, engineering, and technology; security and protective services; construction and mining; and transport operating and related jobs. The female minority group is dominated by management-related jobs. The male minority group is dominated by the two "classical" female occupational Orders; professional and related jobs in education, welfare, and health, and clerical and related jobs.

However, within each occupational Order a further degree of gender segregation is apparent. Even within Orders where men predominate, the women are more heavily concentrated in "residual" categories or in lower status jobs. Conversely, among the Orders where women predominate, men are more heavily concentrated in the higher status jobs within the Order.

TABLE 7.1
Distribution of Men and Women Working Within OPCS 1980 Occupation Groups by "Token Status" of Group

		Number Within Group (Twenty-07 Data)		
Occupational Group	% Women in Group (1991 census figures)	Men Total (Part-time)	Women Total (Part-time)	All
"Female token" groups (up to 20% women)		**150 (2)**	**21 (10)**	**171**
Order 4 Professional and related in science, engineering, technology, and similar fields	11.9	37 (2)	5 (0)	42
Order 8 Security and protective service	12.3	16 (0)	4 (4)	20
Order 12 Processing, making, repairing, and related (metal & electrical)	5.6	58 (0)	8 (5)	66
Order 14 Construction, mining, and related not identified elsewhere	1.8	14 (0)	1 (0)	15
Order 15 Transport operating, materials moving and storing, and related	6.1	25 (0)	3 (1)	28
"Female minority" groups (21-40% women)		**96 (3)**	**48 (2)**	**144**
Order 1 Profession and related supporting management; senior national and local government managers	34.3	34 (1)	9 (0)	43
Order 5 Managerial	31.2	47 (1)	22 (1)	69
Order 11 Materials processing: making and repairing (excluding metal & electrical)	37.1	15 (1)	17 (1)	32
"Male minority" groups (61-80% women)		**76 (2)**	**254 (110)**	**330**
Order 2 Professional and related in education, welfare, and health	71.4	31 (1)	93 (33)	124
Order 6 Clerical and related	79.5	26 (0)	83 (31)	109
Order 7 Selling	65.2	14 (1)	20 (13)	34
Order 9 Catering, cleaning, hairdressing, and other personal service	76.9	5 (0)	58 (33)	63
Total		**322 (7)**	**323 (122)**	**645**

Note. "Token status" of occupational group defined by % of women working within each group according to 1991 census data for the Strathclyde Region (10% sample).

Thus, an examination of the occupational groups occupied by this community sample of 40-year-old men and women reemphasizes two aspects of female employment. The first is the degree to which men and women in general continue to work in different jobs, despite recent changes in labor-force participation and Equal Opportunities legislation. Gender remains entrenched as an axis for the division of labor (an axis all too frequently obvious in spatial organization of the workplace; Ardener, 1981; Spain, 1992). The second point that is highlighted is the deficiencies of the classificatory system for women's jobs (Roberts & Barker, 1986). As Macran, Clarke, Sloggett, and Bethune (1994) have said:

> The conventional occupational classification scheme concentrates a very large number of women into a very small number of groups, mainly in routine non-manual, personal service and semi-skilled jobs. It combines into single groups occupations involving quite diverse activities and work environments and with dissimilar levels of remuneration. (p. 186)

Gender Differences in Health Within "Occupational Token Status" Groups

Two aspects of health are considered here: psychological distress (measured using the 30-item General Household Questionnaire, or GHQ; Goldberg, 1972), with 4/5 as the threshold for "probable cases" following other work (see, for example, Stansfeld, Davey Smith, & Marmot, 1993); and self-assessed health (own rating of general health over the last year, contrasting "fair"/"poor" health with "excellent"/"good" health). Overall (see Table 7.2) women's health was worse than men's on these measures (although the difference only borders on significance for GHQ "caseness").

Looking within occupational gender ratio groups, gender differences among those in female token and male minority occupations were generally slightly less than those observed overall, and were more pronounced in female minority occupations. For GHQ "caseness," particularly, this increased gender difference is attributable to *poorer* health of women in this group (in comparison with other women), rather than to improved men's health in this group. Generally, the percentage reporting poor health varies more by gender ratio group for women than men.

However, these gender ratio categories clearly group together some quite different jobs (see Table 7.1), with differing physical and psychosocial conditions, costs, and rewards (material and psychological). We thus compare gender differences in health taking account of the professional or managerial status of the occupation. In Table 7.3, Orders 1, 2, 4, and 5 are professional/managerial and Orders 6, 7, 8, 9, 11, 12, 14, and 15 are not. Broadly, as expected, the health of those doing professional or managerial jobs is better than the health of same-sex counterparts doing other jobs. Generally

TABLE 7.2
Health Variables by Gender and Occupational "Gender Ratio" Groups

	Male		Female		Gender Difference % Female- % Male	Significance p value
	%	Base n	%	Base n		
% GHQ caseness 4/5 *All employed 10+ hours*	*17*	*324*	*23*	*327*	*6*	*.09*
Female token	15	(147)	19	(21)	4	.87
Female minority	19	(93)	35	(46)	16	.07
Male minority	19	(74)	21	(245)	2	.85
Self-assessed health in last year "fair" or "poor" *All employed 10+ hours*	*21*	*332*	*29*	*337*	*8*	*.02*
Female token	21	(150)	24	(21)	3	.96
Female minority	18	(96)	30	(47)	12	.15
Male minority	24	(76)	28	(254)	4	.55

TABLE 7.3

Gender Differences in Health by Occupational "Gender Ratio" Groups:
Professional/Managerial Jobs and Other Jobs Compared

| | Professional and Managerial Jobs | | | | | Other Jobs | | | | |
| | Men | | Women | | | Men | | Women | | |
	%	(Base n)	%	(Base n)	Sig	%	(Base n)	%	(Base n)	Sig
% GHQ "caseness"										
All employed 10+ hours	17	(146)	21	(126)		17	(168)	24	(186)	
Female token	19	(36)	20	(5)	NV	14	(111)	19	(16)	
Female minority	18	(79)	37	(30)	+	29	(14)	31	(16)	
Male minority	13	(31)	17	(91)		23	(43)	23	(154)	
Self-assessed health in last year "fair" or "poor"										
All employed 10+ hours	17	(149)	20	(128)		23	(173)	33	(194)	*
Female token	22	(37)	20	(5)	NV	20	(113)	25	(16)	
Female minority	16	(81)	33	(30)		27	(15)	24	(17)	
Male minority	16	(31)	16	(93)		29	(45)	35	(161)	

*$p < 0.05$; +$0.01 > p > 0.05$; NV = chi-square invalid.

speaking the gender differences are greater within professional/managerial jobs than amongst other jobs, and the exaggeration of gender differences in female minority jobs is *only* apparent among the professional/managerial jobs. Of these women, 37% are classed as a probable GHQ "case" and 33% rated their health over the last year as "fair" or "poor."

In summary, therefore, comparing aspects of health across the occupational gender ratio groups revealed more variation for women than for men, but this did not conform simply to the predictions that might be made from Kanter's work. Rather than the female tokens (i.e., those who "should," according to Kanter, have been subjected to the greatest pressures), it was women in female minority jobs amongst those working in professional and managerial occupational Orders (although not in other Orders) who tended to fare badly as a group.

We have not yet speculated about the differences in mental and general well-being between women in professional and managerial occupations working in female token and female minority occupations. The former (working in professional and related jobs in science, engineering, technology, and similar fields—Order 4) may have more autonomy, flexibility (e.g., in working hours and working practices, leaving them more able to accommodate demands from other aspects of their lives, including children), prestige and resources, perhaps with relatively little direct responsibility for more junior staff. The female minority professional and managerial jobs are professional and related jobs supporting management, senior national and local government managers (Order 1) and managerial jobs (Order 5). It is plausible that although women may be comparatively well tolerated in male jobs where they have relatively little impact on other employees or the workplace ethos as a whole, they are likely to be far less so when they are in positions that require them to exert a degree of authority over other workers, male and female. Thus women in managerial jobs may be particularly vulnerable, with their presence, work activities and conduct, and demeanor and appearance attracting heightened attention and criticism from other employees, and their managerial position isolating them simultaneously from most female employees. Offermann and Armitage (1993) noted that "the literature on the effects of stress on the health of women managers is not yet well developed, with much speculation and little conclusion" (p. 133), and few studies have compared the experience male and female managers in detail (Wajcman, 1994), although Savage's (1992) work might suggest that women in this occupational Order could be engaged in different types of management, and management jobs that are inherently more stressful. It may also be that these women managers have more commitments external to their paid work, but are in jobs that do not allow them sufficient autonomy or flexibility to carry both roles without some psychological cost; current research is looking at how male and female managers handle their domestic and work commitments (Wajcman, 1994). However, a review of studies of women managers suggests that most are not married; those that are married are less likely to have children, have a career priority lower than their husband's, and have little time for leisure or for themselves (Parasuraman & Greenhaus, 1993). A large study of members of the British Institute of Management came to very similar conclusions. British women managers were better qualified, younger, more likely to be single or divorced, and without children than male managers. And although the women were as likely as the men to be concerned about the opportunity for advancement, they were more concerned than men about having a challenging job with prospects for developments. The women were also more aware than men of the constant personal sacrifices which their commitment to career required. The benefits of work-related fulfillment and achievements that are often cited were more often offset for the women against feelings of isolation, being under close scrutiny, and being "tested by a suspicious audience" (Alban-Metcalfe & West, 1991, p. 167). "Frustration, even depression, and considerable resentment" have been described as "the inevitable price" which many of these women paid (p. 166).

Our own data are subject to number of limitations for this analysis; as we said earlier, this analysis is intended to be exploratory and provocative rather than definitive. First, as only 670 of our respondents are employed for more than 10 hours per week, there are relatively few people in each occupational group. Ideally in assessing the impact of "controlling" for occupation (or the gender mix within occupations) on gender differences in health we would have taken specific occupations. However, few occupations are sufficiently well represented in a random community sample of this size for such an analysis to be possible; only two occupations (schoolteachers and clerks) are represented by more than 50 respondents. The fact that both of these occupations are female-dominated is attributable both to the classificatory system itself and the narrowness of definitions of "appropriate" jobs for women.

Second, we did not collect information directly from respondents about the gender mix in their own workplace (or how they felt about this), but have extrapolated from broader group data. Other quantitative studies (see, for example, Wharton & Baron, 1987) are subject to the same limitation. Gross though our measure of occupational gender ratio is, the overwhelming evidence on gender segregation of work would suggest that, if anything, classifying occupations at the level of OPCS's Occupational Group is likely to underestimate gender segregation. Thus, aggregating to the level of occupational groups may mask a high degree of gender segregation, both spatially and in terms of the content of the jobs themselves.

In this analysis we have also had to ignore other potentially important factors. However, a univariate examination of reported physical and psychosocial conditions at work did not show that women working in female minority professional and managerial jobs simply reported poorer physical and psychosocial aspects of work. If anything, these women report doing slightly less monotonous and repetitive, or hectic, work, and less conflict between home and work life, as well as less time pressure due to work, although slightly more report that the stress of their work has upset their sleep, or their appetite, occasionally or more, or perceive their job as insecure. Also it was not possible to systematically examine the effect of part-time versus full-time employment for the women because only 2 of the 48 women classified as doing female minority jobs were working part time. However, recent work has suggested that women's occupational group has the strongest influence on self-assessed health after controlling for age and longstanding illness or disability; whether the women worked part or full time seemed to have little impact per se (Macran et al., 1994). Another factor that may be important is the process which leads to entry to a gender-atypical job. With the level of gender segregation that exists in the labor market, access to such jobs is likely to be the result of complex selective processes that may have consequences for the aggregate health of the group.

Few data are available to compare with our results; what little there is suggests that this is an important area to pursue. Reported data for employees in the British Civil Service (Stansfeld & Marmot, 1992), a hierarchical organization in which women are most represented at the bottom and decreasingly represented toward the top, are of interest, although they were not reported in the context of tokenism. A more straightforward relationship is apparent. Levels of minor psychiatric disorder (assessed, as here, using the GHQ 30) among women, and the gender difference in "caseness," were highest amongst those in administrative grades (where the percentage of women was lowest) and lowest in clerical and support grades (where the percentage of women was highest). As the percentage of women increased from 12.6%, through 26.9% to 73.3%, the gender difference in those classified as GHQ "cases" declined from 10.4% through 8.4% to 3.6%. The prevalence of psychiatric morbidity was again more affected by occupational level for women than for men (there being a 10% difference between administrative and clerical and support grades for women, but only a 3.2% difference for men). Contemporary work on rates of sick leave in Sweden reported that females in extremely male-dominated groups had the highest rates, but that both female and male sick-leave rates were lower in "more gender-integrated" groups (Alexanderson, Leijon, Akerlind, Rydh, & Bjurulf, 1994). This has also been shown to be true for sick leave due to minor psychiatric morbidity where:

Women in extremely male-dominated groups had the highest incidence of all groups, 4.6%. Men in extremely female-dominated occupations had the highest incidence of all men, 2.9%. Occupations with an equal sex distribution had the lowest sick-leave incidence, 1.2%. (Hensing, Alexanderson, Akerlind, & Bjurulf, 1995, p. 39)

Similarly, the findings reported in this volume by Light and colleagues (chapter 15) are intriguing in this context: Among White and Black women and Black men, high-effort coping styles in those who had high-status jobs were associated with increased diastolic blood pressure at work; no such relationship was seen for White men (Light, Girdler, West, & Brownley, chapter 15, this volume).

CONCLUSION

As yet much of the recent literature in organizational theory has remained separate from research within medical sociology on gender, work, and health, although the additional stresses described for those working in gender-atypical occupations could have obvious etiological relevance. Hearn and Parkin's (1994) comment that "the analysis of sexuality and gender are now both well-established and still strangely invisible within the analysis of organisations" (p. 2) is perhaps even more apt for the sociology of gender, work, and health. Here we have presented a preliminary analysis that sought to compare gender disparities in health between occupational gender ratio groups using data from a community-based sample of young middle-aged employed men and women. The analysis is speculative and limited numbers have not allowed us to take account of some factors that are likely to be implicated. Such questions could only be addressed in a specific study, probably based within a single large organization; such a study is nearing completion (Emslie, 1977; Emslie, Hunt, & Macintrye, in press). We would argue that the literature and data presented here suggest that this is an important area to study in more detail, although it may only have relevance for understanding the impact of paid work on women within certain jobs, namely professional and managerial ones. With the combination of greater female participation in the workforce, pressure for women to gain access to "male" jobs, and the growing obsession with evaluation, performance indicators, and productivity measurement, paying due attention to the gendered structure of the workplace may be important for understanding gender differences in many aspects of work and health, including mental well-being (where a female excess of morbidity is most pronounced; Macintyre et al., 1996), consultation patterns and rates of absenteeism. As yet the relationship between work-related stress and hypertension and coronary heart disease has been less studied in women than men (where links have been demonstrated; Light, 1995), but it seems likely that these additional work stresses may well be implicated in the etiology of cardiovascular disease.

ACKNOWLEDGMENTS

Thanks are due to Mildred Blaxter, Hannah Bradby, Simon Carter, Graeme Ford, Sally Macintyre, and Sally Wyke for comments on an earlier version of this chapter. The authors are financed by the Medical Research Council of Great Britain.

REFERENCES

Acker, J. (1991). Hierarchies, jobs, bodies: A theory of gendered organizations. In J. Lorber & S. A. Farrell (Eds.), *The social construction of gender* (pp. 162–179). London: Sage.

Acker, J., & van Houten, D. R. (1974). Differential recruitment and control: The sex structuring of organizations. *Administrative Science Quarterly, 19*, 152–163.

Alban-Metcalfe, B., & West, M. A. (1991). Women managers. In J. Firth-Cozens & M. A. West (Eds.), *Women at work. Psychological and organizational perspectives* (pp. 154–171). Buckingham, England: Open University Press.

Alexanderson, K., Leijon, M., Akerlind, I., Rydh, H., & Bjurulf, P. (1994). Epidemiology of sickness absence in a Swedish county in 1985, 1986 and 1987. *Scandinavian Journal of Social Medicine, 22*, 27–34.

Allan, J. (1993). Male elementary teachers. Experiences and perspectives. In C. L. Williams (Ed.), *Doing "women's work." Men in nontraditional occupations* (pp. 113–127). Newbury Park, CA: Sage.

Arber, S. (1989). Gender and class inequalities in health: Understanding the differentials. In J. Fox (Ed.), *Health inequalities in European countries* (pp. 250–279). Aldershot, England: Gower.

Arber, S. (1991). Class, paid employment and family roles: Making sense of structural disadvantage, gender and health status. *Social Science and Medicine, 32*(4), 425–436.

Arber, S., & Gilbert, N. (1992). Re-assessing women's working lives: An introductory essay. In S. Arber & N. Gilbert (Eds.), *Women and working lives* (pp. 1–13). London: Macmillan.

Arber, S., Gilbert, G. N., & Dale, A. (1985). Paid employment and women's health: A benefit or a source of role strain? *Sociology of Health & Illness, 7*(3), 375–400.

Ardener, S. (Ed.). (1981). *Women and space.* London: Croom Helm.

Bartley, M., Popay, J., & Plewis, I. (1992). Domestic conditions, paid employment and women's experience of ill-health. *Sociology of Health & Illness, 14*(3), 313–343.

Bradley, H. (1989). *Men's work, women's work.* Cambridge, England: Polity Press.

Bradley, H. (1993). Across the great divide. The entry of men into "women's" jobs. In C. L. Williams (Ed.), *Doing "women's work." Men in nontraditional occupations* (pp. 10–27). Newbury Park, CA: Sage.

Carter, S. (1994a, March). *Risk and masculinity: A case study of scientific theories of risk and male work practices.* Paper presented to the 1994 British Sociological Association Conference, University of Central Lancashire, England.

Carter, S. (1994b). *Risk, masculinity and modernity. Understandings of gender and danger in the modern period.* Unpublished doctoral dissertation, University of Lancaster, England.

Cockburn, C. (1990). Men's power in organizations: "Equal opportunities" intervenes. In J. Hearn & D. Morgan (Eds.), *Men, masculinites and social theory* (pp. 72–89). London: Unwin Hyman.

Collinson, D. L., & Collinson, M. (1990). Sexuality in the workplace: The domination of men's sexuality. In J. Hearn & D. Morgan (Eds.), *Men, masculinites and social theory* (pp. 91–109). London: Unwin Hyman.

Collinson, M., & Collinson, D. (1994, March). "It's only Dick": Men's sexuality and power in the insurance industry. Paper presented to the 1994 BSA Conference, University of Central Lancashire, England.

Davies, C. (1992). Gender, history and management style in nursing: Towards a theoretical synthesis. In M. Savage & A. Witz (Eds.), Gender and bureaucracy (pp. 228–252). Oxford, England: Blackwell.

Ecob, R. (1987). West of Scotland Twenty-07 study: The sampling scheme, frame and procedures for the cohort studies (Working Paper No. 6). Glasgow: MRC Medical Sociology Unit.

Elliot, B. J., & Huppert, F. A. (1991). In sickness and in health: Associations between physical and mental well-being, employment and parental status in a British nationwide sample of married women. Psychological Medicine, 21, 515–524.

Emslie, C. (1977). Banking on good health? Gender differences in minor morbidity amongst men and women working full-time in a British bank. Unpublished doctoral dissertation, University of Glasgow.

Emslie, C. Hunt, K., & Macintyre, S. (in press). Gender, grade or graft? Gender differences in minor morbidity amongst full-time employees in a British bank. Social Science and Medicine.

England, P., & Herbert, M. S. (1993). The pay of men in "female" occupations. Is comparable worth only for women? In C. L. Williams (Ed.), Doing "women's work." Men in nontraditional occupations (pp. 28–48). Newbury Park, CA: Sage.

Feldberg, R., & Glenn, E. N. (1979). Male and female: Job versus gender models in the sociology of work. Social Problems, 26, 524–538.

Floge, L., & Merrill, D. M. (1986). Tokenism reconsidered: Male nurses and female physicians in a hospital setting. Social Forces, 64(4), 925–947.

Game, A., & Pringle, R. (1983). Gender at work. Sydney: George Allen & Unwin.

General Register Office for Scotland. (1993). 1991 census report for Strathclyde Region (Part 2). Edinburgh: Her Majesty's Stationery Office.

Goldberg, D. P. (1972). The detection of psychiatric illness by a questionnaire (Maudsley Monograph No. 21). London: Open University Press.

Grimm, J. W., & Stern, R. N. (1974). Sex roles and internal labor market structures: The "female" semi-professions. Social Problems, 21, 690–705.

Hearn, J., & Parkin, W. (1987). "Sex" at "work." The power and paradox of organisation sexuality. Brighton, England: Wheatsheaf.

Hearn, J., & Parkin, W. (1994, March). Sexuality, gender and organisations: Acknowledging complexities and contentions. Paper presented at the British Sociological Association Annual Conference, University of Central Lancashire, England.

Hensing, G., Alexanderson, K., Akerlind, I., & Bjurulf, P. (1994). Sick-leave due to minor psychiatric morbidity: Role of sex integration. Social Psychiatry and Psychiatric Epidemiology, 30, 39–43.

Hibbard, J. H., & Pope, C. R. (1985). Employment status, employment characteristics, and women's health. Women & Health, 10(1), 59–77.

Hibbard, J. H., & Pope, C. R. (1991). Effect of domestic and occupational roles on morbidity and mortality. Social Science and Medicine, 32(7), 805–811.

Hunt, K., & Annandale, E. (1993). Just the job? Is the relationship between health and domestic and paid work gender-specific? Sociology of Health & Illness, 15(5), 632–664.

Jacobs, J. A. (1993). Men in female-dominated fields. Trends and turnover. In C. L. Williams (Ed.), Doing "women's work." Men in nontraditional occupations (pp. 49–63). Newbury Park, CA: Sage.

Kanter, R. M. (1977a). Men and women of the corporation. New York: Basic Books.

Kanter, R. M. (1977b). Some effects of proportions on group life: Skewed sex ratios and responses to token women. American Journal of Sociology, 82(5), 965–990.

Kauppinen-Torpainen, K., & Lammi, J. (1993). Men in female-dominated occupations. A cross-cultural comparison. In C. L. Williams (Ed.), Doing "women's work." Men in nontraditional occupations (pp. 91–112). Newbury Park, CA: Sage.

Macintyre, S., Annandale, E., Ecob, R., Ford, G., Hunt, K., Jamieson, B., Maciver, S., West, P., & Wyke, S. (1989). The West of Scotland Twenty-07 Study: Health in the community. In C. J.

Martin & D. V. McQueen (Eds.), *Readings for a new public health* (pp. 56–74). Edinburgh: Edinburgh University Press.

Macintyre, S., Hunt, K., & Sweeting, H. (1996). Gender differences in health: Are things really as simple as they seem? *Social Science and Medicine, 42*(4), 617–624.

Macran, S., Clarke, L., Sloggett, A., & Bethune, A. (1994). Women's socio-economic status and self-assessed health: Identifying some disadvantaged groups. *Sociology of Health & Illness, 16*, 182–208.

Mills, A. J., & Tancred, P. (Eds.). (1992). *Gendering organizational analysis.* Newbury Park, CA: Sage.

Morgan, D. (1992). *Discovering men. Critical studies on men and masculinities 3.* London: Routledge.

Nathanson, C. A. (1977). Sex, illness and medical care. A review of data, theory and method. *Social Science and Medicine, 11*, 13–25.

Offerman, L. R., & Armitage, M. A. (1993). Stress and the woman manager: Sources, health outcomes, and interventions. In E. A. Fagenson (Ed.), *Women in management. Trends, issues and challenges in managerial diversity* (pp. 131–161). Newbury Park, CA: Sage.

Office of Population Censuses and Surveys. (1980). *Classification of occupations.* London: Her Majesty's Stationery Office.

Parasuraman, S., & Greenhaus, J. H. (1993). Personal portrait: The life-style of the woman manager. In E. A. Fagenson (Ed.), *Women in management. Trends, issues and challenges in managerial diversity* (pp. 186–211). Newbury Park, CA: Sage.

Patterson, M., & Engelberg, L. (1978). Women in male-dominated professions. In A. H. Stromberg & S. Harkess (Eds.), *Women working. Theories and facts in perspective* (pp. 266–292). CA: Mayfield.

Pringle, R. (1993). Male secretaries. In C. L. Williams (Ed.), *Doing "women's work." Men in nontraditional occupations* (pp. 128–151). Newbury Park, CA: Sage.

Reskin, B. F. (1991). Bringing the men back in: Sex differentiation and the devaluation of women's work. In J. Lorber & S. A. Farrell (Eds.), *The social construction of gender* (pp. 141–161). London: Sage.

Reskin, B. F., & Roos, P. A. (Eds.). (1990). *Job queues, gender queues. Explaining women's inroads into male occupations.* Philadelphia: Temple University Press.

Roberts, H., & Barker, R. (1986). *The social classification of women* (LS Working Paper No. 46). London: Social Statistics Research Unit, City University.

Savage, M. (1992). Women's expertise, men's authority; Gendered organisations and the contemporary middle classes. In M. Savage & A. Witz (Eds.), *Gender and bureaucracy* (pp. 124–151). Oxford, England: Blackwell.

Segal, B. E. (1962). Male nurses: A case study in status contradiction and prestige loss. *Social Forces, 41*, 31–38.

Sorensen, G., Pirie, P., Folsom, A., Luepker, R., Jacobs, D., & Gillum, R. (1985). Sex differences in the relationship between work and health: The Minnesota Heart Survey. *Journal of Health and Social Behavior, 26*, 379–394.

Spain, D. (1992). *Gendered spaces.* Chapel Hill: The University of North Carolina Press.

Spencer, A., & Podmore, D. (1987). Women lawyers—Marginal members of a male-dominated profession. In A. Spencer & D. Podmore (Eds.), *In a man's world* (pp. 113–133). London: Tavistock.

Stansfeld, S. A., & Marmot, M. G. (1992). Social class and minor psychiatric disorder in British Civil Servants: A validated screening survey using the General Health Questionnaire. *Psychological Medicine, 22*, 739–749.

Stansfeld, S. A., Davey Smith, G., & Marmot, M. (1993). Association between physical and psychological morbidity in the Whitehall II study. *Journal of Psychosomatic Research, 37*(3), 227–238.

Verbrugge, L. M. (1989). The twain meet: Empirical explanations of sex differences in health and mortality. *Journal of Health and Social Behavior, 30*, 282–304.

Wajcman, J. (1994, March). *The gender relations of management.* Paper presented to the 1994 British Sociological Association Conference, University of Central Lancashire, England.

Wharton, A. S., & Baron, J. N. (1987). So happy together? The impact of gender segregation on men at work. *American Sociological Review, 52,* 574–587.

Williams, C. L. (1992). The glass escalator: Hidden advantages for men in the "female" professions. *Social Problems, 39*(3), 253–267.

Williams, C. L. (Ed.). (1993). *Doing "women's work." Men in nontraditional occupations.* Newbury Park, CA: Sage.

Witz, A. (1990). Patriarchy and professions: The gendered politics of occupational closure. *Sociology, 24*(4), 675–690.

Witz, A., Halford, S., & Savage, M. (1994, March). *Organised bodies: Gender, sexuality, bodies and organisational culture.* Paper presented to the 1994 British Sociological Association Conference, University of Central Lancashire, England.

Witz, A., & Savage, M. (1992). The gender of organizations. In M. Savage & A. Witz (Eds.), *Gender and bureaucracy* (pp. 3–62). Oxford, England: Blackwell.

Zimmer, L. (1988). Tokenism and women in the workplace: The limits of gender-neutral theory. *Social Problems, 35*(1), 64–77.

MULTIPLE ROLES, SOCIAL SUPPORT, AND COPING IN WOMEN

8

Women's Roles and Health: A Life-Course Approach

Phyllis Moen
Cornell University

Social isolation is a significant risk factor in the development of disease and health impairment. Its obverse, social integration and connectedness to the broader community, can bolster general health over the life course. This chapter considers women's social integration (in the form of multiple role involvements) and health as constituting two dynamic and interdependent life pathways.

KEY CONCEPTS

Social integration is a concept historically applied to collectivities (Williams, 1965), but one that can also describe the multiple roles of individuals. A distinction can be made between social–psychological and structural integration, with structural integration denoting the concrete involvement of individuals with various aspects of a collectivity. Psychological integration, on the other hand, is the subjective experience of that connectedness. Both concepts are related; both may be important in predicting health outcomes. *Multiple roles* is a concept isomorphic with Merton's (1968) *status set*, referring to the "complex of distinct positions assigned to individuals both within and among social systems" (p. 434). The behavior enacted in fulfilling a position with defined rights and responsibilities constitutes a *role* (Linton, 1936; Williams, 1965). Thus, women may occupy the position of worker, wife, churchgoer, friend, club member, volunteer, neighbor—each with its own attendant behavioral (role) expectations. Some roles, such as that of worker, are highly structured, whereas others, such as friend or neighbor, are diffuse, with more vaguely defined obligations and privileges rather than highly specified rights and duties. Presumably, the greater number of roles, the greater the level of social connectedness or integration. This conforms to House and Kahn's (1985) use of the term *social integration* or, conversely, *isolation*, to represent "the existence or quantity of relationships" (p. 85). Multiple role involvements can be seen as a protective mechanism, like socioeconomic status, that is related, broadly, to a variety of different components of health. However, it is not clear whether multiple role occupancy as a life pattern is what contributes to good health or whether it is concurrent integration that matters.

THEORETICAL PERSPECTIVES
ON WOMEN'S ROLES

Social systems use gender as a fundamental basis for social organization, and, despite the push toward gender equality, cultural norms persist in defining sex-appropriate behavior and in shaping distinctive life pathways for women and men (Moen, 1994, 1995a, 1997a, 1997b). It cannot be assumed, therefore, that the effects of multiple roles, or any particular role, are similar for both sexes. Both marriage and parenting can be quite different experiences for women than for men.

Historically, adulthood for women has been synonymous with marriage and motherhood, and, even at the turn of the century, for most women family roles remain extremely salient. Durkheim (1897/1951) observed that women were less involved than men in collective existence and, consequently, less likely to reap either the benefits or the costs of that involvement. As women increasingly take on roles beyond home and family, however, the question is raised about the significance of these changes for their physical and emotional health.

There are two competing views coupling multiple roles with both physical and emotional well-being. The theoretical orientation most supported by empirical evidence is the *role enhancement* perspective. This view points to the way in which multiple roles augment an individual's power, prestige, resources, and emotional gratifications, including social recognition and a heightened sense of identity (Marks, 1977; Sieber, 1974). A key assumption of this perspective holds that there are benefits to be gained through the accumulation of social identities or roles (Marks, 1977; Sieber, 1974; Thoits, 1983).

The notion of multiple roles as promoting resilience is especially pertinent to women's lives, as women traditionally have had less opportunity than men to engage in roles beyond the domestic sphere. In the light of the historical isolation of women from "the main stream of society" (Gavron, 1966, p. 146), employment and other, nondomestic roles have been depicted as mechanisms to promote psychological well-being, health, and a long life. In fact, some scholars argue that men gain advantage from their multiple roles within society, especially their paid work roles—in the form of status, social relationships, and self-esteem. Women, by contrast, have been more vulnerable to psychological distress, hemmed in by their exclusive home-making responsibilities (Gove, 1972; Gove & Geerken, 1977; Oakley, 1974). However, as women become more "like men" (i.e., employed for most of their adult lives), the argument goes, they too will benefit psychologically. Thus, from this *role enhancement* perspective, women engaged in multiple roles should be more resilient, experiencing higher levels of physical and emotional health than those who are less integrated into the broader society.

On the other hand, there are those who favor a *role strain* interpretation and make an opposite argument. According to this view, some role combinations, such as work and family, may be detrimental to women's well-being, introducing competing demands on time, energy, and involvement. This perspective emphasizes the costs rather than the benefits of multiple roles, role obligations that produce overload and strain which, in turn, lead to lower resistance and poor physical as well as emotional health. The "role strain" interpretation necessarily assumes that there is a fixed quantity of time, energy, and commitment available for family and nonfamily role responsibilities (Burr et al., 1979; Coser & Rokoff, 1971; Goode, 1960).

Women are taking on new roles in the marketplace without abandoning old roles and old expectations in the home (see also Berk, 1985; Coverman & Sheley, 1986). Proponents of the role strain position argue that occupying multiple roles is more stressful for women than for men because women take on employment and other roles *over and above* their domestic obligations, whereas men remain free to concentrate almost exclusively on their work.

THE RESEARCH EVIDENCE

There is a considerable body of research linking social integration, or multiple role involvement, with health and well-being. Studies have found that integration into society, in terms of multiple role occupancy, reduces the likelihood of psychological distress among both men and women (Gore & Mangione, 1983; Kandel, Davies, & Raveis, 1985; Moen, 1996; Spreitzer, Snyder, & Larson, 1979; Thoits, 1983, 1986), and similar findings also link multiple roles to physical health (Moen, Dempster-McClain, & Williams, 1992; Nathanson, 1980, 1984; Verbrugge, 1983, 1985), coronary heart disease (Haynes, Feinleib, Devine, Scotch, & Kannel, 1978; Reed, McGee, & Yano, 1983), and

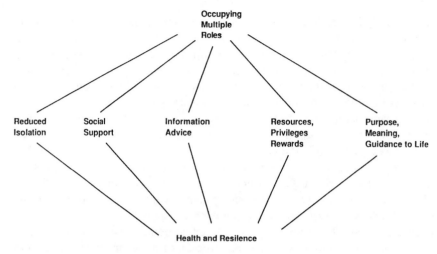

FIG. 8.1. Mechanisms linking multiple roles to women's health.

duration of life (Blazer, 1982; House, Robbins, & Metzner, 1982; Moen, Dempster-McClain, & Williams, 1989; Seeman, Kaplan, Knudsen, Cohen, & Guralnik, 1987). There is also a body of research addressing the significance of one role: employment (see Fig. 8.1).

Employment and Health

The relationship between employment and women's physical health is both straightforward and ambiguous. It is straightforward because employed women are typically more healthy than the nonemployed. At every age level, employed women report fewer chronic conditions and less short- or long-term disability than do full-time homemakers.[1]

Are working women more healthy *because* of their employment, or is it that the more healthy individuals are the most likely to work? Both interpretations are likely to be true. Healthy women are active in a number of roles, including paid work; and being active does promote better health. Some types of employment, however, when combined with marriage and motherhood, may be related to coronary disease. One 10-year study, for example, showed that those most vulnerable to heart disease were married mothers who had three or more children and were employed in clerical occupations (Haynes & Feinleib, 1980). Further adding to our understanding of the employment–health link is Welch and Booth's (1977) finding that married women who had been employed for more than a year were healthier

[1]Data are from the national Health Interview Survey. See Verbrugge (1982, 1983, 1985, 1987). See also Feld (1963), Haynes and Feinleib (1980), Nathanson (1980), Northcutt (1981), Nye (1974), Sharp and Nye (1963), Welch and Booth (1974), Woods and Hulka (1979).

than those who had worked for only a short period of time. According to the study, both groups were healthy enough to work. As those employed longer were healthier, it may be that the positive relationship typically found between employment and health is not due simply to healthy women choosing to work, but to the effects of their work experience as well. Several studies suggest, however, that health affects labor-force entry and exits rather than vice versa (see Kessler & McRae, 1982; Waldron, Herold, Dunn, & Staum, 1982; Waldron & Jacobs, 1989; Wethington & Kessler, 1989).

In the 1980s, scholars began to look at combinations of work and family roles. For example, Verbrugge and colleagues (Verbrugge, 1987, 1989; Verbrugge & Madans, 1985) found that the healthiest women were those who occupied the three roles of wife, mother, and paid worker. Whether employment positively or negatively contributes to women's resilience depends on women's attitudes toward their jobs, their other obligations, the characteristics of the job and the conditions of work. Although women are increasingly present in the labor force, relatively few have come to hold "men's" jobs. Their paid work, of course, is *in addition* to the domestic work they perform in fulfilling their traditional and principal role of caregiving—of children and homes and also of ailing or infirm husbands, parents, and other kin. Although the mental and physical health costs and benefits of employment remain somewhat ambiguous, the existing evidence suggests that the benefits of employment for women's health may well outweigh its costs, and that the ratio of benefits to costs has become more favorable over time.

Multiple Roles and Longevity

Three panel studies have examined the significance of social relationships for mortality. The first, a study of a random sample of 6,928 residents of Alameda County, CA (Berkman & Breslow, 1983; Berkman & Syme, 1979), found that the risk of mortality over the period from 1965 to 1973 was related to social ties in the form of (a) marriage, (b) contacts with close friends and relatives, (c) church membership, and (d) membership in other (nonchurch) organizations. Among those studied, the most isolated were the most prone to death, even after controlling for measures of physical health in 1965 and lifestyle factors such as smoking, alcohol use, obesity, physical activity, and utilization of prevention and health services. Subsequent investigations of longevity over a 17-year period showed that marriage was less important for those 60 or older (Seeman et al., 1987).

The second panel study followed a group of men and women in the Tecumseh, MI community from 1967–1969 to 1978–1979 (House et al., 1982). It found that frequency of church attendance was inversely related to the mortality of female respondents, even after controlling for a range of risk factors. Frequency of attendance in other organizations also proved significant for men, although not for women.

The third panel study examined the longevity of women who were wives and mothers in the 1950s in a midsized upstate New York community (Moen et al., 1989). In the Women's Roles and Well-Being Project we found that the longevity of these wives and mothers over a 30-year period responded to their multiple role occupancy in the 1950s, providing support beyond the evidence presented in the Alameda County study of the significance of multiple roles *in conjunction* with their family role obligations for women.

Multiple Roles, Heart Disease, and General Health

Some investigations have examined the links between social integration and coronary heart disease (CHD; see, for example, Legato & Colman, 1991; Nickels & Chirikos, 1990; Oliver, Vedin & Wilhelmsson, 1986). For example, Reed et al. (1983) found higher rates of angina, myocardial infarction (MI), and heart disease among socially isolated men of Japanese ancestry in California and Honolulu, even after controlling for a number of risk factors. Haynes et al. (1978) reported a link between marital dissatisfaction and CHD among men and women over 65 in the Framingham study.

Occupying multiple roles—such as worker, club member, and church-goer—has also been positively linked to physical health generally (House, Landis, & Umberson, 1988; Menaghan, 1989; Moen, Dempster-McClain, & Williams, 1992; Verbrugge, 1989). Our panel data on women in upstate New York show that multiple role occupancy in earlier adulthood affect both physical health and psychological well-being in the later years, even controlling for earlier health and well-being (Moen, 1997a, 1997b). Panel studies also link the three roles of wife, mother, and paid worker to health, with nonmarried women and Black women with children at home especially benefiting from labor-force participation (Waldron & Jacobs, 1989).

A LIFE-COURSE APPROACH

Research evidence points to the essential simplicity of both the role strain and role enhancement approaches. What is missing is attention to *context* and acknowledgment of *change* on two fronts: (a) across lives (through aging and shifting family responsibilities and life goals); and (b) across society (in the form of structural and normative shifts, both as a result of cohort replacement and individual change). A life-course formulation considers the links between life biography and social history, and the settings that shape, and are shaped by, individual choices (Elder, 1995; Elder et al., 1996).

The life-course, *role context* perspective provides an analytical approach to the relationship between multiple roles and women's resilience that emphasizes continuity and change across the life span as well as the dynamic interplay between historical time and individual lives (Moen, 1992, 1995a, 1995b, 1997a, 1997b; Moen et al., 1989, 1992). The life-course viewpoint integrates the role strain and the role enhancement theoretical perspectives by considering not only the number of role involvements, but their nature, circumstance, and patterning over the life course. This perspective features consideration of (a) *transitions and trajectories*, (b) *historical change*, and (c) *contexts and contingencies*. Thus it can incorporate elements from both the role strain and the role enhancement perspectives; whether multiple roles have deleterious or positive effects on women's resilience depends on their timing and the contexts in which they occur. The life-course approach places role theory in a larger—and dynamic—framework, incorporating the following foci.

Role Transitions, Trajectories, and Timing

The life-course approach attends to the interface of transitions and trajectories in roles and identities across lives (Elder, 1995; Elder et al., 1996). A central trajectory throughout women's adulthood has been the parenting "career," but the adult years are also marked by paid work, volunteer, marital, and caregiving role trajectories. What may matter is not employment (or any other role) at one point in time but entry and exits over the adult years, the duration of employment (or any other role), and its timing in relation to a woman's age as well as other roles she may occupy. These, in turn, are tied to still another trajectory: shifts in health and well-being throughout adulthood.

Most studies linking multiple roles with women's health are cross-sectional and, as such, treat both role occupancy and health as static phenomena, something an individual either has or does not have at a particular time. However, we all know from personal experience and from our own observations that roles and health are fluid rather than constant. Ideally, then, we should measure them not at one point in time, but with reference to stability and change over time. It may not be role occupancy but the timing, sequencing, duration, and number of spells in particular roles that is consequential for health. For example, in the Women's Roles Project and the Cornell Retirement and Well-Being Project, we are charting the patterning of women's marital, family, work, and community roles throughout adulthood. We have found that the experience of particular roles, their timing in the life course, or their persistence affects self-reported health and psychological well-being (Moen et al., 1992; Moen, 1997a, 1997b). Moving out of family, occupational, and community roles in middle and later adulthood, as well as taking on new roles at this time, affects women's health. We know that women experience a decline in roles in midlife as their children leave home, their marriages frequently dissolve, and they move out of the labor force (Esterberg, Moen, & Dempster-McClain, 1994; Moen, 1991, 1992, 1994;

Smith & Moen, 1988). Older women are particularly vulnerable to social isolation. Menaghan (1989) found that for American women aged 50 to 65, 20% had no children, were not married, and not employed, compared to but 3% of men in that age group and 2% of younger women.

Another key life-course theme is how earlier experiences shape the course of lives as well as patterns of health (Elder, 1995; Moen & Erickson, 1995). In my study of working parents in Sweden, I found the dynamics of well-being to include a certain "cumulativeness": Individuals experiencing psychological distress and fatigue in one survey were the most prone to these difficulties in the next survey, 6 years later (Moen, 1989). Life changes in later adulthood, such as taking on caregiving of aging relatives or leaving the labor force, must be considered within this background of emotional resources; those who previously were socially connected are less prone to problems (Moen, 1997a, 1997b; Moen, Robison, & Dempster-McClain, 1995). Merton's (1968) notion of the cummulativeness of advantage or disadvantage is an important consideration when looking at roles and health over the life course; in both cases, the "haves" benefit throughout their lives.

The challenge of research in this area, as Giele (1982) has pointed out, is not only to map out the various life patterns of women, but also to ascertain which of these patterns are the most adaptive. It is also important to recognize that what may promote health at one life phase may or may not be conducive to health at later ages.

A key tenet of the life-course approach is that a transition always occurs in the context of ongoing life history trajectories, which construct and give meaning to the transition (Elder, 1995). Clearly, women's previous health and lifestyle trajectories serve to shape the meaning and experience of the biological changes accompanying aging. However, women's *histories of role participation and commitments* to social roles such as employment, marriage, parenting, and voluntary activities also help to mold their lifestyles and health care practices, as well as their subsequent health and well-being. Researchers and practitioners should focus, therefore, on how different developmental paths throughout adulthood, involving reproductive, employment and other role experiences in interplay with biological transitions and transformations, have an impact on women's stress, their lifestyle-related acquired risks (e.g., obesity, dietary intake, exercise, smoking, substance use) and, consequently, on their health in later adulthood.

Historical Shifts

A life-course approach also calls attention to lives in time, focusing on the way in which societal changes may influence both the nature of the life course and the resources individuals bring to each life stage (Elder, 1995). Consider the changing demography of women's lives. Changes in the timing and duration of women's roles may have important implications for the manner in which roles affect health and well-being. For example, today women expect and are expected to spend much of their adulthood in paid labor; these changing norms may alter the health effects of employment. How women cope with the problems of combining family responsibilities with other nonfamily roles has obvious health implications; however, these modes of adaptation are conditioned in large part by the cultural and social environment. For example, policies providing supports to working parents can reduce the strains of combining various role responsibilities (e.g., Moen, 1989). The hallmark of the life-course perspective is attention to the historical conditions in which lives are lived, and how, as these circumstances change, so do the relationships between variables. It may be that the effects of employment on women's health have changed in conjunction with the progressive transformations that have occurred in society's gender-role prescriptions. Indeed, analysis of a number of surveys from 1957 to 1976 led Kessler and McRae (1981, 1982) to conclude that the benefits of employment for American women increased over the years.

This is corroborated by my findings on the decline in psychological distress in Swedish mothers of young children from 1968 to 1981 (Moen, 1989). It may be that those who perceive the meshing of work and family roles as a personally valued and culturally sanctioned experience, who benefit from supportive employment policies and who are encouraged by an ideology of gender equality, should be the least prone to role conflicts and overloads and, consequently, the most likely to benefit from their labor-force participation. The meaning of women's employment, or other roles, may have been very different in the 1950s, when it was the exception as compared to now at the turn of the century, when it has become the rule. Similarly, employment is vastly different in Sweden, with its array of family supports, than in the United States, with its ambivalence toward maternal employment. This larger social and historical frame needs to be considered in studies of roles and resilience in women's lives.

Contexts and Contingencies

The life-course orientation keys in on the heterogeneity of women's life paths, how they differ among various subgroups within society, and how they are shaped by life contexts and contingencies. This emphasis on context, including the quality of roles and women's subjective evaluation of them, is crucial to linking women's roles to their health. Some women are more able to choose and manage their roles than others within the constraints of the larger social and economic structural context.

Certain role contexts can prove advantageous. For instance, more informal roles involving primary groups, such as the roles of relatives, friends and neighbors, may offer emotional support that is beneficial to health (Litwak et al., 1989). Participation in these roles also may serve as a source of information and advice, as well as more concrete forms of assistance (House & Kahn, 1985). Such social bonds have been found to both promote mental health (Aneshensel & Frerichs, 1982; Brown & Harris, 1978) and reduce mortality (Berkman & Breslow, 1983; House et al., 1982). These findings suggest that roles providing social support, rather than the total number of roles, are important facilitators of health.

A similar approach posits that particular roles, such as employment, matter, rather than their aggregate number. As reported earlier, employment has been shown to be positively linked to women's mental and physical health (e.g., Gove & Geerkin, 1977; Kessler & McRae, 1982; Nathanson, 1980; Verbrugge, 1983, 1985) and may have a greater impact on health than other roles.

Still another possibility is that the *level of participation* in a particular role might be conducive to health (House & Kahn, 1985). Women with many friends or those who attend church frequently may have a high degree of social connectedness, regardless of what other roles they may occupy. Three contexts and contingencies cannot be ignored in linking roles to women's health: individual dispositions and resources; family structure; stresses and supports, and other role contexts, including the larger opportunity structure.

Individual Dispositions and Resources. Psychosocial stress can be defined any number of ways, from "the experience of unfulfilled need" (Kaplan, 1983, p. 196) to a "mismatch—actual or perceived—between the person and his or her environment" (Menaghan, 1983, p. 158). Many women are particularly susceptible to just such a mismatch, because they face daily cross-pressures of work and family responsibilities. However, the mismatch can be subjective as well as objective, as when individual dispositions make some roles more desirable or more valued than others.

Researchers like Ross and colleagues have suggested that the development of more egalitarian gender roles can prove beneficial to both men and women, decreasing tensions between husbands and wives, and providing for multiple and socially valued roles for both. However, these benefits are likely to accrue only to the extent that behavior is congruent with attitudes; when husbands and wives not only share provider and domestic roles but also agree that this is their preferred arrangement (Ross, Mirowsky, & Huber, 1983).

The more personal resources women posses in their early years, the more likely they are to experience both higher levels of social integration and health. These resources include education, income, prior health and emotional well-being (Brown & Harris, 1978). For example, Cleary and Mechanic (1983) pointed out the importance of socioeconomic context: They found that employed wives with children under 18 at home and with low family incomes had lower levels of depression than those with children at home but with higher family incomes, or those who were not employed. Baruch et al. (1987) found that employment was more important to women with higher levels of education than those with less education. Women with family responsibilities and little education or money may have a restricted number of roles. Older, recently widowed women may find themselves in similar circumstances. Women (and men) at any age who find themselves trapped in roles, for example, in dead-end, low-paying jobs, are also vulnerable to role strain.

The challenge is to identify the individual dispositions and experiences that promote social integration and health or that place women at risk of role strain and disease and to chart their variations over the life course.

Family Context. Particular family contingencies can either promote or hamper health, but the maternal role itself has been depicted as having potentially harmful effects. For example, both Gove and Hughes (1979) and Veroff, Douvan, and Kulka (1981) suggested that women's responsibility for the welfare of children, husbands, and ailing relatives may have deleterious consequences for their own health and well-being. Gove and Hughes (1979) offered a notion of nurturant role obligations, which they described as "role obligations that require constant ongoing activities vis-à-vis spouse, children and others (such as parents) living in the home" (p. 133). They argued that these obligations prevent women from taking proper care of themselves and, consequently, impair their health. Because these nurturant role obligations are of an ongoing nature, caregiving of others may have a negative effect on self-care and personal health. Indeed, Nathanson (1980) found that the presence of children adversely affects women's appraisal of their own health. Race may operate as a contextual factor here. For example, the presence of children produced higher distress among White women, whereas children actually reduced the distress of Black men and women in a national survey in the early 1960s (Reskin & Coverman, 1985). The presence of children, marriage, or both may interact with other roles to affect women's health. Kandel et al. (1985) found parenthood exacerbates occupational stress, and Gove and Geerken (1977) found that symptoms of psychological distress among employed women increase as a function of the number of children present in the home. Other studies also link the presence of children with higher levels of psychological distress (McLanahan & Adams, 1987; Radloff, 1975). In terms of physical health, a prospective study analyzing data over an 8-year period (the Framingham study) found that women with three or more children who were working outside the home were more likely to experience CHD than either homemakers with three children or working women with no children (Haynes & Feinleib, 1980; Haynes, Feinleib, & Kannel, 1980).

Waldron and Jacobs (1989) found that employment was more beneficial to the health of unmarried rather than married women. The quality of marriage is also important. Employed wives with low marital strain experienced lower depression levels than those nonemployed with low strain, or employed with high marital strain. The significance of various permutations in roles can be complex. For example, the Haynes and Feinleib (1980) study found that women in clerical jobs married to blue-collar husbands were especially vulnerable to CHD.

Clearly, single parents or women with several children are more vulnerable to role overloads and strains than are those who share family responsibilities with a spouse or partner or have few children (Cherlin, 1981; Garfinkel & McLanahan, 1986). My Swedish Parents Study pointed to the importance, for well-being, of the emotional support of a partner, whether a spouse or a cohabitant. Single-parent women lacking this support were particularly disadvantaged (Moen, 1989).

A life-course approach challenges the researcher to place multiple roles within the family context of stressors and social support, locating women not only by their age, but the ages of their children, and by the presence of a supportive spouse. Family transitions, into and from marriage, into and out of active parenting, into and out of caregiving for infirm husbands or parents, may be consequential for women's health, not only directly but indirectly, in moderating the impacts of other roles.

Role Contexts and the Opportunity Structure. The organization and conditions of work have been shown to be directly related to the mental as well as the physical health of workers.[2] In the Swedish Parents Study, I found that parents who occupied psychologically and physically demanding jobs were, understandably, more likely to experience strains than were those whose occupations were less hectic, monotonous, or exhausting (Moen, 1989; Moen & Forest, 1990). It is also true that some job features can enhance well-being. For example, some discretion and opportunity for individual control over working hours was positively related to well-being. The majority of working women in the United States remain clustered in low-paid, low-status jobs; as more women move into jobs that offers opportunity for self-direction the health effects may be more beneficial.

Educational achievement and occupational prestige have been shown to be highly correlated with subjective health appraisals (Nathanson, 1980) and mortality (Nathanson & Lopez, 1987). Moreover, lifestyles incorporating risk factors such as smoking have been linked to social class, with working-class women slightly more likely to smoke than higher status women. The circum-

---

[2]For documentation of the physical and psychological impacts of conditions at work see Karasek and Theorell (1991), Levi (1974), Levi, Frankenhauser, and Gardell (1982), Miller, Schooler, Kohn, and Miller (1979), Moen (1989).

stances in which women become involved in other roles, such as community service, also need to be considered. In the Women's Roles Project as well as the Cornell Retirement and Well-Being Study we found that volunteer and community activities are positively related to physical health and longevity, as well as to psychological well-being. The life-course challenge is to understand the circumstances under which roles may, or may not, be beneficial to women's health.

MECHANISMS

By documenting the links between multiple roles and health, well-being, and longevity the research evidence provides strong support for the Durkheimian notion of the protective function of social integration. It is important to ask, is it number of roles or certain types of roles that are most conducive to health? Although the social support literature suggests that certain roles should be more beneficial than others, in the Women's Roles and Retirement Studies we found both the number of roles that women possessed, as well as particular types of roles, promoted health and longevity. What is it about occupying multiple roles that might promote women's resilience to disease and debilitation?

Social integration appears to operate, at least in part directly, by *reducing isolation* (Fig. 8.1) and, hence, anomie (Durkheim, 1897/1951). Occupying multiple roles serves to build and maintain extended social networks (Eckenrode & Gore, 1990).

Being integrated in such networks offers the opportunity for *social support* (Nathanson, 1980; Thoits, 1982). Participation in informal roles extends emotional support that is beneficial to health (Litwak et al., 1989). Such social bonds have been found to both promote mental health (Aneshensel & Frerichs, 1982; Brown & Harris, 1978) and reduce mortality (Berkman & Breslow, 1983; House et al., 1982). These findings suggest that those roles providing social support are important facilitators of health.

Participation in multiple roles also serve as a source of *information and advice*, as well as more concrete forms of assistance (House & Kahn, 1985). Being integrated within a web of social networks promotes information, choice, and guidance about health-related matters, in terms of individual behaviors (diet, exercise, smoking, drinking) and the propensity to seek professional health care.

Social roles offer *resources, privileges, and rewards*, all of which may affect preventative health behavior and enhance health-related resources and choices (Sieber, 1974; Verbrugge, 1985). The multiple roles effect could reflect the value of a diverse social network in promoting health-related behavior. Women with few roles may either be more vulnerable to risk factors or more exposed to hazardous lifestyles than those more socially integrated.

Multiple roles give *purpose, meaning and guidance to life*, promoting self-esteem and autonomy, and discouraging disordered conduct (Coser, 1975; Pearlin, Lieberman, Menaghan, & Mullan, 1981; Thoits, 1986). For example, multiple role attachments may lessen the distress produced by the loss or strains accompanying any particular role (Sieber, 1974). This calls forth Coser's (1975) notion of roles as a "seedbed of complexity," wherein varied social ties promote autonomy and, conceivably, health.

An important research issue is the link between roles and subjective identities, how roles become internalized and how both identities and roles feed into one another and change over the life course. The relationship between role occupancy and personal control is also relevant (Downey & Moen, 1987; Rosenfield, 1989). The process by which roles enhance health—as a source of identity, efficacy, and self-esteem, as a source of social support and social control, or both—needs fuller explication.

The Importance of Social Participation

In many of the studies of women's roles in relation to health a focus on their social participation is missing. There is some evidence that church membership and frequency of church attendance is inversely related to women's mortality, after controlling for a range of risk factors (Berkman & Breslow, 1983; House et al., 1982). Frequent church attendance has been associated with less psychological distress as well. The Women's Roles and the Retirement Studies demonstrate how important participation in clubs and voluntary organizations is for both longevity and health. We found that club membership and volunteering are especially consequential for both women's health and psychological well-being, and that participation in clubs and organizations earlier in life has long-term health consequences (Moen, 1997a, 1997b; Moen, Dempster-McClain, & Williams, 1989, 1992, 1994). What is not clear is under what conditions, or why, this is so.

Kohn and Schooler (1982) and Karasek and Theorell (1991) described workplace conditions—jobs that are routinized and not substantively complex—that undermine a sense of self-direction and that negatively affect health. Social participation in clubs and volunteer work, on the other hand, may be extremely facilitative of a sense of self-direction, in that women have greater opportunity to choose the amount and type of their activity than they do on their paid jobs.

The Importance of Choice

Research is needed that specifically examines the relevance of *choice* of role attachments for health, and again invokes Coser's (1975) emphasis on autonomy. Magnusson (1995) pointed out that some events are in effect "chance" occurrences, such as widowhood, a health crisis, war, or economic downturns. Other events are "purposive," as individuals choose to marry or divorce, to move, to buy a new house, to take on or leave a job, to return to school. He also noted that the effects of these changes may either be immediately visible, constituting a "turning point" (Clausen, 1995), or develop slowly over time. Participation in clubs and voluntary activities is typically discretionary. That very discretion may well lead to the salutary consequences we have observed in the Women's Roles and Retirement Studies.

PATHWAYS TO WOMEN'S HEALTH

Health is more than a consequence of biology and of aging; research provides ample evidence that social integration, in the form of multiple role involvements, can promote resilience in the face of the biological and environmental risks accompanying aging. Both the sheer number of roles occupied and roles related to social participation—active involvement in organizations, churches, volunteering—seem to have salutary consequences. However, little is known about the *processes* by which women retain, lose, or achieve multiple role involvements and health as they age (see Fig. 8.2).

A life-course, role context approach (Moen et al., 1989, 1992; Spitze, Logan, Joseph, & Lee, 1994) draws on role theory and temporal considerations to suggest that the *contexts* of roles, as well as the dynamics of role transitions and trajectories, matter. Thus both earlier social integration as a young adult

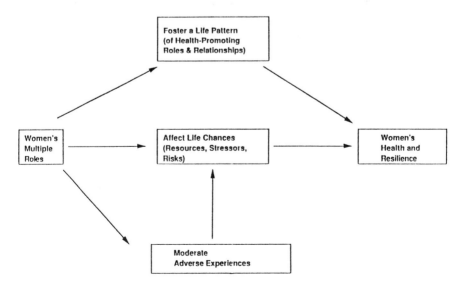

FIG. 8.2. Pathways from role occupancy to women's health.

and the patterning of roles throughout adulthood affect subsequent resilience in midlife and old age (Moen, 1997a, 1997b).

Differences in health by involvement in any particular role status may be a composite function of five sets of factors:

1. Self-selection—those individual predispositions and experiences drawing women into or out of roles.
2. Conditions of the role—for example, the impacts of the employment role are tempered by time at work and workplace flexibility as well as the job's physical and psychological demands.
3. Role definition or quality.
4. Structural options—the modes of adaptation available to women, such as flexible work-time options, as well as the constraints within society that push or pull women into or out of certain roles.
5. Family situation—including care responsibilities and as the presence of a (supportive) spouse. The findings from the best research in this area direct attention to the dynamic interplay among these elements in promoting or reducing women's health.

One can envision, then, three routes by which social integration could shape older women's health (Fig. 8.2). First, there could be a *life pattern* of multiple role occupancy and its health-promoting aspects. In my own research I find a certain cumulativeness in advantage over time; those women who are socially integrated and healthy in their early years of adulthood are also apt to be both more integrated and healthier in their later years. Women with initial good health both participate in more roles, and, in turn, reap the benefits of such role participation.

Second, early social integration can *shape life chances* of individuals, affecting pathways and practices that, in turn, shape the psychosocial resources, stressors, and risk factors with which individuals confront old age. The health and resilience of older women is influenced by their own life biographies including their roles earlier in life (Kohn, 1995; Moen & Erickson, 1995; Rutter, Champion, Quinton, Maughan, & Pickles, 1995). An important proposition of the life-course paradigm is that earlier resources affect both life pathways and psychosocial resources later in life (Elder, 1995).

Third, early social integration can also *moderate* the impacts of life experiences on health and resilience later in life. Social forces, such as significant life events, can reshape not only the direction of one's life course but also one's psychosocial resources, fostering (or inhibiting) resilience (such as preventative health care) as individuals age. Role participation and commitments could interact with objective symptomatology in affecting health behaviors and treatment choices, and, ultimately, health.

The life-course challenge to research and to practice is to recognize the dynamic interplay between women's health and social integration, how their altered roles and behavior patterns affect health, and how health, in turn, produces alterations in roles and behavior patterns. A life-course orientation offers rich insights, not simple explanations. This more complicated but more enriched view can help to unravel the web of forces linking gender, family, multiple roles, and health.

ACKNOWLEDGMENTS

Work on this chapter and the author's studies described here were supported by Research Grant R01 AG05450 to Phyllis Moen and Research Grant 1 P50 AG11711–01 to Karl Pillemer and Phyllis Moen from the National Institute on Aging, U.S. Department of Health and Human Services.

REFERENCES

Aneshensel, C. S., & Frerichs, R. R. (1982). Stress, support and depression: A longitudinal causal model. *Journal of Community Psychology, 10*, 363–376.

Barnett, R. C., & Baruch, G. K. (1985). Women's involvement in multiple roles, and psychological distress. *Journal of Personality and Social Psychology, 49*, 135–145.

Baruch, G. K., Biener, L., & Barnett, R. C. (1987). Women and gender in research on work and family. *American Psychologist, 42*, 130–136.

Bernard, J. (1972). *The future of marriage.* New York: Bantam.

Berk, S. F. (1985). *The gender factory: The apportionment of work in American households.* New York: Plenum.

Berkman, L. F., & Breslow, L. (1983). *Health and ways of living: The Alameda County study.* New York: Oxford University Press.

Berkman, L. F., & Syme, S. L. (1979). Social networks, host resistance and mortality: A nine-year follow-up study of Alameda County residents. *American Journal of Epidemiology, 109*, 186–204.

Blazer, D. G. (1982). Social support and mortality in an elderly community population. *American Journal of Epidemiology, 115*, 684–694.

Brown, G. W., & Harris, T. (1978). *Social origins of depression.* New York: The Free Press.

Burr, W. R., Leigh, G. K., Day, R. D., & Constantine, J. (1979). Symbolic interaction and the family. In W. R. Burr, R. Hill, F. I. Nye, & I. L. Reiss (Eds.), *Contemporary theories about the family* (Vol. 11, pp. 42–112). New York: The Free Press.

Cherlin, A. (1981). *Marriage, divorce, and remarriage: Changing patterns in the post war United States.* Cambridge, MA: Harvard University Press.

Clausen, J. A. (1995). Gender, contexts, and turning points in adults' lives. In P. Moen, G. H. Elder, Jr., & K. Luscher (Eds.), *Examining lives in context: Perspectives on the ecology of human development* (pp. 365–391). Washington, DC: American Psychological Association.

Cleary, P., & Mechanic, D. (1983). Sex differences in psychological distress among married people. *Journal of Health and Social Behavior, 24*, 111–121.

Coser, R. L. (1975). The complexity of roles as a seedbed of individual autonomy. In L. A. Coser (Ed.), *The idea of social structure: Papers in honor of Robert Merton* (pp. 237–265). New York: Harcourt Brace Jovanovich.

Coser, R. L., & Rokoff, G. (1971). Women in the occupational world: Social disruption and conflict. *Social Problems, 18*, 535–554.

Coverman, S., & Sheley, J. F. (1986). Change in men's housework and child-care time, 1965–1975. *Journal of Marriage and the Family, 48*, 413–422.

Downey, G., & Moen, P. (1987). Personal efficacy and income: A longitudinal study of women heading households. *Journal of Health and Social Behavior, 28*, 320–333.

Durkheim, E. (1951). *Suicide: A study in sociology* (J. A. Spaulding & G. Simpson, Trans.). New York: The Free Press. (Original work published 1897)

Eckenrode, J., & Gore, S. (1990). *Stress between work and family.* New York: Plenum.

Elder, G. H., Jr. (1995). The dynamics of individual development. In P. Moen, G. H. Elder, Jr., & K. Luscher (Eds.), *Examining lives in context: Perspectives on the ecology of human development* (pp. 15–17). Washington, DC: American Psychological Association.

Elder, G. H., Jr., George, L. K., & Shanahan, M. J. (1996). Psychosocial stress over the life course. In H. B. Kaplan (Ed.), *Psychosocial stress: Perspectives on structure, theory, life course, and methods* (pp. 247–291). Orlando, FL: Academic Press.

Esterberg, K. G., Moen, P., & Dempster-McClain, D. (1994). Transition to divorce: A life-course approach to women's marital duration and dissolution. *The Sociology Quarterly, 35*, 289–307.

Feld, S. (1963). Feelings of adjustment. In F. I. Nye & L. W. Hoftman (Eds.), *The employed mother in America* (pp. 331–352). Chicago: Rand McNally.

Forest, K. B., Moen, P., & Dempster-McClain, D. (1996). The effects of childhood family stress on women's depressive symptoms: A life course approach. *Psychology of Women Quarterly, 20*, 81–100.

Garfinkel, I., & McLanahan, S. S. (1986). *Single mothers and their children: A new American dilemma.* Washington, DC: Urban Institute Press.

Gavron, H. (1966). *The captive wife: Conflicts of housebound mothers.* London: Routledge & Kegan Paul.

Giele, J. Z. (1982). Women's work and family roles. In J. Z. Giele (Ed.), *Women in the middle years* (pp. 115–150). New York: The Free Press.

Goode, W. I. (1960). A theory of role strain. *American Sociological Review, 25*(4), 483–496.

Gore, S., & Mangione, T. (1983). Social roles, sex roles, and psychological distress: Additive and interactive models of sex differences. *Journal of Health and Social Behavior, 24*, 300–312.

Gove, W. R. (1972). The relationship between sex roles, marital status, and mental illness. *Social Forces, 56*, 67–76.

Gove, W. R., & Geerken, M. R. (1977). The effect of children and employment on the mental health of married men and women. *Social Forces, 56*, 66–76.

Gove, W. R., & Hughes, M. (1979). Possible causes of the apparent sex differences in physical health: An empirical investigation. *American Sociological Review, 44*, 126–146.

Hall, D. T. (1972). A model of coping with role conflict: The role behavior of college educated women. *Administrative Science Quarterly, 17*, 471–489.

Haynes, S. G., & Feinleib, M. (1980). Women, work and coronary heart disease: Prospective findings from the Framingham heart study. *American Journal of Public Health, 70*(2), 133–141.

Haynes, S. G., Feinleib, M., Devine, S., Scotch, N., & Kannel, W. B. (1978). The relationship of psychosocial factors to coronary heart disease in the Framingham study. *American Journal of Epidemiology, 107*, 384–402.

Haynes, S., Feinleib, M., & Kannel, W. B. (1980). The relationship of psychological factors to coronary heart disease in the Framingham study pt. III. *American Journal of Epidemiology, 3*, 37–54.

Herman, J. B., & Gyllstrom, K. K. (1977). Working men and women: Inter- and intra-role conflict. *Psychology of Women Quarterly, 1*, 319–333.

House, J. S., & Kahn, R. L. (1985). Measures and concepts of social support. In S. Cohen & S. L. Syme (Eds.), *Social support and health.* New York: Academic Press.

House, J. S., Landis, K. R., & Umberson, D. (1988). Social relationships and health. *Science, 241*, 540–545.

House, J. S., Robbins, C., & Metzner, H. L. (1982). The association of social relationships and activities with mortality: Prospective evidence from the Tecumseh community health study. *American Journal of Epidemiology, 116*, 123–140.

Kandel, D., Davies, M., & Raveis, V. (1985). The stressfulness of daily social roles for women: Marital, occupational, and household roles. *Journal of Health and Social Behavior, 26*, 64–78.

Kaplan, H. B. (1983). *Psychosocial stress: Trends in theory and research.* New York: Academic Press.

Karasek, R., & Theorell, T. (1991). *Healthy work: Stress, productivity, and the reconstruction of working life.* New York: Basic Books.

Kasl, S. V. (1986). The detection and modification of psychosocial and behavioral risk factors. In L. A. Aiken & D. H. Mechanic (Eds.), *Applications of social science to clinical medicine and health policy* (pp. 359–391). New Brunswick, NJ: Rutgers University Press.

Kessler, R. C., & McRae, J. A. (1981). Trends in the relationship between sex and psychological distress: 1957–1976. *American Sociological Review, 46*, 443–452.

Kessler, R. C., & McRae, J. A. (1982). The effects of wives' employment on the mental health of men and women. *American Sociological Review, 27*, 216–227.

Kohn, M. L. (1995). Social structure and personality through time and space. In P. Moen, G. H. Elder, Jr., & K. Luscher (Eds.), *Examining lives in context: Perspectives on the ecology of human development* (pp. 141–168). Washington, DC: American Psychological Association.

Kohn, M. L., & Schooler, C. (1982). Job conditions and personality: A longitudinal assessment of their reciprocal effects. *American Journal of Sociology, 87*(6), 1257–1286.

Legato, M. J., & Colman, C. (1991). *The female heart.* New York: Simon & Schuster.

Levi, L. (1974). Psychosocial stress and disease: A conceptual model. In E. K. Gunderson & R. H. Rahe (Eds.), *Life stress and illness* (pp. 8–33). Springfield, IL: Thomas.

Levi, L., Frankenhauser, M., & Gardell, B. (1982). Report on work stress related to social structures and processes. In G. R. Elliott & G. Eisdorfer (Eds.), *Stress and human health* (pp. 119–146). New York: Springer.

Linton, R. (1936). *The study of men.* New York: Appleton Century.

Litwak, E., Messeri, P., Wolfe, S., Gorman, S., Silverstein, M., & Guilarte, M. (1989). Organizational theory, social supports, and mortality rates: A theoretical convergence. *American Sociological Review, 54*(1), 49–66.

Magnusson, D. (1995). Individual development: A holistic, integrated model. In P. Moen, G. H. Elder, Jr., & K. Luscher (Eds.), *Examining lives in context: Perspectives on the ecology of human development* (pp. 19–60). Washington, DC: American Psychological Association.

Marks, S. R. (1977). Some notes on human energy, time and commitment. *American Sociological Review, 42*(6), 921–936.

McLanahan, S., & Adams, J. (1987). Parenthood and psychological well-being. *Annual Review of Sociology, 13*, 237–257.

Menaghan, E. G. (1983). Individual coping efforts: Moderators of the relationship between life stress and mental health outcomes. In R. E. Smith (Ed.), *The subtle revolution: Women at work* (pp. 31–61). New York: Academic Press.

Menaghan, E. G. (1989). Role changes and psychological well-being: Variations in effects by gender and role repertoire. *Social Forces, 67*, 693–714.

Merton, R. K. (1968). *Social theory and social structure.* New York: The Free Press.

Miller, J., Schooler, C., Kohn, M. L., & Miller, K. A. (1979). Women & work: The psychological effects of occupational conditions. *American Journal of Sociology, 85*(1), 66–94.

Moen, P. (1989). *Working parents: Transformations in gender roles and public policies in Sweden.* Madison: University of Wisconsin Press.

Moen, P. (1991). Transitions in mid-life: Women's work and family roles in the 1970s. *Journal of Marriage and the Family, 53*, 135–150.

Moen, P. (1992). *Women's two roles: A contemporary dilemma.* Westport, CT: Greenwood.

Moen, P. (1994). Women, work, and family: A sociological perspective on changing roles. In M. W. Riley, R. L. Kahn, & A. Foner (Eds.), *Age and structural lag: Society's failure to provide meaningful opportunities in work, family, and leisure* (pp. 151–170). New York: Wiley.

Moen, P. (1995a). Gender, age, and the life course. In R. H. Binstock & L. George (Eds.), *Handbook of aging and the social sciences* (4th ed., pp. 171–187). San Diego, CA: Academic Press.

Moen, P. (1995b). A life course approach to post-retirement roles and well-being. In L. A. Bond, S. J. Cutler, & A. E. Grams (Eds.), *Promoting successful and productive aging* (pp. 239–256). Newbury Park, CA: Sage.

Moen, P. (1996). A life course perspective on retirement, gender, and well-being. *Journal of Occupational Health Psychology, 1,* 131–144.

Moen, P. (1997a). A life course perspective. In E. Blechman & K. Brownell (Eds.), *Behavioral medicine for women: A comprehensive handbook.* NY: Guilford. (forthcoming)

Moen, P. (1997b). Pathways to women's resilience. In I. H. Gotlib & B. Wheaton (Eds.), *Stress and adversity over the life course: Trajectories and turning points.* New York: Cambridge University Press. (forthcoming)

Moen, P., Dempster-McClain, D., & Williams, R. W., Jr. (1989). Social integration and longevity: An event history analysis of women's roles and resilience. *American Sociological Review, 54,* 635–647.

Moen, P., Dempster-McClain, D., & Williams, R. W., Jr. (1992). Successful aging: A life course perspective on women's roles and health. *American Journal of Sociology, 97*(6), 1612–1638.

Moen, P., & Erickson, M. A. (1995). Linked lives: A trans-generational approach to resiliency. In P. Moen, G. H. Elder, Jr., & K. Lüscher (Eds.), *Examining lives in context: Perspectives on the ecology of human development* (pp. 169–210). Washington, DC: American Psychological Association.

Moen, P., & Forest, K. B. (1990). Working parents, workplace supports, and well-being: The Swedish experience. *Social Psychology Quarterly, 53*(2), 117–131.

Moen, P., Robison, J., & Dempster-McClain, D. (1995). Caregiving and women's well-being. *Journal of Health and Social Behavior, 36*(3), 259–273.

Moen, P., Robison, J., & Fields, V. (1994). Women's work and caregiving roles: A life course approach. *Journal of Gerontology: Social Sciences, 49*(4), S176–S186.

Nathanson, C. (1980). Social roles and health status among women: The significance of employment. *Social Science and Medicine, 14,* 463–471.

Nathanson, C. (1984). Sex differences in mortality. In R. H. Turner & J. F. Short, Jr. (Eds.), *Annual review of sociology* (Vol. 10, pp. 191–213). Palo Alto, CA: Annual Reviews Inc.

Nathanson, C., & Lopez, G. (1987). The future of sex mortality differentials in industrialized countries: A structural hypothesis. *Population Research and Policy Review, 6*(2), 123–136.

Nickels, J. T., & Chirikos, T. N. (1990). Functional disability of elderly patients with long-term coronary heart disease: A sex stratified analysis. *Journal of Gerontology: Social Sciences, 45,* S60–S68.

Northcutt, H. C. (1981). Women, work, health and happiness. *International Journal of Women's Studies, 4*(3), 268–276.

Nye, F. I. (1974). Effect on mother. In L. W. Hoffman & F. I. Nye (Eds.), *Working mothers* (pp. 207–225). San Francisco: Jossey-Bass.

Oakley, A. (1974). *The sociology of housework.* New York: Pantheon.

Oliver, M., Vedin, A., & Wilhelmsson, C. (Eds.). (1986). *Myocardial infarction in women.* New York: Churchill Livingstone.

Pearlin, L. I. (1975). Sex roles and depression. In D. N. Ginsberg (Ed.), *Normative life crises* (pp. 191–207). New York: Academic Press.

Pearlin, L. I. (1983). Role strains and the self. In H. B. Kaplan (Ed.), *Psychosocial stress: Trends in theory and research* (pp. 26–32). New York: Academic Press.

Pearlin, L. I., Lieberman, M. A., Menaghan, E., & Mullan, J. T. (1981). The stress process. *Journal of Health and Social Behavior, 22*, 337–356.

Radloff, L. (1975). Sex differences in depression: The effect of occupation and marital status. *Sex Roles, 1*(3), 249–265.

Reed, D., McGee, D., & Yano, K. (1983). Psychosocial processes and general susceptibility to chronic disease. *American Journal of Epidemiology, 119*, 356–370.

Reskin, B. F., & Coverman, S. (1985). Sex and race in the determinants of psychophysical distress: A reappraisal of the sex-role hypothesis. *Social Forces, 63*(4), 1038–1059.

Robison, J., Moen, P., & Dempster-McClain, D. (1995). Women's caregiving: Changing profiles and pathways. *Journal of Gerontology: Social Sciences, 50B*, S362–S373.

Rosenfield, S. (1989). The effects of women's employment: Personal control and sex differences in mental health. *Journal of Health and Social Behavior, 30*, 77–91.

Ross, C. E., Mirowsky, J., & Huber, J. (1983). Dividing work, sharing work, and in-between: Marriage patterns and depression. *American Sociological Review, 48*, 809–823.

Russell, S. (1974). Transition to parenthood: Problems and gratifications. *Journal of Marriage and the Family, 36*, 294–302.

Rutter, M., Champion, L., Quinton, D., Maughan, B., & Pickles, A. (1995). Understanding individual differences in environmental-risk exposure. In P. Moen, G. H. Elder, Jr., & K. Luscher (Eds.), *Examining lives in context: Perspectives on the ecology of human development* (pp. 61–96). Washington, DC: American Psychological Association.

Seeman, T. E., Kaplan, G. A., Knudsen, L., Cohen, R., & Guralnik, J. (1987). Social network ties and mortality among the elderly in the Alameda County Study. *American Journal of Epidemiology, 126*(4), 714–723.

Sharp, L., & Nye, F. I. (1963). Maternal mental health. In F. Nye & L. Hoffman (Eds.), *The employed mother in America* (pp. 309–319). Chicago: Rand McNally.

Sieber, S. D. (1974). Toward a theory of role accumulation. *American Sociological Review, 39*, 567–578.

Smith, K. R., & Moen, P. (1988). Passage through midlife: Women's changing family roles and economic well-being. *Sociological Quarterly, 29*, 503–524.

Spitze, G., Logan, J. R., Joseph, G., & Lee, E. (1994). Middle generation roles and the well-being of men and women. *Journal of Gerontology: Social Sciences, 49*, S107–116.

Spreitzer, E., Snyder, E. E., & Larson, D. L. (1979). Multiple roles and psychological well-being. *Sociological Focus, 12*, 141–148.

Thoits, P. A. (1982). Conceptual, methodological, and theoretical problems in studying social support as a buffer against life stress. *Journal of Health and Social Behavior, 23*, 145–159.

Thoits, P. A. (1983). Multiple identities and psychological well-being: A reformulation and test of the social isolation hypothesis. *American Sociological Review, 48*, 174–187.

Thoits, P. A. (1986). Multiple identities: Examining gender and marital status differences in distress. *American Sociological Review, 51*, 259–272.

Verbrugge, L. M. (1982). Women's social roles and health. In P. Berman & E. Ramey (Eds.), *Women: A developmental perspective* (Rep. No. 82-2298, pp. 49–78). Bethesda, MD: National Institutes of Health.

Verbrugge, L. M. (1983). Multiple roles and physical health of women and men. *Journal of Health and Social Behavior, 24*, 16–30.

Verbrugge, L. M. (1985). Gender and health: An update on hypotheses and evidence. *Journal of Health and Social Behavior, 26*, 156–182.

Verbrugge, L. M. (1987). Role burdens and physical health of women and men. In F. Crosby (Ed.), *Spouse, parent, worker: On gender and multiple roles* (pp. 154–166). New Haven, CT: Yale University Press.

Verbrugge, L. M. (1989). Gender, aging and health. In K. S. Markides (Ed.), *Aging and health* (pp. 23–78). Newbury Park, CA: Sage.

Verbrugge, L. M., & Madans, J. H. (1985, Fall). Social roles and health: Trends of American women. *Milbank Memorial Fund Quarterly, Health and Society, 63*(4), 691–735.

Veroff, J., Douvan, E., & Kulka, R. A. (1981). *The inner American.* New York: Basic Books.

Waldron, I., Herold, J., Dunn, D., & Staum, R. (1982). Reciprocal effects of health and labor force participation among women: Evidence from two longitudinal studies. *Journal of Occupational Medicine, 24*(2), 126–132.

Waldron, I., & Jacobs, J. A. (1989). Effects of multiple roles on women's health—Evidence from a national longitudinal study. *Women and Health, 15,* 3–19.

Welch, S., & Booth, A. (1977). Employment and health among married women with children. *Sex Roles, 3*(4), 385–397.

Wethington, E., & Kessler, R. C. (1989). Employment, parenting responsibility and psychological distress: A longitudinal study of married women. *Journal of Family Issues, 10,* 527–546.

Williams, R. M., Jr. (1965). *American society: A sociological interpretation.* New York: Knopf.

Woods, N. F., & Hulka, B. S. (1979). Symptom reports and illness behavior among employed women and homemakers. *Journal of Community Health, 5*(1), 36–45.

9

Well-Being Among Swedish Employed Mothers With Preschool Children

Ulla Björnberg
Göteborg University

This chapter addresses the psychological aspects of reconciliation of employment and family life. The focus is on the double burden of women and the relative importance of working conditions and conditions in the home for the well-being of women and men, with particular emphasis placed on the role of the family situation for the psychological well-being of employed mothers. The point of departure for the chapter is a theoretical framework for analysis of constraints in contemporary family life. The empirical analysis is based on data collected in Sweden from 670 parents with preschool children.

The assumption behind this study is that the problems connected with women's health must be approached from a broad perspective and include more thoroughly what postmodern family life means and how it influences the well-being of women and men. Several indices suggest that stress related to their responsibility for home and family is important for understanding the psychological well-being of women.

Research has suggested that employment in itself does not have a negative impact on the psychological health of women. In fact, comparisons between housewives and employed women indicate that housewives have more health problems than employed women. Longitudinal data for women between 1968 and 1981 provide no evidence of deterioration in health status for those women who entered the labor market during the studied period. These conclusions are supported by other results which demonstrate that the degree of integration within different spheres of society has a positive impact on the psychological well-being of women, as well as among men (Axelsson, 1992; Lundberg, 1990; Vågerö, 1994).

Several studies have pointed out that psychologically, as well as physically, demanding jobs have a similar impact on the health of men and women. Taken into consideration that women often have a second shift at home, it is reasonable to assume that psychological health is a combined effect of both working conditions and the home situation for women (Hall, 1990; Moen, 1989). Women's greater responsibility for the household and family explains their lower psychological health status (Lundberg, 1990). This conclusion generates questions concerning the particular aspects of household labor that are detrimental to women's health. Is it a question of quantity—that is, the amount of housework, number of children, age of children—or are there other aspects, irrespective of the objective quantity of the work load that can explain why women so often feel stress and fatigue?

According to time-budget studies in Sweden, time spent for cleaning has been reduced heavily during the last decades. Between 1950 and 1980, cleaning was reduced by 7.5 hours per week. Time spent for child care has, however, increased (Nyberg, 1989). Another investigation reveals that "active time" with the children is equal among families where both parents are employed compared with families where one parent works in the home (Gustafsson & Kjuhlin, 1992). Recent time-budget studies in Sweden indicate that women do twice as much work as men within the household and with children, even when they have small children and are employed full time (Rydenstam, 1993). Subsequently, there is reason to believe that the women's double burden contributes to their reported symptoms of fatigue.

The growth of the dual earner family in Sweden during the last 30 years has had considerable implications for the ways in which couples negotiate their responsibilities toward employment, children, and family life in general. On the basis of several studies it seems reasonable to conclude that parents in Sweden give high priority to their children during their free time. Their ambitions to try to have as much time as possible with their children seems to be high (Björnberg, 1992; Lundén-Jacoby & Näsman, 1987).

Private life and intimate relationships have a fundamental importance for the identity construction of both men and women. This is far more important than the sphere of work and employment for the identity of a majority of both men and women (Björnberg, 1994). Family life and household labor occupy a large proportion of an individual's time and energy. Expectations regarding what family life should provide are high, but the image of the "good family life" is different for men and women. Subsequently, there are discrepancies between dreams and reality that are often difficult to negotiate. Households are increasingly being regarded as arenas of potential conflicts, where the division of household labor, childrearing, child care, and financial matters are some of the main sources of disputes. The rising divorce rates in most industrial countries is a clear indication of this problem. Longitudinal data suggest that the increase in divorces can be traced to the growth in employment among women (Axelsson, 1992; Morris, 1990). Apart from their lower rates of psychological well-being, women are increasingly choosing to break up families. Women take divorce initiatives at a much higher rate than men (Koch-Nielsen, 1983; Moxnes, 1990; Wadsby & Svedin, 1993).

In her book *Brave New Families*, Stacey (1990) described postmodern family life, that is, family forms which have developed since the 1970s. The "new" families are, according to Stacey, both insecure and undemocratic when evaluated against the ideals that feminists and visionary intellectuals had for family life in transition, where a new gender order of companionship, equal partnership, and parenthood was envisioned. In this model, gender relations would be less asymmetrical without patriarchal subordination, replacing the older male "breadwinner models." These ideals are supported in theory by most men and women in society today. Women, on the one hand, entered the labor market in order to assume their share of the economic support of families. On the other hand, men did not assume their share in the household labor and the care of family members. Instead of the model of companionship, the realities of postmodern families is a gender order free of norms. Everything is subject for negotiations—parenthood, sexuality, the division of labor, the allocation of money. This situation has brought with it insecurity and conflicts on unequal terms. Rather than sensible negotiations, family members are caught in a power struggle.

Family negotiations concern not only the division of labor between partners, they also concern educational values and styles of relating to one another within the family. In the discourse of the implications of postmodernity many authors have emphasized the process of individualization and the loosening of traditional social relationships within the family and local communities (Beck, 1986; Melucci, 1991). Many parents feel that their own upbringing can only to a very limited extent serve as a model for how they should deal with situations they confront today. The parents' own experiences are perceived as inadequate or insufficient in many new types of situations. They are also unsure as to what norms and judgments others have (Zoll & Oechsle, 1992). In the late-modern family ideal, the importance of democratic relationships based on mutual respect is emphasized. Emotional relations assume a central position and individual needs and demands are awarded more space among all of the family members. The role of parents toward their children is that of counselors, and even friends. They are responsible for their children and are also advice partners. The relationships between parents and children are individualized and open in order to be susceptible to new information and to reflect, or at least try to mentally digest and interpret, the overflow of information directed toward families

(Dencik, Bäckström, & Larsson, 1988). In this late-modern context, both children and parents feel a need to move toward autonomy and self-reflection. Children and parents both in the course of their relationships feel a demand to argue and provide reasons for actions (Bjerrum Nielsen & Rudberg, 1991). Against this briefly summarized stock of knowledge on problems regarding the ambiguities faced by post- or late-modern dual-earner families, it can be assumed that dimensions of conflict within families and a sense of insecurity in parenting are important factors to take into consideration in understanding the psychological well-being among women and men.

EMPIRICAL DATA AND RESULTS

During the autumn of 1992, interviews were conducted with men and women in their homes. They were interviewed separately. Five-year-old children were sampled and their mothers and the male partner in the home were interviewed (90% of the men were the biological father of the children). Among the selected families, 60% had children under 5 years of age. The number of individuals interviewed was 670, among them 215 men and 146 single mothers.

Three indicators were used to illuminate the well-being of women and men:

1. Psychological well-being.[1]
2. Perception of the work at home as a burden or not, labeled as "home stress."[2]
3. Subjective evaluations of their ability to balance job and family.[3]

As explanatory variables, the following were applied:

A. *Circumstances of employment.*

    1. Working conditions.[4]

---

[1]The measure is a summary index based on replies to the following question: "How would you judge your state of health at present (with reference to the last fortnight) considering the health factors listed: fatigued; stressed; aches, such as neck, head, shoulders; slightly depressed; feelings of insufficiency; cold?"

[2]The measure is a summary index based on replies to the following question: "Bearing in mind the last fortnight, do you think that your share of the responsibility for the family has felt easy or strenuous for you?" (4-point scaled answers.)

[3]The question was formulated as follows: "How well do you think that you succeed in balancing the demands of your family and those of your job?" (5-point scaled answer.)

[4]Working conditions is a summary index based on subjective evaluations on a 5-point scale with the following indicators: stressful–calm; physically heavy–easy; unhygienic–clean; monotonous–stimulating; risky–safe; insecure employment–secure employment. In the summary index the respondents have been classified as having *strenuous jobs, somewhat strenuous jobs,* and *not strenuous jobs.*

2. Amount of time in paid labor—short, normal and long.[5]

B. *Circumstances at home.*

1. Number of children.

2. Degree of conflicts in the home.

3. Parental identity as secure or insecure.

An index for "conflict family" was constructed on the basis of questions concerning struggles over division of household chores, allocation of household money, child care and childrearing.[6] Among the women 24% and among the men 18% were categorized as living in conflict families. An index of "parental identity" was constructed on the basis of questions measuring the extent of control in balancing the children's needs against one's own needs, the urge to compensate the child for not being at home during the workday, and to which extent parents have feelings of helplessness toward the child and have feelings of not providing enough support to the child.[7] Respondents were categorized into three groups—one being labeled as having a "secure parental identity," one as having an "insecure parental identity," and one as being "in between." Among the women sampled, 13%, and among the men, only 3%, have been attributed with an "insecure parental identity," whereas 62% of the women and 86% of the men are classified as having a "secure parental identity."

Psychological Well-Being

The results support findings from other studies which indicate that women have a lower degree of psychological well-being than men. They are more

---

[5]Working hours: Short < 35 hours per week, no extra work, no overtime; Normal: > 35 hours per week, no extra work, overtime < 5 hours per week; Long: > 35 hours per week, overtime > 11 hours per week.

[6]"Conflict family" is a summary index based on replies to the following questions: "Does it occur that the household labor or work with the children leads to disputes between you and your partner?" "Does it occur that issues on child rearing lead to disputes between you and your partner?" "Does it occur that questions on how your incomes should be used lead to disputes between you and your partner?" Options were daily; sometimes; every week; rarely; never. "Do you feel that you are usually able to balance the needs and wishes of your children against your own or do you think that you often have to give up your own wishes and needs for the sake of theirs?" (5-point scale.)

[7]The index was constructed on the basis of the following questions: "Are there situations in your everyday life when you feel helpless or insecure as a mother/father?" Options were often; sometimes; rarely; never. "Do you feel that you are usually able to balance the needs and wishes of your children against your own or do you think that you often have to give up your own wishes and needs for the sake of theirs?" (5-point scale.) "Do you think that your children are frustrated, satisfied, or overindulged as far as the following factors are concerned—respect; affiliation; attention; appreciation; trust; tenderness; love?" (4-point scale.) "Does it occur that you feel obliged to compensate your 5-year-old for the time he or she does not spend at home?" Options were daily; sometimes; every week; rarely; never.

TABLE 9.1
Subjective Evaluationof Well-Being/Psychological Health Among Women and Men. Percentages

	Men	Women
Good psychological health	48	27
Certain flaws	45	55
Poor psychological health	7	18
Total	100	100
N	215	435

Note. Chi-square $p = .0001$.

fatigued, more often have head-, shoulder, and backaches, and feel more depressed, and so forth (see Table 9.1).

The results suggest a positive interaction between stressful work situations and low psychological well-being for both men and women. In the sample, 45% of both sexes perceive their jobs as stressful.[8] The results also suggest that women with an insecure job position report a lower psychological well-being than those who consider that their jobs are secure. The results are significant for women, but not for men.

Other working conditions measured suggest a weak interaction with psychological health, in particular among women. Among women with a strenuous work load, 24% indicate poor psychological health, in contrast to 13% among those without a strenuous work load. The differences between the groups are not significant for either women or men.

Conflicts in the family have a strong impact on the psychological well-being for both men and women, and the results are highly significant. Having an insecure parental identity is also a strong factor influencing the health of women. Very few men revealed an insecure parental identity in the study; subsequently, comparisons between men and women in regard to this variable are impossible.

Home Stress

Home stress measures the extent to which responsibility for home and family is felt to be a burden. Women feel home stress to a much higher degree than men (see Fig. 9.1). Working conditions do not influence the degree of home stress felt by either sex, nor does the number of children. However, conflicts in the family and insecure parental identity play a significant role.

---

[8]Those who stated 1–2 on a 5-point scale have been classified as having stressful jobs.

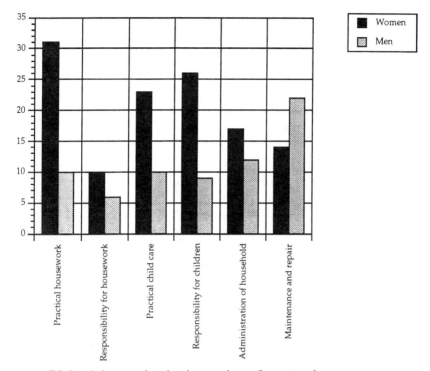

FIG. 9.1. Judgments of work at home as heavy (home stress) among women and men, by percentages. From the 1994 project on "Parental Employment and Family Life," Department of Sociology, Göteborg University. Project leader: Ulla Björnberg.

Balancing Family and Employment

Around one fourth of both the men and the women sampled have a low self-evaluation of their ability to balance family and employment. The evaluation is particularly low among highly qualified men and women. This socioeconomic group has both demanding jobs and high ambitions for family life (Andersson, 1993; Björnberg & Bäck-Wiklund, 1990; Roman, 1994). In this group, 40% of the men and 35% of the women stated that they do not manage very well in this respect. For women, but not for the men, stressful jobs have a significant impact on low evaluations. Other working conditions have no significant impact.

Living in a conflict family weighs heavily in relation to their evaluation as to how well they balance family and paid labor for the men, but not for the women studied. Among men living in conflict families, 47% stated that they manage less than well compared to 16% among those who live in nonconflict families. For women, an insecure parental identity also has an impact on their judgment as to being able to balance family and employment. Women with an insecure parental identity manage less than well to a greater extent than women with a secure parental identity—a difference of 16%.

Interactions Between Psychological Well-Being, Home Stress and Evaluations of Ability to Balance Family and Employment

Contrary to what could have been expected, the results do not suggest any significant interaction between feelings of balancing job and family on the one hand, and feeling of home stress on the other, for either sex. The results are surprising in the sense that it could have been expected that work at home would have been felt as a burden to a greater extent among those who did not find a satisfactory balance between paid labor and the family.

However, there are strong interactions between feelings of home stress and psychological health (see Table 9.2). The data also suggest that both men and women who feel that they do not manage to balance paid labor and family have a low degree of psychological well-being. Both interactions are highly significant for women, as well as for men.

Respondents with a low evaluation of their ability to manage a balance between their families and their jobs were asked to mention at whose expense the lack of balance was struck. The respondents felt that the lack of balance was detrimental for their own personal well-being, with almost 50% of the women and 35% of the men expressing this opinion. Around one fourth considered that it is primarily their children who suffer from this lack of balance. Another interesting result is that men, to a much greater extent than women, claim that their partner suffers (26% of the men and 8% of the women).

Very few individuals expressed the opinion that their colleagues or work suffered. One can interpret the results so that work is awarded the highest

TABLE 9.2
Psychological Health and Home Stress Among Women and Men

	Good Health		Certain Flaws		Poor Health	
	Women	Men	Women	Men	Women	Men
Home stress	11	2	23	9	42	21
N	92	99	172	87	45	13

Note. Women $P = .0023$; Men $P = .0073$.

priority, whereas personal well-being is given the lowest priority among those individuals who do not manage to find a proper balance.

Conflicts in the Home

The results of the study do not suggest any interaction between living in conflict families and independent variables such as working conditions, number of hours at work, or number of children. Thus, having a demanding burden does not, as such, increase the probability of experiencing conflicts. These results are surprising and should be judged as highly suggestive. More in-depth analysis is needed to sort out strategic factors behind conflicts in families. Such factors are to be located within a framework of gender power relations within families, and later in the chapter a theoretical interpretation is developed regarding the gender aspects of contemporary family life.

Insecure Parental Identity

On issues concerning parent–child relationships the results of the study suggest that there is a high degree of insecurity and disagreement in parenting. Many women feel that they have little support from the fathers and this is experienced as highly unsatisfactory. Twenty-six percent of the women and 19% of the men reply that responsibilities for the children lead to conflicts with their partner every week. Fifty-seven percent of the mothers and only 15% of the fathers admit feelings of insecurity, either often or sometimes.[9] Almost 50% of the women and 38% of the men express every week or daily a need to compensate the child for the time which he or she does not spend at home.

In the study, women and men have been asked to compare themselves with their partner on different aspects of parenting.[10] The purpose has been to study to what extent men and women judge their partner as different, passive, or impatient in their approach to their children. The results suggest that women and men have different views on childrearing and about what responsibility for children implies. More than 40% of both genders report that their partner has a different approach toward their children. For example, 53% of the women state that their partner plays more with the child,

---

[9]Question asked: "Are there everyday situations when you feel helpless or insecure as a mother or a father?"

[10]The full question was: "If you compare yourself with your partner regarding aspects of relating to your 5-year-old child, how would this comparison look?" *Different:* "He/she has another view on childrearing than I. Plays more with the child than I; He/she has a better hand with the child than I." *Passive:* "He/she is passive with the child, demands too little; He/she devotes too little time to the children; He/she doesn't care about the child, wants to stay neutral." *Impatient:* "He/she is often impatient and demands too much from the children; He/she is often irritated in front of the children."

compared to 47% of the men. Women (33%) judge their partner to be passive in contrast to 15% of the men. More than 30% of the women find that the father devotes too little time to their children. Only 8% of the men have the same opinion about their female partners. 27% of the women find their partner to be impatient compared to 20% of the men.

In those families where the partners have many conflicts, men and women evaluate their partner as different, especially on issues concerning child-rearing. Parents with an insecure parental identity consider their partner as different, passive, and impatient to a much greater extent than parents with a secure parental identity.

Summary

The results from the study suggest that the family's situation is an important dimension in connection with how employed parents perceive their work load in the family, as well as for their psychological health. Women who have stressful working conditions also tend to experience domestic responsibilities as a burden—that is, feel home stress—as well as work stress. Other working conditions measured did not seem to have a similar impact. The results also suggest that concrete stress factors in family life, particularly conflicts in the family and insecure parental identity, are hidden factors behind psychological well-being, feelings of home stress and subjective evaluations as to their ability to find a satisfying balance between family and paid labor.

Individuals who have jobs judged as stressful by the individuals themselves have a lower measure of psychological well-being. Stressful jobs have a negative impact on the parents' ability to balance family and job in a satisfactory way. The psychological well-being of women is also strongly influenced by insecure job situations. These factors seem to influence women and men in similar ways, but they are particularly important for women, because more women indicate feeling home stress and have a lower level of psychological well-being than men. Thus, the results suggest that stress factors, rather than work load (i.e., number of children, full-time employment, physically demanding or dirty working conditions) are important factors to consider in further analysis.

The results do not suggest any interaction between conflicts in the family and working conditions or number of working hours. Thus the employment situation does not seem to be of importance for conflicts between the partners in the family; nor do working conditions or work hours seem to have any impact on an insecure parental identity. The results from this study support other research results which indicate that women's "double burden" is the primary factor behind their poor psychological health (Lundberg, 1990).

On the basis of the results, it is concluded that it is important to look more closely into the implications and meanings of domestic work and care responsibilities for women and men. A deeper analysis of the role of household labor, care, and responsibility for family life in contemporary partnerships is needed. For many years the economic value of unpaid labor in the home has been discussed; however, the labor as such has seldom been analyzed on equal terms with paid labor. It might appear as a trivial fact that people become exhausted and stressed in conflictual situations. Conflicts concerning domestic work and care, however, are not in themselves trivial, but have to be considered as a problematic aspect in dual-earner households in contemporary everyday life, especially when partners are not able to handle their conflicts in a constructive way. The division of labor in the home is the subject of continuous negotiations within the context of dual-earner families and these negotiations have to be understood in terms of gender power relations.

GENDERED NEGOTIATIONS OVER DOMESTIC WORK AND PARENTING IN CONTEMPORARY FAMILIES

Negotiations between partners in the family as to how everyday life activities should be organized are carried out on the basis of different premises for men and women. In marriage relationships, women and men have different rationales and different views regarding their roles in the mutual family project with which they initiate their negotiations and on which their coexistence is constructed. Women tend to have a quite clear view that marriage implies a radical change in their lives. Men tend to be unaware of the amount of time consumed by domestic chores and children. Men are inclined to be set on carrying on with their existence as before, and to interpret that equality means that each person can do whatever he or she wishes. Thus, men tend to insist on continuing as before, thereby making it impossible for the women to make choices in the same way (Moxnes, 1990).

Thus marriages are regulated by "the invisible marriage contract" where women and men have contradictory starting points for life in couple relationships and families. For most women, the family constitutes a goal that is perceived as superior to all other goals. For the man, the family constitutes one of many interests, and is not always awarded the highest priority. Negotiations between the spouses revolve around how high on the list of priorities he is willing to place marriage and the family. In Moxnes' (1990) study, most spouses were, however, unaware of their different perceptions regarding marriage and the family. Negotiations had taken place where the women expected that their spouses would award as much priority to the marriage and the family as they did.

Regarding domestic work and care there is in general a tacit presumption that women bear the main responsibility for the work, for the well-being and the overall maintenance of the home, and for the social networks surrounding the home. Whereas men share to a certain extent the chores that have to be undertaken, women want men to share both the responsibility and practical tasks in the household, and try in different ways to involve men. Men become involved, but in between his involvement and her involvement there is a high degree of tension and the potential for conflict is acute. Women's legitimacy is low in their negotiations over the distribution of labor and women have a low rate of control over their own autonomy, within, as well as outside of, the home.

Autonomy for Men, Responsibility of Care for Women

According to Chodorow (1978), the social construction of male identity presupposes their acquisition of autonomy. The young boy separates himself from his mother, and during this process he strengthens his ability to represent himself. Intimacy—physiological and psychological closeness—is not developed in the same way as it is for the young girl, because she develops psychologically in a close relationship with her mother. Men will perceive the normal order in such a way that he maintains his autonomy while securing love, care and service from a woman—his mother and later his female partners. This is "the male project." To a certain extent men regard care and service as expressions of love.

In a corresponding way women develop their potentials for intimacy and capacities to satisfy the needs of others, primarily their children and their husband. The social construction of the female gender presupposes that the woman unconditionally assumes the responsibility for family and household—her commitment and love will be taken for granted. Both partners depart from this tacitly perceived female unconditional and male conditional division of labor in their mutual negotiations.

In their actions, women are inclined to refer to a rationality of responsibility, whereas men to a greater extent will refer to a technical rationality. The rationality of responsibility implies that actions are viewed in connection to the consequences they have for others—that is, the premises of others are taken into consideration (Sörensen, 1982). Technical rationality, on the other hand, is connected to a means–end rationale and anchored in a contractual mode of thinking (Haavind, 1987). If a woman refrains from assuming responsibility for others, she, in turn neglects them and creates guilt for herself. Subsequently, this responsibility is perceived as a "burden." Women are relatively powerless in relation to this responsibility because they have very little control over the conditions for it (Haavind, 1982). With the expression "the female burden," the rationality of responsibility is given further meaning, perceived within the context of the gender power relations that permeate the family and society in general.

Although men are prepared to undertake a share in the chores, they will nevertheless resist assuming a share of the responsibility that would result in a loss of their autonomy. Consequently, they may apply a strategy that leaves her with the "control," that is, does not interfere in what should be done and how it should be done. She retains responsibility for the definition of standards and the distribution of labor. Thus, she will be blamed by him, as well as by herself, if the family is not properly cared for (Haavind & Andenaes, 1994). If he starts to interfere with her standards of performance, her routines, or both and become involved he will run the risk of losing his autonomy (Stjernelund, 1995). For men, abandoning responsibility is a safer strategy. When they negotiate over a more equal division of labor in the home, his share will be defined, whereas her share remains undefined, as the underlying responsibility rests with her. In negotiations, which she must initiate, her partner occupies a stronger position in regards to the terms of negotiation. The more she demands, the more she runs the risk of appearing to be a "nag."

Leaving her with all control implies that he will be dependent on her for the services and care that he expects her to perform. However, his being dependent on her is not equivalent to her having power over him. On the contrary, her surplus work at home frees him to use his time at his own discretion and makes her time use dependent on his (Stjernelund, 1995). Time allocation, the planning and coordination of family projects of the family members, becomes primarily a woman's problem, often at her own expense (Björnberg, 1992; Friberg, 1990).

The implicit rationality behind "assuming a share" of the work load which rests with someone else is that it should be "worth" something. Male involvement in home and family is regarded by men as an investment toward a good relationship. It is an investment in time and it is a gift that is received with appreciation by the children and his wife. By getting involved he will give up some of his autonomy, but on the whole men resist binding their time and energy into commitments that will significantly reduce their autonomy. This is a potential source of conflict, both among men themselves, but also between men and other family members (Haavind & Andeneas, 1994).

Contemporary women's struggle for emancipation has spiraled around their efforts to expand their own possibilities to choose—that is, control over their own lives. In practice, this has implied that women themselves decide how they should adapt to others. Failures are perceived as personal, because the choice was personal. Women assume sole responsibility for how they use their possibilities. A woman sees it as her task to make the best of the possibilities over which she in effect has very little control (Haavind, 1987). This is the potential source of conflict, both among women themselves, and between them and their family members. For example, when the woman takes the responsibility for making sure that everyone in the family (particularly the children) are all right, she risks becoming fixed in a circle of demands. She is receptive to the external pressures that contribute to pushing up the demands for what a good mother should do. On television, polished kitchen and bathroom surfaces are presented as something worthwhile and attainable with the help of an effective detergent. In magazines, on television and radio, new knowledge concerning child development are proffered. It is here that insecure parental identity comes into the picture. The criteria that women set for what is good can as a rule be infinite and are not necessarily related to how other family members value their situation. To the extent that women live up to unreasonable expectations, they also run the risk of increasing their "debt."

The subordination of women has changed direction and form. When women acknowledge their own needs and demands, the men have, in turn, been able to use this in such a way that they have been able to free themselves from emotional and economic responsibilities. When men assume their share of the responsibility, they experience it as something they actively give, and for which they should be given "credit."

Household responsibilities carry different symbolic meanings for men and women according to the interaction and the sense or togetherness that they create in the marriage. Work in the household is part of a "game of love," ethics of giving, debts, and retribution. Negotiations are a question of deciding on a reasonable division of labor between the partners in accordance with their views on gender roles, the couple relationship, and the family. This is a problematic situation in that the spouses do not share the same views or they value their actions differently. In an exchange perspective, what is being exchanged can be of a different quality, and it is therefore often difficult to evaluate efforts in accordance with what is "fair."

A home can not be compared with a place of employment. Hierarchies of power and incentives are different in the home and at the work place. In families there is an "economy of gifts" that is not present in a work place (Kauffmann, 1992). There are, however, dimensions within the work situation at home which on a theoretical level can be comparable to those at a work place. In a theoretical model of a psychosocial work environment, Karasek and Theorell (1990) identified two dimensions: the rate of expectations or claims on work performance, and the rate of control. Combined in the model are four groups that result in two opposite poles—the first is a high degree of performance with a high rate of control, which is classified as a stimulating and active psychosocial environment. The other is a combination of job demands with a low rate of control, which is classified as an environment that creates a high degree of negative stress. This model could be applied to the psychosocial analysis of labor in the household. In the home, responsibility for the well-being of the family members is combined with control over the work that has to be done. As women bear most of the responsibility, they subsequently in an objective sense have a high rate of control. Thus, according to the model, they should feel stimulated and active. The empirical results presented in this chapter point in the opposite direction, that is, women have a low rate of control, because their work performance is dictated by the needs of other family members. In domestic work women assume a greater responsibility, but have little power to delegate tasks. The ability of women to control work performance is also limited, because the conditions for their work are set by others. The urge to adapt to conditions set by others is part of women's identity as homemakers. A woman has difficulties in negotiating better conditions for herself because this would restrict the project of autonomy of her husband. The more women become adapted to a mode of life as a paid laborer, the more they will demand their share of free time and autonomy. The division of labor and responsibility in contemporary households is, according to the theory presented here, a tension between autonomy and dependency for both men and women. It is an issue of drawing borderlines and setting the limits for commitments and responsibilities between spouses and between parents and children. Although women want to set limits for their own work load in the family, they are not prepared to give up their commitments. They prefer to share the burden of responsibility more equally with men, and would like men to perceive needs in the same way as they do. However, although their "need perception" is tacit, taken for granted, it is not shared by men. Conflicts and home stress evolve from these dilemmas connected to power inequalities in the home.

REFERENCES

Andersson, G. (1993). Leva för jobbet och jobba för livet [To live for the job and to work for life]. Stockholm: Symposion.

Axelsson, C. (1992). Hemmafrun som försvann. Övergången till lönearbete bland gifta kvinnor i Sverige 1968–1981 [The vanished housewife. Transition to employment among married women in Sweden 1968–1981]. Stockholm: University of Stockholm, Swedish Institute for Social Research.

Beck, U. (1986). Risikogesellschaft. Auf dem Weg in eine andere Moderne. Frankfurt: Suhrkamp.

Beck, U. (1994). Risk society. Towards a new modernity. London: Sage.

Bjerrum Nielsen, H., & Rudberg, M. (1991). Historien om flickor och pojkar. Könssocialisation i ett utvecklingsperspektiv [The history of girls and boys. Gender socialization from a developmental-psychological perspective]. Lund: Studentlitteratur.

Björnberg, U. (1992). Parents and their ideals in everyday life. In U. Björnberg (Ed.), European parents in the 1990s. Contradictions and comparisons (pp. 83–102). New Brunswick, NJ: Transaction.

Björnberg, U. (1994). Mäns familjeorientering i förändring [Men's family orientation in a process of change]. In U. Björnberg, A.-K. Kollind, & A. Nilsson, (Eds), *Janus & genus. Om kön och social identitet i familj och samhälle* [Janus & gender. On gender and social identity in family and society] (pp. 49–71). Stockholm: Brombergs.

Björnberg, U., & Bäck-Wiklund, M. (1990). *Vardagslivets organisering i familj och närsamhälle* [Organization of everyday life in family and community]. Göteborg: Daidalos.

Chodorow, N. (1978). *The reproduction of mothering.* Berkeley: University of California Press.

Dencik, L., Bäckström, C., & Larsson, E. (1988). *Barnens två världar* [Children's two worlds]. Stockholm: Esselte.

Gustafsson, B., & Kjuhlin, U. (1992). *Barnomsorg och hushållsarbete. Den offentliga barnomsorgens effekter på föräldrarnas hushållsarbete och fördelning av subventioner från densamma* [Child care and housework. Distribution of subsidies and effects on domestic work and public child care]. Göteborg, Sweden: Göteborg University, Department of Economics.

Friberg, T. (1990). *Kvinnors vardag. Om kvinnors arbete och liv* [Everyday lives of women. On women's work and lives]. Lund, Sweden: Lund University Press.

Haavind, H. (1982). Makt og kjærlighet i ekteskapet [Power and love in marriage]. In R. Haukaa, M. Hoel, & H. Haavind (Eds.), *Kvinneforskning. Bidrag til samfunnsteori* [Women's research. Contribution to a theory on women] (pp. 138–171). Oslo: Universitetsforlaget.

Haavind, H. (1987). *Liten og Stor* [Small and big]. Oslo: Universitetsforlaget.

Haavind, H., & Andeneas, A. (1994, April). *Care and the responsibility for children: Creating the life of women creating themselves.* Paper presented at "Men's Families" seminar, Copenhagen, Denmark.

Hall, E. (1990). *Women's work. An inquiry into the health effects of invisible and visible labour.* Stockholm: Karolinska Institute.

Karasek, R., & Theorell, T. (1990). *Healthy work. Stress, productivity and the reconstruction of working live.* New York: Basic Books.

Kauffman, J. C. (1992). *La trame conjugale. Analyse du couple par son ligne* [The conjugal drama. Analysis of the couple through their tissues]. Paris: Éditions Nathan.

Koch-Nielsen, I. (1983). *Skilsmisser* [Divorces] (Pub. No. 118). Copenhagen, Denmark: Institute for Social Research.

Lundén-Jacoby, A., & Näsman, E. (1987). *Mamma, pappa, jobb* [Mama, papa, job]. Stockholm: National Institute for Working Life.

Lundberg, O. (1990). *Den ojämlika ohälsan. Om klass- och könsskillnader i sjuklighet* [Unequal poor health. On differences of class and gender for sickness]. Stockholm: Swedish Institute for Social Research.

Melucci, A. (1991). *Nomader i nuet. Sociala rörelser och individuella behov i dagens samhälle* [Nomads of the present. Social Movements and individual needs in contemporary society]. Göteborg, Sweden: Daidalos.

Moen, P. (1989). *Working parents.* Madison: The University of Wisconsin Press.

Morris, L. (1990). *The workings of the household.* Cambridge, England: Polity Press.

Moxnes, K. (1990). *Kjernesprengning i familien? Familieforandring ved samlivsbrudd og dannelse av nye samliv* [The eruption of the nuclear family? Family change after divorce and the reconstitution of families]. Oslo: Universitetsforlaget.

Nyberg, A. (1989). *Tekniken—kvinnornas befriare? Hushållsteknik, köpevaror, gifta kvinnors hushållsarbetstid och förvärvsdeltagande 1930–talet–1980–talet* [Household technology—liberation of women? Household technology, consumer goods, hours of household work and employment among married women 1930–1980]. Linköping, Sweden: University of Linköping, Department of Technology and Social Change.

Roman, C. (1994). *Lika på olika villkor. Könssegregering i kunskapsföretag* [Similar on dissimilar terms. Gender segregation in knowledge companies]. Stockholm: Symposion.

Rydenstam, L. (1993). *I tid och otid. Om kvinnors och mäns tidsanvändning 1990/1991* [Time use among women and men] (Rep. No. 79). Levnadsförhållanden, Stockholm: Statistics Sweden.

Sörensen, B. (1982). Ansvarsrationalitet. Om mål-middeltenking blant kvinner [The rationality of responsibility. On logics of goals and means from a feminist perspective]. In H. Holter (Ed.), *Kvinner i Felleskap* [Women and community] (pp. 392–403). Oslo: Universitetsforlaget.

Stacey, J. (1990). *Brave new families. Stories of domestic upheaval in late twentieth century America.* New York: Basic Books.

Stjernelund, P. I. (1995). Könsrolle-kommunikasjon sett fra en manns ståsted [Gender role communication from a male perspective]. *Fokus På Familjen, 3,* 136–151.

Wadsby, M., & Svedin, C. (1993). Skilsmässa—bakgrund, orsaker och följder [Divorce—causes and consequences]. In A. Agell, B. Arve-Parès, & U. Björnberg (Eds.), *Om modernt familjeliv och familjeseparationer* [On modern family life and family separation] (pp. 177–186). Stockholm: Council for Social Research.

Vågerö, D. (1994). Ha contribuido la creciente participacion de la mujer en el mundo laboral a mejorar su salud o no? [Has the increasing labour market participation among women contributed to better health or not?]. *Quadern CAPS, 21,* 17–23.

Zoll, R., & Oechsle, M. (1992). Young people and their ideas on parenthood. In U. Björnberg (Ed.), *European parents in the 1990s. Contradictions and comparisons* (pp. 45–58). New Brunswick, NJ: Transaction.

10

Psychosocial Aspects of Women's Recovery From Heart Disease

Susan M. Czajkowski
National Heart, Lung, and Blood Institute

Cardiovascular disease (CVD) is the leading cause of death for women in the industrialized world. Diseases of the heart and blood vessels kill over 3 million women per year in developed countries alone (World Health Organization [WHO], 1995), and coronary heart disease (CHD) accounts for the greatest percentage of these deaths, causing more than one third of CVD deaths in these countries (WHO, 1995). In the United States alone, 2.5 million women are hospitalized annually for cardiovascular disorders (National Hospital Discharge Survey, 1995), and it is estimated that 7% of the population of adult women in the United States have CHD (NHANES III, 1995).

In addition to its effects on the duration of women's lives, CVD also takes a significant toll on women's quality of life and daily functioning. Unfortunately, much of our knowledge about the psychosocial factors involved in treatment for and recovery from CHD has been derived from studies of men. However, evidence is accumulating regarding the psychosocial factors involved in recovery from CHD in women. In recent years, measures of health-related quality of life (HQL) and psychosocial functioning have been incorporated into studies of heart disease patients, many of which include substantial numbers of women. The findings from this growing database allow us to construct HQL profiles of women with heart disease in order to characterize the psychosocial sequelae of CHD events and procedures in women. These data also permit the identification of psychosocial factors that are associated with better recovery in women with heart disease, ultimately leading to the design of psychosocial interventions to enhance the recovery process in women.

This chapter provides an overview of findings regarding psychosocial aspects of recovery for women following myocardial infarction (MI) and coronary artery bypass graft (CABG) surgery, including the psychosocial factors that best predict survival and recovery. First, data regarding women's physical recovery from MI and CABG surgery are briefly reviewed. This will be followed by a review of the findings concerning women's psychosocial recovery and the psychosocial predictors of recovery from CHD in both women and men.

PHYSICAL RECOVERY IN WOMEN WITH CHD

Evidence suggests that women who develop CHD fare less well than men (Wenger, 1993). Although MI is the initial manifestation of CHD in women less often than in men, a number of studies have shown that women are more likely to die following an MI than are men (Greenland, Reicher-Reiss, Goldbourt, Behar & the Israeli SPRINT Investigators, 1991; Kannel, Sorlie, & McNamara, 1979; Tofler et al., 1987). Women also report greater morbidity following an MI than men, including more chronic illness, poorer health, and more days of reduced activity (Conn, Taylor, & Abele, 1991).

A number of studies have also shown that women have a higher operative mortality during CABG surgery than men (Douglas et al., 1981; Khan, 1991; Loop et al., 1983). Although operative mortality is higher for women than for men, studies show similar rates of mortality at 5 and 10 years post-surgery for men and women (Killen, Reed, Arnold, McCallister, & Bell, 1982; Hall et al., 1983; Eaker et al., 1989). However, women report less improvement in symptoms, mainly angina, and have lower rates of graft patency than men following CABG (Bolooki, Vargas, Green, Kaiser, & Ghahramani, 1975; Douglas et al., 1981; Khan et al., 1990; Loop et al., 1983; Tyras et al., 1978).

The less favorable medical consequences of an MI or CABG surgery in women may be due to a number of factors. One explanation for women's poorer prognosis is that, on average, women develop heart disease 10 years later than men. Because they are older than men when they experience their first CHD event or treatment, women are more likely to have other comorbid conditions (e.g., diabetes, hypertension) that can negatively impact prognosis (Eysmann & Douglas, 1993; Welty, 1994). However, some studies have found a less favorable prognosis for women CHD patients even when controlling for their older age and poorer clinical status (Greenland et al., 1991; Tofler et al., 1987).

Other factors cited as potential influences on women's heart disease outcomes include the nature of the CHD detection, referral, and treatment process in women; the underutilization of cardiac rehabilitation programs by women with CHD; and the poor HQL and psychosocial profiles of female heart disease patients. These are addressed in turn in the following sections.

Identification, Referral, and Treatment of CHD in Women

Concerns have been raised that women with CHD are managed less aggressively, that is, they are referred for CABG and other invasive procedures later in the course of their disease than men. Evidence supporting this hypothesis includes several recent studies that documented the less frequent referral of women for cardiac catheterization, percutaneous transluminal coronary angioplasty (PTCA), and CABG surgery following hospitalization for MI and angina, even after controlling for age and disease severity (Ayanian & Epstein, 1991; Steingart et al., 1991; Tobin et al., 1987). Although it is not clear from these data whether these invasive procedures are underutilized in women or overutilized in men, some have cited the less aggressive management and later referral of women as a factor in women's greater risk of operative death during CABG (Khan et al., 1990).

Unfortunately, there is relatively little information available on the factors, including psychosocial factors, which may affect the identification of CHD and the clinical management of women with cardiac symptoms. Available evidence suggests that the perception of cardiac symptoms by women and their physicians influences detection of CHD, as well as the selection of diagnostic and treatment strategies.

Women with CHD who experience chest pain have been shown to seek care less frequently than men, and women with severe chest pain wait longer than men before seeking emergency care (Moser & Dracup, 1994). Delayed care seeking in women may occur because of a lack of knowledge about the significant risks posed by CVD to women's health. One study found that, when women were asked about the most important risks to their health, only 6% cited diseases of the heart, blood vessels, diabetes, and arthritis, whereas 76% cited cancer as the greatest health risk women face (Frank & Taylor, 1993). Because CVD is by far the leading cause of death and disability for women, these findings reveal a troubling lack of awareness of and concern about the importance of heart disease as a risk among women, which may lead to a discounting of CHD symptoms by women and their partners.

Physicians' attitudes and behaviors may also contribute to gender differences in the detection and treatment of heart disease. Physicians may refer women less often for invasive interventions due to a belief that these procedures are relatively less effective in women than in men, or because they believe some diagnostic procedures (e.g., exercise ECGs) are less reliable in women than men. Additionally, physicians may not interpret women's symptoms as cardiac symptoms as early in the disease process as in men. Regarding the latter hypothesis, one study showed that physicians were less likely to refer women for certain medical procedures than men, even when the women presented the same symptoms as men (McKinlay, Crawford, McKinlay, & Sellers, 1994).

More studies are needed to determine to what extent psychosocial factors, such as women's and physicians' beliefs about heart disease in women, misinterpretation of symptoms, and factors that delay care seeking in women, play a role in the detection and management of women with CHD and in the poorer prognosis of women following CHD events and treatments. These studies should include research on the decision-making process by women in seeking care, and by their physicians in ordering diagnostic tests and referring women for invasive procedures.

Women's Participation in Cardiac Rehabilitation Programs

Formal exercise rehabilitation programs represent an underutilized resource for women with heart disease, and the lack of attendance by women in these programs may hinder their physical as well as their psychosocial recovery. Evidence shows that women are less likely to participate in cardiac rehabilitation programs relative to men following an MI or CABG surgery, and have excessive dropout rates from such programs (Ades, Waldman, Polk, & Coflesky, 1992; Boogard & Briody, 1985; Conn, Taylor, & Abele, 1991; Schuster & Waldron, 1991). However, when they do participate, women have been shown to derive equivalent benefits to men. In one study, although women had poorer risk factor profiles and greater impairment than men prior to entry into a post-MI rehabilitation program, they showed similar improvements as men in exercise duration, oxygen consumption, and depression; in fact, older women (over age 60) showed the greatest improvements in exercise capacity (Downing & Littman, 1994).

Given the importance of cardiac rehabilitation programs in the recovery process, it is disturbing that relatively few women attend and adhere to these programs. It is possible that women's lower participation rates reflect lifestyle constraints for women, who are often the primary source of care for other family members, such as elderly parents. Also, transportation and other practical constraints may pose logistical problems, especially for older women, that affect their attendance. Finally, physician attitudes and behaviors have been shown to be an important determinant of patient participation in cardiac rehabilitation programs. One study found physician recommendations to be the most powerful predictor of attendance in these programs (Ades et al., 1992). Thus, to maximize women's participation and therefore the benefits of these programs for women, physicians should emphasize women's participation, and the programs should be designed with increased flexibility to better meet women's needs.

PSYCHOSOCIAL PROFILES OF WOMEN WITH CHD

In addition to the poorer medical profile in women with CHD, a number of studies have now documented a poorer psychosocial profile for women CHD patients relative to men. The psychosocial profiles for two categories of CHD patients, women who survive an MI and those who undergo CABG surgery, are described next.

Myocardial Infarction

Research shows that women experience greater psychosocial dysfunction than men following MI. Women return to work less often than men and take longer to recuperate physically after MI (Boogard & Briody, 1985; Chirikos & Nickel, 1984; Murdaugh & O'Rourke, 1988; Stern, Pascale, & Ackerman, 1977). In addition, women MI patients have been found to experience more negative affect and mood disturbance, especially depression, than men (Byrne, 1979; Conn, Taylor, & Abele, 1991; Conn, Taylor, & Wiman, 1991; Guiry, Conroy, Hickey, & Mulcahy, 1987; Mayou, 1979; Stern, 1984; Stern et al., 1977). Although women begin household activities sooner than men post-MI, they feel more guilty than men about limitations in their abilities to perform household chores (Boogard, 1984; Boogard & Briody, 1985). Finally, women resume sexual activity later than men post-MI, are more fearful of resuming sexual activity, and participate in sexual activity less frequently than men (Boogard & Briody, 1985; Papadopoulos, Beaumont, Shelley, & Larrimore, 1983; Stern, Pascale, & Ackerman, 1977).

A study by Stern et al. (1977) provided evidence of gender differences in HQL and psychosocial functioning following MI. These researchers followed 53 men and 13 women for one year following MI, collecting data on mortality, hospital readmission, and on various aspects of HQL such as sexual, emotional, and occupational functioning. The differences between men and women were striking, with women demonstrating a much poorer profile in all areas of functioning and in the medical status variables as well. Women were half as likely as men to be alive at one year post-MI, and those surviving were about half as likely as men to be free of anxiety and depression, and to have resumed work and sexual activity.

Although the findings from a number of studies have been consistent regarding women's lower levels of HQL and psychosocial functioning following MI relative to men, most of these studies have used very small sample sizes and have not controlled for women's worse physical profile at the time of the MI. Thus, any decrements in psychosocial functioning during recovery may simply reflect women's older age, more severe disease, and the presence of comorbid conditions that occur more frequently for women MI patients than for men. However, evidence that women's poorer psychosocial profile following MI exists independently of their physical status is provided by the findings from a large multicenter, double-blind, placebo-controlled trial involving post-MI patients—the Cardiac Arrhythmia Suppression Trial, or CAST—which included a large sample of women (about 20% of the sample were women), and collected data on patients' medical status and HQL and psychosocial factors, including their physical, social, and emotional functioning. In this study, with the exception of physical functioning, women were found to have a worse psychosocial profile than men following an MI, even when taking into account their older age, comorbidities, and medications (Schron, Pawitan, Shumaker, & Hale, 1991).

The finding that women's poorer psychosocial functioning post-MI is not solely attributable to their less favorable medical profile is an important one, because it suggests that disparities in psychosocial functioning between men and women with CHD may be related to gender differences in societal role functioning and the stresses associated with women's roles. However, it is unclear from these studies whether the poorer psychosocial profiles of women MI patients are specific to women with heart disease, or merely reflect gender differences in emotional status and psychosocial functioning in the broader population. For example, data show that even otherwise healthy women are more likely to be depressed than men (Nolen-Hoeksema, 1990). Furthermore, regardless of their health status, women are more likely to act as caregivers than men, and therefore are more likely to experience multiple role demands and the stresses associated with these demands than are men.

Coronary Artery Bypass Graft (CABG) Surgery

Women undergoing CABG surgery demonstrate psychosocial decrements similar to those found in female MI patients. Following CABG, women report less improvement in physical functioning, fewer days of restricted activity, and more days in bed due to cardiac symptoms than men (Bass, 1984; Brown & Rawlinson, 1977; Douglas et al., 1981; Stanton, Jenkins, Savageau, & Thurer, 1984; Zyzanski, Rouse, Stanton et al., 1982; Zyzanski, Stanton, Jenkins, & Klein, 1981). Women have also been reported as having greater anxiety, depression, and sleep disturbance following CABG than men (Stern, 1984; Stanton, 1987), although the finding of poorer emotional functioning in women has not been confirmed in some studies (Rankin, 1989, 1990; Sokol et al., 1987). However, women with multiple bypasses have been found to have poorer psychological functioning than men one year postsurgery, independent of their medical status (Stanton, Zyzanski, Jenkins et al., 1982; Zyzanski et al., 1981).

There are inconsistent findings regarding return to work for women following CABG (Almeida, Bradford, Wenger et al., 1983; Altof, Coffman, & Levine, 1984; Barnes, Raj, Oberman, & Kouchoukos, 1977; Niles, Vandersalm, & Cotler, 1980; Stanton, Zyzanski, Jenkins et al., 1982; Westaby, Sapsford, & Bental, 1979; Wilson-Barnett, 1981). This may reflect the fact that many studies use paid employment as a measure of work status, and do not include homemaking and other productive, but non-compensated, work as employment. Nevertheless, those women who are forced to retire following CABG surgery have been found to have poorer psychosocial adjustment than men (Zyzanski, Rouse, Stanton et al., 1982). Furthermore, men have better self-reported health following CABG, and perceive greater benefits for surgery than do women (Gortner et al., 1989; Yates, 1987).

These data appear to show fewer benefits of CABG for women than for men; however, it is not clear whether these differences reflect poorer psychosocial and physical risk profiles for women CABG patients at the time of surgery, or whether the surgery itself is less effective in women than in men.

A recent multicenter cohort study of 759 male and female CABG surgery patients, the POST CABG Biobehavioral Study, has documented preoperative gender differences in CABG patients on medical, sociodemographic, and psychosocial variables prior to CABG surgery (Czajkowski, Terrin, Lindquist, et al., 1997). The findings from this study confirm that women are in poorer health than men prior to CABG surgery: Female patients selected for enrollment in the Biobehavioral Study were more likely than men to die prior to being enrolled, and of those enrolled, women were more likely to have a medical condition which precluded preoperative psychosocial assessment (Czajkowski, Terrin, Lindquist, et al., 1997).

The findings of this study indicate that women CABG surgery patients are at greater risk not only from a physical health standpoint, but from a psychosocial standpoint as well, and that these decrements in pychosocial functioning exist prior to CABG surgery. At the time of surgery, female CABG patients in the Biobehavioral study were less educated, with lower incomes, and more likely to be unmarried and to live alone than men. Furthermore, women were less able to perform activities of daily living prior to surgery than were men, including basic self-care activities, social and recreational activities, and activities necessary to maintain a household. Women were also more anxious and reported more depressive symptoms than men (Czajkowski, Terrin, Lindquist, et al., 1997). These findings suggest that perioperative and convalescent care for women undergoing CABG surgery should take into account their less favorable psychosocial and physical status relative to men.

PSYCHOSOCIAL PREDICTORS OF CHD RECOVERY IN WOMEN

The data in the studies reviewed earlier indicates that women with CHD fare more poorly, both in terms of their physical health and their psychosocial recovery, than men. This raises the possibility that women's worse psychosocial profile is responsible, at least partly, for the more negative physical outcomes that have been reported for women with CHD. If this is so, it would be useful to identify the psychosocial factors that best predict survival and physical recovery in women with heart disease, so that interventions can be designed to target these factors.

Several large-scale, epidemiologic studies have tested associations between psychosocial factors and health outcomes in heart disease patients. The psychosocial factors that have been implicated as being most associated with mortality following CHD diagnosis or treatment, for both men and women, are social isolation, or lack of social support, and depression.

Social Isolation

A number of studies have shown that social isolation predicts cardiac morbidity and mortality in both men and women with existing heart disease. Williams et al. (1992) found significantly lower 5-year mortality for patients with documented coronary artery disease who identified themselves as being married, as having a close confidant, or both relative to those patients who were unmarried and had no such close relationship. Case, Moss, Case, McDermott, and Eberly (1992) found an increased rate of cardiac occurrences for MI patients who lived alone relative to those who lived with others. Unfortunately, although these two studies did include women, the numbers of women were relatively small—the samples consisted of about 80% men. Although both studies tested for gender effects and found none, they may not have had sufficient power to detect gender differences.

Social isolation has also been found to predict cardiac events and mortality in studies with larger samples of women. In a study by Berkman, Leo-Summers, and Horwitz (1992), which included approximately equal numbers of men and women (110 men and 94 women), the number of patients dying within 6 months of an MI was related to the number of sources of emotional support that patients identified. In fact, insufficient emotional support was the most powerful and consistent predictor of mortality in-hospital and during 6- and 12-month follow-up periods. At the end of 12 months, 55% of patients without a source of emotional support had died, whereas only 27% of patients with two or more sources of support died during this period. Thus, the importance of emotional support to survival following an MI appears to be the same for men and women, suggesting that providing social support to women, as well as men, with existing CHD may improve prognosis.

Depression

Depression is common among persons with heart disease, with prevalence estimates ranging from 18 to 25% (Carney et al., 1987; Forrester, Lipsey, Teitelbaum, DePaulo, & Andrzejewski, 1992; Schleifer et al., 1989). Studies have shown that depression is associated with increased risk for cardiac events, such as reinfarction and mortality. Independent of disease severity, high levels of depressive symptoms have been associated with increased mortality and cardiac arrest, for both men and women (Ahern et al., 1990; Carney et al., 1988; Falgar & Appels, 1982; Follick et al., 1988; Frasure-Smith, Lesperance, & Talajic, 1993; Silverstone, 1987). Recently, this finding has been confirmed in a reanalysis of the data from the Systolic Hypertension in the Elderly Program (SHEP), a large multicenter clinical trial that examined the efficacy of antihypertensive treatment for isolated systolic hypertension in elderly men and women. In the reanalysis of data from SHEP, Wassertheil-Smoller (1994) found that an increase in symptoms of depression, measured via self-report or ratings of depressive symptoms, was associated with increased risk of stroke, MI, or death in both men and women. These findings suggest that treatment of depression may be efficacious in lowering the risk of CHD events and death in both women and men with existing heart disease or at high risk for heart disease (e.g., hypertensive patients in SHEP).

CONCLUSIONS

Women have been shown to have a worse prognosis than men following certain CHD events and treatments, but the reasons are not fully understood. The less favorable physical recovery of women following MI and CABG may be due to women's older age and worse medical status relative to men at the time of an MI or CABG surgery; the use of less aggressive referral and treatment strategies for women with heart disease; women's lower rates of participation in cardiac rehabilitation programs; and the worse psychosocial and HQL profiles for women who experience an MI or undergo CABG surgery.

The studies reviewed here point to two major conclusions concerning the role of psychosocial factors in the recovery of women with heart disease. First, based on data from both small-scale and larger, more rigorous studies, women MI and CABG surgery patients demonstrate poorer HQL and psychosocial functioning than men following heart disease diagnosis and treatment. Second, the psychosocial factors that are most consistently related to both women's and men's recovery from heart disease are social isolation and depression. With this knowledge, the next steps involve gaining a better understanding of the mechanisms through which these psychosocial factors affect recovery, and designing and implementing interventions to address psychosocial deficits and enhance recovery in women with heart disease.

An example of a study designed to test such interventions is the Enhancing Recovery in Coronary Heart Disease (ENRICHD) Patients Study, a multicenter, randomized clinical trial funded by the National Heart, Lung, and Blood Institute. ENRICHD is designed to evaluate the effects of a psychosocial intervention that lessens depression and increases social support on reinfarction and mortality in 3,000 post-MI patients at high psychosocial risk (i.e., depressed and/or socially isolated patients). Since 50% of the patients to be enrolled in ENRICHD are expected to be women, this study, which will be completed in 2001, will provide important information on the clinical value of psychosocial interventions in women with heart disease.

REFERENCES

Ades, P. A., Waldmann, M. L., Polk, D. M., & Coflesky, J. T. (1992). Referral patterns and exercise response in the rehabilitation of female coronary patients aged ≥ 62 years. *American Journal of Cardiology, 69*, 1422–1425.

Ahern, D., Gorkin, L., Anderson, J., Tierney, C., Hallstrom, A., Ewart, C., Capone, R., Schron, E., Kornfeld, D., Herd, J., Richardson, D., & Follick, M. (1990). Biobehavioral variables and mortality or cardiac arrest in the Cardiac Arrhythmia Pilot Study (CAPS). *American Journal of Cardiology, 66*, 59–62.

Almeida, D., Bradford, J. M., Wenger, N. K., King, S. B., & Hurst, J. W. (1983). Return to work after coronary bypass surgery. *Circulation, 68*(suppl II), 205–213.

Altof, S. E., Coffman, C. B., & Levine, S. B. (1984). The effects of coronary bypass surgery on female sexual, psychological and vocational adaptation. *Journal of Sex and Marital Therapy, 10*, 176–184.

Ayanian, J. Z., & Epstein, A. M. (1991). Differences in the use of procedures between women and men hospitalized for coronary heart disease. *The New England Journal of Medicine, 325*(4), 221–225.

Barnes, G. K., Raj, M. J., Oberman, A., & Kouchoukos, M. (1977). Changes in working status of patients following coronary bypass surgery. *Journal of the American Medical Association, 238*, 1259–1262.

Bass, C. (1984). Psychosocial outcome after CAB surgery. *British Journal of Psychiatry, 145*, 526–532.

Berkman, L. F., Leo-Summers, L., & Horwitz, R. I. (1992). Emotional support and survival after myocardial infarction. *Annals of Internal Medicine, 117*, 1003–1009.

Bolooki, H., Vargas, A., Green, R., Kaiser, G. A., & Ghahramani, A. (1975). Results of direct coronary artery surgery in women. *Journal of Thoracic and Cardiovascular Surgery, 69*, 271–277.

Boogaard, M. (1984). Rehabilitation of the female patient after myocardial infarction. *Nursing Clinics of North America, 19*, 433–440.

Boogaard, M., & Briody, M. (1985). Comparison of the rehabilitation of men and women post-myocardial infarction. *Journal of Cardiopulmonary Rehabilitation, 5*, 379–384.

Brown, J. S., & Rawlinson, M. E. (1977). Sex differences in sick role rejection and in work performance following cardiac surgery. *Journal of Health and Social Behavior, 18*, 276–292.

Byrne, D. (1979). Anxiety as state and trait following myocardial infarction. *British Journal of Social and Clinical Psychology, 18,* 417–423.

Carney, R. M., Rich, M. W., Freedland, K. E., Saini, J., teVelde, A., Simeone, C., & Clark, K. (1988). Major depressive disorder predicts cardiac events in patients with coronary artery disease. *Psychosomatic Medicine, 50,* 627–633.

Carney, R. M., Rich, M. W., Tevelde, A., Saini, J., Clark, K., & Jaffe, A. S. (1987). Major depressive disorder in coronary artery disease. *American Journal of Cardiology, 60,* 1273–1275.

Case, R. B., Moss, A. J., Case, N., McDermott, M., & Eberly, S. (1992). Living alone after myocardial infarction. *Journal of the American Medical Association, 267*(4), 515–519.

Chirikos, T. N., & Nickel, J. L. (1984). Work disability from coronary heart disease in women. *Women and Health, 9*(1), 55–71.

Conn, S., Taylor, S. G., & Abele, P. B. (1991). Myocardial infarction survivors: Age and gender differences in physical health, psychosocial state and regimen adherence. *Journal of Advanced Nursing, 16,* 1026–1034.

Conn, V. S., Taylor, S. G., & Wiman, P. (1991). Anxiety, depression, quality of life, and self-care among survivors of myocardial infarction. *Issues in Mental Health Nursing, 12*(4), 321–331.

Czajkowski, S. M., Terrin, M., Lindquist, R., Hoogwerf, B., Dupuis, G., Shumaker, S. A., Gray, R., Herd, J. A., Treat-Jacobson, D., Zyzanski, S., & Knatterud, G. L. for the POST CABG Biobehavioral Study Investigators. (1997). Comparison of preoperative characteristics of men and women undergoing coronary artery bypass grafting (The POST Coronary Artery Bypass Graft [CABG] Biobehavioral Study. *American Journal of Cardiology, 79,* 1017–1024.

Douglas, J. S., King, S. B., Jones, E. L., Craver, J. M., Bradford, J. M., & Hatcher, C. R., Jr. (1981). Reduced efficacy of coronary bypass surgery in women. *Circulation, 164*(suppl II), II11–II16.

Downing, J., & Littman, A. (1994). Gender differences in response to cardiac rehabilitation. In S. M. Czajkowski, D. R. Hill, & T. B. Clarkson (Eds.), *Women, behavior and cardiovascular disease.* Proceedings of a National Heart, Lung, and Blood Institute sponsored conference. NIH Publication No. 94-3309.

Eaker, E. D., Kronmal, R., Kennedy, J. W., & Davis, K. (1989). Comparison of the long-term postsurgical survival of women and men in the Coronary Artery Surgery Study (CASS). *American Heart Journal, 117,* 71–81.

Eysmann, S. B., & Douglas, P. S. (1993). Coronary heart disease: Therapeutic principles. In P. S. Douglas (Ed.), *Cardiovascular health and disease in women.* Philadelphia: Saunders.

Falgar, P., & Appels, A. (1982). Psychological risk factors over the life course of myocardial infarction patients. *Advances in Cardiology, 29,* 132–139.

Follick, M. J., Gorkin, L., Capone, R. J., Smith, T. W., Ahern, D. K., Stablein, D., Niaura, R., & Visco, J. (1988). Psychological distress as a predictor of ventricular arrhythmias in a post-myocardial infarction population. *American Heart Journal, 116,* 32–36.

Forrester, A. W., Lipsey, J. R., Teitelbaum, M. L., DePaulo, J. R., & Andrzejewski, P. L. (1992). Depression following myocardial infarction. *International Journal of Psychiatry in Medicine, 22,* 33–46.

Frank, E., & Taylor, C. B. (1993). Psychosocial influences on diagnosis and treatment plans of women with coronary heart disease. In N. K. Wenger, L. Speroff, & B. Packard (Eds.), *Cardiovascular health and disease in women* (pp. 231–237). Greenwich, CT: Le Jacq.

Frasure-Smith, N., Lesperance, F., & Talajic, M. (1993). Depression following myocardial infarction: Impact on 6-month survival. *Journal of the American Medical Association, 270,* 1819–1825.

Gortner, S. R., Rankin, S., Gillis, C. L., Sparacio, P. A., Paul, S. M., Shinn, J. A., & Leavitt, M. B. (1989). Expected and realized benefits from cardiac surgery: An update. *Cardiological Nursing, 25,* 19–24.

Greenland, P., Reicher-Reiss, H., Goldbourt, U., Behar, S., & the Israeli SPRINT Investigators. (1991). In-hospital and 1-year mortality in 1,524 women after myocardial infarction. *Circulation, 83,* 484–491.37.

Guiry, E., Conroy, R., Hickey, N., & Mulcahy, R. (1987). Psychological response to an acute coronary event. *Journal of Cardiology, 10,* 256–260.

Hall, R. J., Elayda, M. A., Gray, A., Mathur, V. S., Garcia, E., deCastro, C. M., Massumi, A., & Cooley, D. (1983). Coronary artery bypass: Long-term follow-up of 22,284 consecutive patients. *Circulation, 68*(suppl II), II20–II25.

Kannel, W. B., Sorlie, P., & McNamara, P. M. (1979). Prognosis after myocardial infarction: The Framingham Study. *American Journal of Cardiology, 44,* 53–59.

Khan, S. S., Nessim, S., Gray, R., Czer, L. S., Chaux, A., & Matloff, J. (1990). Increased mortality of women in coronary artery bypass surgery: Evidence for referral bias. *Annals of Internal Medicine, 112,* 561–567.

Khan, S. S. (1991). Why women have a significantly higher bypass surgery mortality rate. *Cardiology Board Review, 8,* 54–67.

Killen, D. A., Reed, W. A., Arnold, M., McCallister, B. D., & Bell, H. H. (1982). Coronary artery bypass in women: Long-term survival. *Annals of Thoracic Surgery, 34,* 559–563.

Loop, F. S., Goulding, L. R., MacMillan, J. P., Cosgrove, D. M., Lyttle, B. W., & Sheldon, W. C. (1983). Coronary artery surgery in women compared with men: Analyses of risk and long-term results. *Journal of the American College of Cardiology, 1,* 383–390.

Mayou, R. (1979). Psychological reactions to myocardial infarction. *Journal of the Royal College of Physicians, 13,* 103–105.

McKinlay, J. B., Crawford, S., McKinlay, S. M., & Sellers, D. E. (1994). On the reported gender difference in coronary heart disease: An illustration of the social construction of epidemiologic rates. In S. M. Czajkowski, D. R. Hill, & T. B. Clarkson (Eds.), *Women, behavior and cardiovascular disease.* (NIH Publication No. 94-3309, pp. 223–252).

Moser, D. K., & Dracup, K. (1994). Gender differences in symptom recognition and health care seeking behavior in acute myocardial infarction. In S. M. Czajkowski, D. R. Hill, & T. B. Clarkson (Eds.), *Women, behavior and cardiovascular disease.* (NIH Publication No. 94-3309, pp. 261–278).

Murdaugh, C. L., & O'Rourke, R. A. (Eds.). (1988). Coronary heart disease in women: Special considerations. *Current Problems in Cardiology, 13*(2).

National Hospital Discharge Survey: Annual Summary Vital and Health Statistics. (1995). Series 13: Data from the National Health Survey No. 121. PHS, National Center for Health Statistics.

NHANES III prevalence. (1988–1991). From C. Sempos (12/22/95). Bureau of Census, from T. Dunn, NCHS.

Niles, N. W., II, Vander Salm, T. J., & Cotler, B. S. (1980). Return to work after coronary artery bypass. *Journal of Thoracic and Cardiovascular Surgery, 79,* 916–921.

Papadopoulos, C., Beaumont, C., Shelley, S., & Larrimore, P. (1983). Myocardial infarction and sexual activity of the female patient. *Archives of Internal Medicine, 143,* 1528–1530.

Nolen-Hoeksema, A. (1990). *Sex differences in depression.* Stanford, CA: Stanford University Press.

Rankin, S. H. (1989). Women's recovery from cardiac surgery. *Circulation, 80*(suppl II), II-391.

Rankin, S. H. (1990). Differences in recovery from cardiac surgery: A profile of male and female patients. *Heart and Lung, 19,* 481–485.

Schleifer, S. J., Macari-Hinson, M. M., Coyle, D. A., William, W. R., Kahn, M., Gorlin, R., & Zucker, H. D. (1989). The nature and course of depression following myocardial infarction. *Archives of Internal Medicine, 149,* 1785–1789.

Schron, E., Pawitan, Y., Shumaker, S. A., & Hale, C. for the CAST Investigators. (1991). Health quality of life differences between men and women in a postinfarction study. *Circulation, 84*(4)(suppl II), II-976.

Schuster, P. M., & Waldron, J. (1991). Gender differences in cardiac rehabilitation patients. *Rehabilitation Nursing, 16*(5), 248–253.

Silverstone, P. H. (1987). Depression and outcome in acute myocardial infarction. *British Medical Journal, 294,* 219–220.

Sokol, R. S., Folks, D. G., Herrick, R. W., & Freeman, A. M., III. (1987). Psychiatric outcome in men and women after coronary bypass surgery. *Psychosomatics, 28*, 11–16.

Stanton, B. A. (1987). Psychosocial aspects of coronary heart disease in women: Implications and expectations for rehabilitation. In E. D. Eacker, B. Packard, N. K. Wenger, T. B. Clarkson, & H. A. Tyroler (Eds.), *Coronary heart disease in women* (pp. 257–263). New York: Haymarket Douma.

Stanton, B. A., Jenkins, C. D., Savageau, J. A., & Thurer, R. L. (1984). Functional benefits following coronary artery bypass graft surgery. *Annals of Thoracic Surgery, 37*, 286–290.

Stanton, B. A., Zyzanski, S. J., Jenkins, C. D. et al. (1982). Recovery after major heart surgery: Medical, psychological and work outcomes. In R. Becker, J. Catz, & M. J. Polonius et al. (Eds.), *Psychopathological and neurological dysfunction following open-heart surgery* (pp. 217–226). Heidelberg: Springer-Verlag.

Steingart, R. M., Packer, M., Hamm, P., Coglianese, M. E., Gersh, B., Geltman, E. M., Sollano, J., Katz, S., Moye, L., Basta, L. L., Lewis, S. J., Gottlieb, S. S., Bernstein, V., McEwan, P., Jacobson, K., Brown, E. J., Kukin, M. L., Kantrowitz, N. E., & Pfeffer, M. A. (1991). Sex differences in the management of coronary artery disease. *New England Journal of Medicine, 325*, 226–230.

Stern, M. (1984). Psychosocial rehabilitation following myocardial infarction and CABG surgery. In N. K. Wenger & H. K. Hellerstein (Eds.), *Rehabilitation of the coronary patient* (pp. 453–471). New York: Wiley.

Stern, M., Pascale, L., & Ackerman, A. (1977). Life adjustment post-myocardial infarction. *Archives of Internal Medicine, 137*, 1680–1685.

Tobin, J. N., Wassertheil-Smoller, S., Wexler, J. P., et al. (1987). Sex bias in considering coronary bypass surgery. *Annals of Internal Medicine, 107*, 19–25.

Tofler, G. H., Stone, P. H., Muller, J. E., Willich, S. N., Davis, V. G., Poole, W. K., Strauss, W., Willerson, J. T., Jaffe, A. S., Robertson, T., Passamani, E., Braunwald, E., & The MILIS Study Group. (1987). Effects of gender and race on prognosis after myocardial infarction: Adverse prognosis for women, particularly Black women. *Journal of American College of Cardiology, 9*(3), 473–482.

Tyras, D. H., Barner, H. B., Kaiser, G. C., Codd, J. E., Laks, H., & Willman, V. L. (1978). Myocardial revascularization in women. *Annals of Thoracic Surgery, 25*, 449–453.

Wassertheil-Smoller, S. for the SHEP Cooperative Research Group. (1994). Change in depression as a precursor of cardiovascular events. *Circulation, 89*, 6.

Welty, F. K. (1994). Gender differences in outcome after diagnosis and treatment of coronary heart disease. In S. M. Czajkowski, D. R. Hill, & T. B. Clarkson (Eds.), *Women, behavior and cardiovascular disease*. (NIH Publication No. 94-3309, pp. 285–310).

Wenger, N. K. (1993). Coronary heart disease: Diagnostic decision-making. In P. S. Douglas (Ed.), *Cardiovascular health and disease in women* (pp. 25–42). Philadelphia: Saunders.

Wenger, N. K. (1994). Coronary heart disease in women: Needs and opportunities. In S. M. Czajkowski, D. R. Hill, & T. B. Clarkson (Eds.), *Women, behavior and cardiovascular disease*. (NIH Publication No. 94-3309, pp. 7–18).

Wenger, N. K., Speroff, L., & Packard, B. (1993). Cardiovascular health and disease in women. *New England Journal of Medicine, 329*, 247–256.

Westaby, S., Sapsford, R. N., & Bental, H. H. (1979). Return to work and quality of life after surgery for coronary artery disease. *British Medical Journal, 2*, 1028–1031.

Williams, R. B., Barefoot, J. C., Califf, R. M., Haney, T. L., Saunders, W. B., Pryor, D. B., Hlatky, M. A., Siegler, I. C., & Mark, D. B. (1992). Prognostic importance of social and economic resources among medically treated patients with angiographically documented coronary artery disease. *American Medical Association, 267*, 520–524.

Wilson-Barnett, J. (1981). Assessment of recovery: With special reference to a study with post-operative cardiac patients. *Journal of Advanced Nursing, 6*, 435–445.

World Health Organization. (1995). *World health statistics annual, 1994*. World Health Organization, Geneva: Author.

Yates, B. C. (1987). Gender differences in compliance behaviors and health perceptions of coronary bypass surgery patients. *Progress in Cardiovascular Nursing, 2,* 105–112.

Zyzanski, S. J., Rouse, B. A., Stanton, B. A., & Jenkins, C. D. (1982). Employment changes among patients following coronary bypass surgery: Social, medical and psychological correlates. *Public Health Reports, 97,* 558–565.

Zyzanski, S. J., Stanton, B. A., Jenkins, C. D., & Klein, M. D. (1981). Medical and psychosocial outcomes in survivors of major heart surgery. *Journal of Psychosomatic Research, 25,* 213–221.

11

Social Support and Heart Disease in Women: Implications for Intervention

Margaret Chesney
University of California, San Francisco

Lynae Darbes
University of Colorado, Boulder

Coronary heart disease (CHD) is the leading cause of death among adult women in most developed countries. Although CHD is perceived to be a predominantly male condition, the number of female CHD deaths since 1989 has surpassed those for men (Wenger, 1994). Moreover, women who survive myocardial infarction (MI) are more likely to be functionally impaired than men (Nickel & Chirikos, 1990). Given the prevalence of CHD among women, it has been predicted that older female heart patients will contribute disproportionately to an already increasing population of elderly people with disabilities. This subpopulation may provide a significant challenge for public health policy makers. The paucity of studies that concentrate on the unique needs of women with CHD renders interventions tailored toward women's experiences imperative.

The evidence that social support, and its converse, social isolation, are associated with CHD morbidity and mortality calls attention to the need for interventions to increase social support and to decrease the negative effects of social isolation. Developing these interventions will be served by an understanding of the pathways by which social isolation exerts its influence. This understanding is particularly necessary for women, where these pathways can be extremely complex.

This chapter proposes a model that portrays social isolation as increasing CHD risk through two different, but related pathways—namely, through depressed mood and health behaviors (see Fig. 11.1). Individuals who are socially isolated are more likely to become depressed than those with adequate social support networks. Depressed mood, in turn, is a significant predictor of mortality in women and men following MI. There are also significant associations between lower levels of social support and damaging health behaviors, such as cigarette smoking, poor diet, and inactivity. These health behaviors are well-known risk factors for CHD. Conversely, those with higher levels of support are more likely to avoid health damaging behavior. Although social isolation is associated with both depressed mood and adverse health behaviors, there are also linkages between depressed mood and health behavior that may further elevate risk. The model also presents a final pathway by which this cluster consisting of social isolation, depressed mood, and adverse health behaviors increase CHD risk through sympathetic and parasympathetic nervous system activity.

This model has important implications for intervention. To the extent that social isolation, depressed mood, and health behaviors have reciprocal relationships, interventions that focus on any one of these components in isolation, such as a program to encourage smoking cessation alone, may prove less than optimally successful. Alternatively, an intervention that captures the interplay among these components and addresses the potential psychological and social barriers to smoking cessation would prove

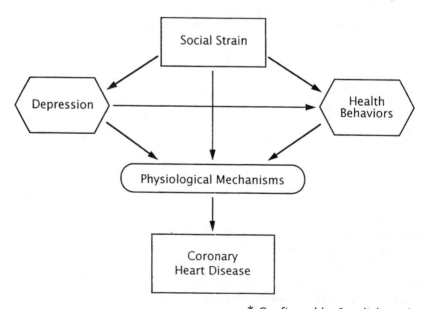

FIG. 11.1. Proposed model showing pathways linking social isolation to coronary heart disease.

more successful and more likely to lead to sustained change. In particular, we propose that interventions should address the extent to which adverse health behaviors, such as smoking, are influenced by depressed mood and social factors. In this chapter, we first review the relationship between social isolation and CHD. We then in turn review other relationships within the model, including physiological mechanisms between social isolation and CHD; the association between social isolation, depressed mood, and CHD; the relationship between social isolation and health behaviors; and the relationships between depressed mood and health behaviors. After completing the review of these relationships we conclude by discussing implications for intervention and describing interventions that take advantage of these important reciprocal relationships, including approaches that strive to reduce risk behaviors by focusing directly on increasing social support.

SOCIAL ISOLATION AND CHD RISK

Social isolation, limited social networks, and low levels of social support are associated with numerous adverse health outcomes, including CHD (see Fig. 11.2). House, Landis, and Umberson (1988) proposed that the degree of health risk associated with low social support is equal to that of cigarette smoking. Mor-Barak and Miller (1991) demonstrated in a longitudinal study

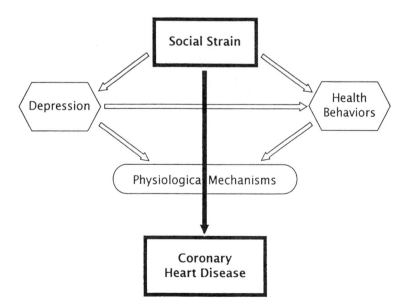

FIG. 11.2. Social isolation is associated with increased CHD morbidity and mortality.

that limited social networks adversely affect health, as opposed to low social interaction being a result of poor health. Numerous studies have specifically focused on the relationship between social isolation and CHD morbidity and mortality.

One of the first associations between social isolation and CHD was described by Orth-Gomér and Unden (1990). This study demonstrated that in a sample of Type A men, low social support was an independent predictor of mortality. There was an interaction between Type A and social isolation such that men who were both Type A and socially isolated had the highest mortality (69%) compared to men who were type B and socially isolated (44%). Both socially isolated groups had higher mortality rates than those men who were socially integrated.

Williams et al. (1992) reported that low social support is an independent risk factor for cardiovascular mortality among patients with coronary artery disease (CAD). Those patients (82% were male) who were unmarried without a confidant were found to have more than a threefold increase for the risk of death within 5 years, compared to those patients who were either married or reported having a close confidant. The investigators conclude that independent of important medical considerations (e.g., history of hypertension or MI), high levels of social support function as a protective factor from risks due to long-term coronary disease.

Further evidence of the protective function of social support was provided by Case et al. (1992). In a follow-up study of 1,234 male and female post-MI patients, Case and his colleagues linked social isolation to both mortality and recurrence of MI. Living alone was a risk for recurrent cardiac events independent of the associated variables of age and disrupted marriage. The influence of living alone persisted despite other variables often associated with recurrence, including severity of myocardial damage, gender, drug compliance, use of beta-blocker therapy, subsequent angioplasty, or bypass grafting. The investigators point out that this study is significant in that it is living alone, a discrete variable, that is associated with disease endpoints, whereas other studies have used numerous measures of social integration that might be argued to be more subjective (e.g., Ruberman, Weinblatt, Goldbert, & Chaudhary, 1984). The investigators also emphasize the positive potential for early intervention that could alleviate the possible morbidity and mortality which they showed to result from living alone.

In a prospective study of the elderly, Berkman, Leo-Summers, and Horwitz (1992) reported that low social support predicted mortality post-MI for both women and men. There was a clear linear relationship between the number of sources of support and percentage of people who died (for sources of emotional support = 0, 1 or ≥ 2: percentages of people who died = 59%, 41%, 23% respectively, for men, and 43%, 32%, 22% respectively, for women). Emotional support was an independent predictor for mortality in the 6 months following MI, controlling for severity of MI, comorbidity, and risk factors such as smoking and hypertension.

PHYSIOLOGICAL MECHANISMS BETWEEN SOCIAL ISOLATION AND CHD RISK

The evidence of a causal relationship between social support and CHD raises the question of possible physiological mechanisms that would increase the risk associated with social isolation (see Fig. 11.3). Ruberman (1992) has suggested that insufficient social support may increase the likelihood of experiencing stressful life events, which then may be exacerbated by the lack of social support. These circumstances in tandem could produce a greater risk of ventricular fibrillation among those who are more vulnerable by the presence of coronary disease.

There is some evidence of a "direct pathway" from a number of laboratory studies. Kamarck, Manuck, and Jennings (1990) posited that social support may moderate psychophysiological responses to stress. Kamarck and his colleagues tested this theory by having women undergo a mental arithmetic and concept formation task either alone (no support condition) or in the company of a female friend (support condition). In the support condition, the companion could touch the subject's wrist, but did so while

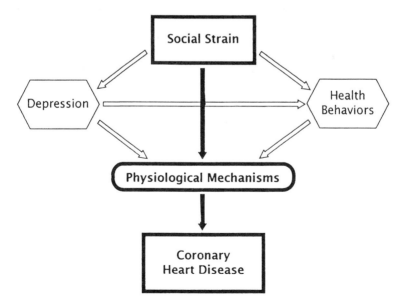

FIG. 11.3. Low social support is associated with increased physiological responses to stress which have been implicated in CHD risk.

wearing a headset and completing questionnaires, in order to prevent distracting or evaluation apprehension in the subject. The women who were supported by a friend showed less BP and HR increases to the lab challenge than the nonsupported women.

Gerin, Pieper, Levy, and Pickering (1992) attempted to incorporate aspects of Social Comparison theory and to lessen the laboratory quality of similar studies in their study of social support and reactivity. Women were brought into a lab and were placed with three confederates. Two of the confederates argued with the subject over a controversial issue. Half of the subjects had a third confederate who agreed with the subject's position (support condition), whereas for the other half of the subjects the third confederate simply sat quietly (no support condition). The women supported by the confederate showed smaller BP and HR increases than the nonsupported women. It is possible, however, that the differences in groups could have been a product of increased reactivity in the subjects in the harassment–no-support condition as opposed to reduced reactivity in the harassment–support condition.

Lepore, Mata Allen, and Evans (1993) attempted to address some of the shortcomings of the aforementioned studies in the following ways: The support manipulation was checked such that they examined whether the subjects in the support condition actually perceived the confederate to be more supportive than subjects in the no support condition; the manipulation was designed to reflect naturalistic situations; and support was offered by a stranger rather than a friend. This design also tested the alternative explanation offered for the Gerin et al. (1992) study described earlier in that it also tested a group of individuals who experienced stress alone. Including this condition tested whether or not support reduced the reactivity to harassment. With this design, it was possible to test whether or not stress appraisals mediated the buffering effects of social support. Subjects who were supported by a confederate showed less BP increase to public speaking than women alone or nonsupported. All of the aforementioned studies found no association between social support and self-reports of perceived stress. This indicates that support was not changing the subjects' appraisal of stress, but rather was affecting the subjects' physical responses to stress.

COMPLEXITIES OF WOMEN'S SOCIAL RELATIONSHIPS

The findings discussed thus far imply a positive benefit from social support for women with regard to CHD. It is important to view these results with caution because social support and CHD risk in women is complex. Marriage could be viewed as the very essence of social support. However, given women's multiple social roles, it is not clear that marriage confers the same health benefits on women as it does on men. In a study of 246 post-MI patients, Young and Kahana (1993) found that women, including those who were married, received less assistance with meals and household tasks than men, where both had a history of MI. At one year post-MI, 20% of women had died compared to 12% of men (Relative Risk = 1.7). When age was controlled, the Relative Risk of death for women compared to men remained significant, and women who were married had 3 times the risk of death as that observed in men. Similarly, Moritz and Satariano (1993) found that women who lived with a spouse had a higher odds ratio (2.02) of being diagnosed with more advanced breast cancer than did women living alone. They suggested that "the presence of a spouse may detract from the attention a woman pays to her own health" (p. 451).

The aforementioned studies demonstrate that, in the context of women's lives, social relationships are not a proxy for social support. Marriage, rather than being the buffer against adverse health effects that it can be for men, appears to have some detrimental effects for women. Women could be at risk for later diagnosis of disease, as well as greater risk of death as compared to either women living alone (Moritz & Satariano, 1993) or to men (Young & Kahana, 1993).

The exact mechanisms by which social support or isolation might influence CHD risk are not known. The studies suggesting protective effects of social support (e.g., Berkman et al., 1992; Lepore et al., 1993) may be reflecting neurohormonal effects of social contact, or advantages of larger social support networks (beyond the spouse) during rehabilitation. The studies pointing to adverse effects associated with marriage may be illustrative of the contextual variables and competing demands associated with role expectations in marriage for women. As discussed by Shively and her colleagues in chapter 13 of this volume, social isolation and strain may be associated with increased risk for CAD through impaired ovarian function.

SOCIAL ISOLATION, DEPRESSED MOOD, AND CHD

One important pathway by which social isolation increases CHD risk may be through its relationship to depressed mood (see Fig. 11.4). Low levels of social support are associated with depressive symptoms (George, Blazer, Hughes, & Fowler, 1989; Monroe, Bromet, Connell, & Steiner, 1986). In a population-based survey of over 1,600 adults over 65 years of age, Palinkas, Wingard, and Barrett-Connor (1990) found that a smaller network size, greater distance to primary support, and low participation in church and community organizations were associated with depressive symptoms. These findings prompted Palinkas and colleagues to conclude, "At any age, the deterioration of social networks is a risk factor for depression" (p. 441).

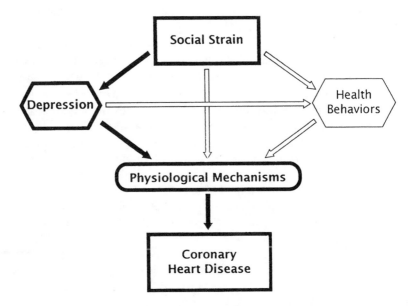

FIG. 11.4. Social isolation is associated with depression which may increase
CHD risk by increasing neuroendocrine responses to stress.

Russell and Cutrona (1991) posited that low levels of social support are
associated both directly and indirectly to later depression in the elderly.
Indirectly, low social support is associated with the incidence of minor
stressful events, which is in itself a significant predictor of subsequent
depression. A more direct relationship was also observed by Russell and
Cutrona, who found that lower levels of support at baseline are associated
with the higher levels of depression 12 months later. This predictive relationship remained significant even when initial levels of depression were
taken into account.

The relationship between depressed mood and social networks is reciprocal with either factor adversely affecting the other. For example, Cerhan
and Wallace (1993) conducted a prospective longitudinal study of rural
elderly in which they found that depressive symptoms predicted a decline
in social relationships after a 3-year period. Cross-cultural confirmation was
obtained by Woo et al. (1994), who found similar results in an elderly Chinese
population. Depressive symptoms may exert influence on social support
through the following pathways: (a) by discouraging members of a social
network from providing support, (b) by reducing a person's ability to become involved with others, and (c) by affecting a person's perception of the
availability and adequacy of support (Palinkas et al., 1990).

Although much of the early focus on psychosocial risk factors was concentrated on coronary-prone behavior, some studies provided evidence that

depression (as well as depressed mood and hopelessness) were associated with increased risk for CHD (Ahern et al., 1990; Kaplan, 1985). Booth-Kewley and Friedman (1987) utilized meta-analysis to examine psychological predictors of heart disease, including Type A behavior and anxiety. They reported that of the variables studied, depression showed the strongest prospective relationship to CHD. In fact, the effect size for depression was greater than that for Type A personality. Two considerations render this finding all the more remarkable: (a) as the authors pointed out, there is a vast difference between the number of studies examining Type A behavior and those investigating the role of depression in CHD; and (b) the majority of subjects were men.

A recent longitudinal study presented noteworthy evidence of the significant predictive power of depression on mortality 6 months post-MI. Frasure-Smith, Lesperance, and Talajic (1993) reported that depressed patients had a fivefold greater risk of mortality compared to nondepressed patients. As prior studies investigating the role of depression have been hampered by methodological problems, this study is compelling given its prospective nature as well as its use of the NIMH Diagnostic Interview Schedule. Concurrent with the publication of the aforementioned study, a reanalysis of the Recurrent Coronary Prevention Project was presented. Depression was reported to be an independent predictor of both mortality and recurrence of cardiac events in women (Powell et al., 1993).

Freedland and Carney (1994) have suggested that (a) the appearance of depression can precede the clinical onset of CHD; (b) major depression often continues for months or years unabated in patients if left untreated; and (c) depression heightens the risks of additional cardiac morbidity and mortality, in addition to functional disability and poor psychosocial adjustment to illness. These problems are particularly relevant to women who are significantly more likely than men to have major or minor depression post-MI (Schleifer et al., 1989). In a study of post-MI patients, M. Stern, Pascale, and Ackerman (1977) reported that 50% of the women were depressed at the initial assessment. At the one-year follow-up, women had a higher post-MI mortality rate than men, with 80% of the deaths occurring among women. Freedland and Carney (1994) suggested that the prevalence rate of depression among women with CAD, which is at least twice as high as that among men with CAD, may explain the observed sex differential in mortality rates associated with acute MI.

Intervening to lessen depression and social isolation may prevent both incidence of CHD and increase survival post-MI. The majority of studies, however, have reported that it is most often the case that neither depression nor anxiety are diagnosed or treated in cardiac patients (T. Stern, 1985). An important next step is to determine what degree of depressive symptoms are clinically significant in relation to CHD. That is, is it only major depression that influences cardiac events, or does depressed mood also increase risk for adverse CHD outcomes (Carney, Freedland, Smith, Rich, & Jaffe, 1994)?

What are the mechanisms through which depression might increase CHD risk? A number of neuroendocrine pathways have been proposed. Depression has been found to be associated with increased norepinephrine, and increased norepinephrine response to orthostatic challenge. Weaker parasympathetic function has also been observed. All of these factors are associated with decreased CNS serotenergic functioning, which is observed in depression (Williams, 1994).

SOCIAL ISOLATION AND HEALTH BEHAVIORS

We next turn to another pathway through which social isolation may influence CHD—that of health behaviors (see Fig. 11.5). Associations between social relationships and health behaviors have been found in numerous studies (Berkman & Breslow, 1983; Langlie, 1977; Umberson, 1987). Broman (1993) reported several pieces of evidence that documented an association between changes in social ties and health behaviors. For example, he reported that a decrease in social ties predicted an increase in health-damaging behavior, and gains in social ties were associated with increases in health-

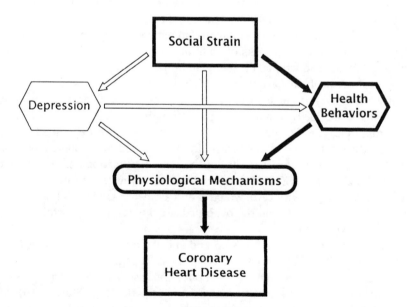

FIG. 11.5. Social isolation is associated with adverse health behaviors which increase CHD risk through known physiological mechanisms.

protective behavior. Consistent with these findings, and focusing on one health behavior—exercise—A. King, Taylor, and Haskell (1990) found that being either divorced or separated has also been observed to place an individual at increased risk for poor exercise adherence. Conversely, greater levels of social support have been reported to be a significant correlate of both exercise adoption and maintenance in women and men (Dishman, Sallis, & Orenstein, 1985; A. King, Young, Oka, & Haskell, 1992). Social relationships may also influence health behaviors directly by providing tangible resources or intangible support for adverse health behaviors. For example, friends who smoke may provide cigarettes to fellow smokers, or pressure members of group who smoke together to not attempt to quit because doing so would disrupt the group's cohesion. Social relationships also influence health behavior indirectly through depressed mood (Franks, Campbell, & Shields, 1992). In studies of major disruptions in social relationships, such as divorce, depression is associated with smoking and alcohol (Broman, 1993). It may be that women attempt to cope with social stressors and its accompanying distressed mood by turning to substances such as alcohol. The association between depression and health behaviors are discussed in the next section.

DEPRESSION AND HEALTH BEHAVIORS

Previous sections have documented the relationships between social isolation, depression, and adverse health behaviors. There is also an important cross-association between depression and health behaviors (see Fig. 11.6). In a community sample, depression was significantly associated with current smoking and the use of alcohol among women (Cohen, Schwartz, Bromet, & Parkinson, 1991). In particular, a history of depression, negative life events, working full time and marital conflict were associated with current smoking. A history of depression and the presence of marital conflict were also associated with alcohol use among women. Franks et al. (1992) also found a relationship between depressive symptoms and current smoking.

In addition to the relationships described earlier, it is possible that depressed persons exhibit a lack of adherence to both medication and recommendations for behavior change. In studies of post-MI patients, including women, depression has been significantly related to nonadherence to exercise, diet, medication, and recommendations to stop smoking (Conn, Taylor & Wiman, 1991). Finnegan and Suler (1985) found, for example, that depressive symptoms in post-MI women predicted poorer maintenance to exercise and weight-loss recommendations that are integral to cardiac rehabilitation. Major depression is also predictive of poor adherence to a prescribed regimen of prophylactic aspirin following the diagnosis of CAD (Carney, Freedland, Eisen, Rich, & Jaffe, 1995). Although the research noted thus far

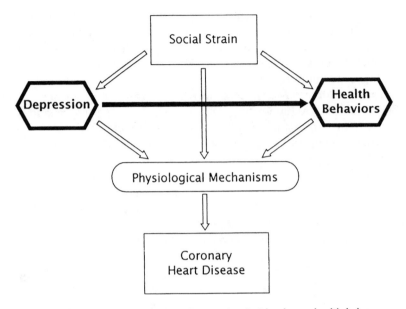

FIG. 11.6. Depression is significantly associated with adverse health behaviors.

emphasizes the adverse effects of depression, it is important to note that the reciprocal relationship between mood and health behaviors can be positive. Regular physical activity decreases depressive mood and anxiety, and can buffer psychological and physiological responses to stress (Taylor, Sallis, & Needle, 1985).

Thus far, we have attempted to trace a number of pathways by which social isolation exerts its influence on CHD in women—including direct effects on reactivity to stress as well as reciprocal pathways involving depression and health behaviors. These pathways have important implications for intervention, and suggest that there exists dynamic relationships among social isolation, moods, and adverse health behaviors that must be taken into account if an intervention is to be successful in lowering the risk of CHD, particularly the risk conferred by stress or health behaviors.

IMPLICATIONS OF THE MODEL FOR INTERVENTION

Efforts to lower risk for CHD in women often focus either on primary prevention or prevention of recurrence of cardiac events through reducing risk factors such as smoking. The model described in this chapter suggests that these efforts to change health behaviors need to address the psychological and social contexts in which these behaviors occur. For example, with regard to the psychological context, smoking and alcohol use often occur in the context of negative moods, such as depressed affect. Programs to effectively modify smoking need to include strategies for coping with this affect. In the context of post-MI patients, these reciprocal relationships are of utmost importance, given that living with chronic conditions such as CAD is often associated with substantial increases in emotional distress. Nickel and Chirikos (1990) observed this increase in distress in a longitudinal studies of chronically ill heart patients and urged future interventions to increase attention to emotional states.

The model described in this chapter also suggests that interventions targeted toward changing health behaviors need to consider the social context surrounding the behaviors. This entails a recognition that existing social networks may encourage such risk factors as unhealthy diets, inactivity, and smoking. Specifically, women's social roles may create barriers to change. Women may be encouraged to cook unhealthy foods to match family preferences and discouraged from taking time to exercise. Women have been observed to return to household activities sooner and feel guilty that they cannot resume the chores they once did sooner (Sharpe, Clark, & Janz, 1991). We need to examine support processes and intervene to engender positive social support in order to establish and maintain positive health changes. Mor-Barak and Miller (1991) have suggested strengthening social networks of poor elderly as a way to reinforce positive health behaviors.

The model suggests that CHD risk can be decreased by targeting social isolation. Programs are needed that strengthen indigenous ties and meaningful role activities (Heller, Thompson, Vlachos-Weber, Steffen, & Trueba, 1991). This may be no easy task given that social withdrawal and isolation may not have occurred voluntarily, but rather are often an aspect of aging. Special considerations need to be made for individuals who may have health or mobility restrictions. Effort must be expended in order to create useful social roles for elderly women who are coping with CAD. Examples of programs that may be effective include becoming companions in day-care nurseries, or participation in reconstructed family programs. One creative role intervention consisted of a peer-education program that sought to increase knowledge regarding cardiovascular disease in the elderly (Rose, 1992). Peer leaders were trained in the relationship between risk factors and heart disease, and given training in teaching others strategies to reduce risk behaviors. The peer leaders also received training in communication skills. In addition to providing a meaningful role for the peer leaders, the intervention demonstrated an increase in overall knowledge of heart disease, dietary self-efficacy, and exercise self-efficacy in the participants. Modern technologies including telecommunications may also be used to maintain social support directed toward health benefits (Heller et al., 1991).

Drawing definitive recommendations about interventions addressing the relationships among social isolation, health behaviors, and heart disease in women with established disease is handicapped by the dearth of research on women with CHD. Studies conducted in male patient populations cannot be extrapolated to women. Nickel and Chirikos (1990) observed that "factors traditionally associated with prognosis for male heart patients are not found to be as predictive for females" (p. 567). K. King, Porter, and Rowe (1994) investigated gender differences in recovery from coronary artery bypass graft (CABG) surgery. Women participants reported greater disruption than men during physical recovery in the initial postsurgery period, although the investigators caution that this is not necessarily due to the surgery itself being more difficult for women. Rather, they suggested that it is differences in role expectations and availability of social support that render postoperative disruption more salient for women. They concluded:

> We contend that these differences represent the experience of women and do not necessarily indicate poor recovery. Caution must be taken not to use the experience of men as the gold standard for comparison. Rather, expectations for recovery in women should be based on the usual experience of women and not the usual experience of men. (p. 353)

Findings that women exhibit poor adherence for exercise rehabilitation programs following MI or CABG have prompted investigators to ask if the typical elderly woman is enrolled in a program structured and designed for men (Boogard & Briody, 1985). Programs should take into account the different modes of activity that women may prefer (e.g., aerobic dance and videotaped exercise programs; A. King, Taylor, Haskell, & Debusk, 1990) and settings in which women might prefer to engage in these activities. Additional considerations to factor into designing interventions for women include the complexity and convenience of the physical activity regimen, monetary and psychological costs (e.g., embarrassment), and regimen structure and flexibility (A. King et al., 1992). Sharpe et al. (1991) found that both men and women conceded the importance of exercise, but women were significantly less likely to adhere to a prescribed regimen (41% of men vs. 19% of women). It is possible that women experience more barriers to exercise than men; for instance, they do not feel safe when walking. Integrating these findings into future interventions would be likely to enhance their effectiveness.

A positive example of the increased benefits of combining exercise with social connections is evident from work conducted at the Melpomene Institute in Minneapolis, which examined the effects of an exercise program for elderly women. Older women who exercise reported that they continued with the program not only to feel and look better but for a significant social payoff. One participant observed that a friend who starts off as an exercise partner "becomes not just someone to walk with, but to share joys and frustrations with. And someone from whom you get new invitations." They reported that a lack of discipline is the biggest barrier to exercise, but that having a "buddy" was effective in combating the lack of discipline. This intervention demonstrated multiple benefits for the women involved—increased social support, increased exercise, and increased well-being (Jaffee, Lutter, & Wu, 1996).

CONCLUSIONS

We hope that the model presented in this chapter will aid in conceptualizing future interventions. Future interventions that are targeted for primary prevention of CHD risk in women, or on improving the survival in women with heart disease, need to take into account the psychological and social contexts within which risk behavior occurs. The research which has demonstrated that social isolation increases CHD risk is compelling evidence of the importance of these contextual factors. The model described herein traces the network of behavioral and physiological mechanisms by which these contextual variables become converted into increased heart disease risk and events. Further research is needed to document the precise neuroendocrine pathways by which variables such as social support become expressed as arterial damage or coronary events. However, we need not wait for explication of these pathways before making recommendations for their adoption in interventions. Ruberman (1992) stated:

> It is well to remember that not every important public health development is preceded by complete understanding of its mode of action. Cigarette smoking and hypertension, two of the big three risk factors for CHD operate through unknown mechanisms, but their reduction is universally advised. Adoption of health education practices that further the development of social support could well be added to such advice. (p. 560)

We suggest that interventions may be enhanced by the inclusion of the aforementioned considerations, and that given the current risk to the health and well-being of women coping with CHD, the challenge of preventing needless suffering is rendered all the more imperative.

REFERENCES

Ahern, D., Gorkin, L., Follick, M., Anderson, J., Hollstrom, A., Tierny, C., Ewart, C., Capone, R., Schron, E., Kornfeld, D., Herd, J., & Richardson, D. (1990). Biobehavioral variables and mortality or cardiac arrest in the Cardiac Arrhythmia Pilot Study (CAPS). *American Journal of Cardiology, 66,* 59–62.

Berkman, L. F., & Breslow, L. (1983). *Health and ways of living: The Alameda County study.* New York: Oxford University Press.

Berkman, L. F., Leo-Summers, L., & Horwitz, R. I. (1992). Emotional support and survival after myocardial infarction. *Annals of Internal Medicine, 117,* 1003–1009.

Boogard, M. A. K., & Briody, M. E. (1985). Comparison of the rehabilitation of men and women post-myocardial infarction. *Journal of Cardiopulmonary Rehabilitation, 5,* 379–384.

Booth-Kewley, S., & Friedman, H. S. (1987). Psychological predictors of heart disease: A quantitative review. *Psychological Bulletin, 101,* 343–362.

Broman, C. L. (1993). Social relationships and health-related behavior. *Journal of Behavioral Medicine, 16,* 335–350.

Carney, R. M., Freedland, K. E., Eisen, S. A., Rich, M. W., & Jaffe, A. S. (1995). Major depression and medication adherence in elderly patients with coronary artery disease. *Health Psychology, 14,* 88–90.

Carney, R. M., Freedland, K. E., Smith, L. J., Rich, M. W., & Jaffe, A. S. (1994). Depression and anxiety as risk factors for coronary heart disease in women. In S. Czajkowski, D. R. Hill, & T. B. Clarkson (Eds.), *Women, behavior, and cardiovascular disease* (NIH Publication No. 94–3309, pp. 117–126). Washington, DC: U.S. Department of Health and Human Services.

Case, R. B., Moss, A. J., Case, N., McDermott, M., & Eberly, S. (1992). Living alone after myocardial infarction. *JAMA, 267,* 515–519.

Cerhan, J. R., & Wallace, R. B. (1993). Predictors of decline in social relationships in the rural elderly. *American Journal of Epidemiology, 137,* 870–880.

Cohen, S., Schwartz, J. E., Bromet, E. J., & Parkinson, D. K. (1991). Mental health, stress, and poor health behaviors in two community samples. *Preventive Medicine, 20,* 306–315.

Conn, V. S., Taylor, S. G., & Wiman, P. (1991). Anxiety, depression, quality of life, and self-care among survivors of myocardial infarction. *Issues in Mental Health Nursing, 12,* 321–331.

Dishman, R. K., Sallis, J. F., & Orenstein, D. R. (1985). The determinants of physical activity and exercise. *Public Health Reports, 100,* 158–171.

Finnegan, D. L., & Suler, J. R. (1985). Psychological factors associated with maintenance of improved health behaviors in postcoronary patients. *Journal of Psychology, 119,* 87–94.

Franks, P., Campbell, T. L., & Shields, C. G. (1992). Social relationships and health: The relative roles of family functioning and social support. *Social Science and Medicine, 34,* 779–788.

Frasure-Smith, N., Lesperance, F., & Talajic, M. (1993). Depression following myocardial infarction. *JAMA, 270,* 1819–1825.

Freedland, K. E., & Carney, R. M. (1994, July). *Depression as a risk factor for coronary heart disease.* Paper presented at the Third International Congress of Behavioral Medicine, Amsterdam, The Netherlands.

Gerin, W., Pieper, C., Levy, R., & Pickering, T. G. (1992). Social support in social interaction: A moderator of cardiovascular reactivity. *Psychosomatic Medicine, 54,* 324–336.

George, L. K., Blazer, D. G., Hughes, D. C., & Fowler, N. (1989). Social support and the outcome of major depression. *British Journal of Psychiatry, 154,* 478–485.

Heller, K., Thompson, M. G., Vlachos-Weber, I., Steffen, A. M., & Trueba, P. E. (1991). Support interventions for older adults: Confidante relationships, perceived family support, and meaningful role activity. *American Journal of Community Psychology, 19,* 139–146.

House, J. S., Landis, K. R., & Umberson, D. (1988). Social relationships and health. *Science, 241,* 540–545.

Jaffee, L., Lutter, J., & Wu, P. (1996). Motivation to be physically active in a work setting. *Melpomene Journal, 15,* 23–29.

Kamarck, T. W., Manuck, S. B., & Jennings, J. R. (1990). Social support reduces cardiovascular reactivity to psychological challenge: A laboratory model. *Psychosomatic Medicine, 52,* 42–58.

Kaplan, G. (1985). Psychosocial aspects of chronic illness: Direct and indirect associations with ischemic heart disease mortality. In R. Kaplan & M. Crique (Eds.), *Behavioral epidemiology and disease prevention* (pp. 237–269). New York: Plenum.

King, A. C., Taylor, C. B., & Haskell, W. L. (1990). Smoking in older women: Is being female a "risk factor" for continued cigarette use? *Archives of Internal Medicine, 150*, 1841–1846.

King, A. C., Taylor, C. B., Haskell, W. L., & DeBusk, R. F. (1990). Identifying strategies for increasing employee physical activity levels: Findings from the Stanford/Lockheed exercise survey. *Health Education Quarterly, 17*, 269–285.

King, A. C., Young, D. R., Oka, R. K., & Haskell, W. L. (1992). Effects of exercise format and intensity on two-year health outcomes in the aging adult (abstract). *Gerontologist, 32*, 190.

King, K. B., Porter, L. A., & Rowe, M. A. (1994). Functional, social, and emotional outcomes in women and men in the first year following coronary artery bypass surgery. *Journal of Women's Health, 3*, 347–354.

Langlie, J. K. (1977). Social networks, health beliefs, and preventive health behavior. *Journal of Health and Social Behavior, 18*, 244–259.

Lepore, S. J., Mata Allen, K. A., & Evans, G. W. (1993). Social support lowers cardiovascular reactivity to an acute stressor. *Psychosomatic Medicine, 55*, 518–524.

Monroe, S. M., Bromet, E. J., Connell, M. M., & Steiner, S. C. (1986). Social support, life events, and depressive symptoms: A 1-year prospective study. *Journal of Consulting and Clinical Psychology, 54*, 424–431.

Mor-Barak, M. E., & Miller, L. S. (1991). A longitudinal study of the causal relationship between social networks and health of the poor frail elderly. *The Journal of Applied Gerontology, 10*, 293–310.

Moritz, D. J., & Satariano, W. A. (1993). Factors predicting stage of breast cancer at diagnosis in middle aged and elderly women: The role of living arrangements. *Journal of Clinical Epidemiology, 46*, 443–454.

Nickel, J. T., & Chirikos, T. N. (1990). Functional disability of elderly patients with long-term coronary heart disease: A sex-stratified analysis. *Journal of Gerontology, 45*, S60–S68.

Orth-Gomér, K., & Unden, A. L. (1990). Type A behavior, social support and coronary risk: Interaction and significance for mortality in cardiac patients. *Psychosomatic Medicine, 52*, 59–72.

Palinkas, L. A., Wingard, D. L., & Barrett-Connor, E. (1990). The biocultural contest of social networks and depression among the elderly. *Social Science and Medicine, 30*, 441–447.

Powell, L., Shaker, L., Jones, B., Vaccarino, L., Thoresen, C., & Pattillo, J. (1993). Psychosocial predictors of mortality in 83 women with premature acute myocardial infarction. *Psychosomatic Medicine, 55*, 426–433.

Rose, M. A. (1992). Evaluation of peer-education program on heart disease prevention with older adults. *Public Health Nursing, 9*, 242–247.

Ruberman, W. (1992). Psychosocial influences on mortality of patients with coronary heart disease. *JAMA, 267*, 559–560.

Ruberman, W., Weinblatt, E., Goldberg, J. D., & Chaudhary, B. S. (1984). Psychosocial influences on mortality after myocardial infarction. *New England Journal of Medicine, 311*, 552–559.

Russell, D. W., & Cutrona, C. E. (1991). Social support, stress, and depressive symptoms among the elderly: Test of a process model. *Psychology and Aging, 6*, 190–201.

Schleifer, S. J., Macari-Hinson, M. M., Coyle, D. A., Slater, W. R., Kahn, M., Gorlin, R., & Zuc, H. D. (1989). The nature and course of depression following myocardial infarction. *Archives of Internal Medicine, 149*, 1785–1789.

Sharpe, P. A., Clark, N. M., & Janz, N. K. (1991). Differences in the impact and management of heart disease between older women and men. *Women & Health, 17*, 25–43.

Stern, M. J., Pascale, L., & Ackerman, A. (1977). Life adjustment post myocardial infarction: Determining predictive variables. *Archives of Internal Medicine, 137*, 1680–1685.

Stern, T. A. (1985). The management of depression and anxiety following myocardial infarction. *Mt. Sinai Journal of Medicine, 52*, 623–633.

Taylor, C. B., Sallis, J. F., & Needle, R. (1985). The relation of physical activity and exercise to mental health. *Public Health Reports, 100*, 195–201.

Umberson, D. (1987). Family status and health behaviors. *Journal of Health and Social Behavior,*
    28, 306–319.
Wenger, N. K. (1994). Coronary heart disease in women: Needs and opportunities. In S.
    Czajkowski, D. R. Hill, & T. B. Clarkson (Eds.), *Women, behavior, and cardiovascular disease*
    (NIH Publication No. 94–3309, pp. 7–18). Washington, DC: U.S. Department of Health and
    Human Services.
Williams, R. B. (1994, July). *Hostility, depression and CHD: A common biological mechanism?* Paper
    presented at the the Third International Congress of Behavioral Medicine, Amsterdam, The
    Netherlands.
Williams, R. B., Barefoot, J. C., Califf, R. M., Haney, T. L., Saunders, W. B., Pryor, D. B., Hlatky,
    M. A., Siegler, I. C., & Mark, D. B. (1992). Prognostic importance of social and economic
    resources among medically treated patients with angiographically documented coronary
    artery disease. *JAMA, 267,* 520–524.
Woo, J., Ho, S. C., Lau, J., Yuen, Y. K., Chiu, H., Lee, H. C., & Chi, I. (1994). The prevalence of
    depressive symptoms and predisposing factors in an elderly Chinese population. *Acta Psy-
    chiatrica Scandinavia, 89,* 8–13.
Young, R. F., & Kahana, E. (1993). Gender, recovery, from late life heart attack, and medical
    care. *Women & Health, 20,* 11–31.

PSYCHOPHYSIOLOGY OF CORONARY HEART DISEASE IN WOMEN

12

Reproductive Hormone Effects on the Cardiovascular System in Women

Karin Schenck-Gustafsson
Faris Al-Khalili
Karolinska Institute and Hospital, Stockholm

Myocardial infarction is the most common cause of death among women and men in Sweden as in the rest of the world. A 50-year-old woman has a 46% risk of contracting coronary heart disease (CHD) in the remaining years of her life and a 31% risk of dying of CHD. The incidence of and the risk of dying from breast cancer over the same time period are 10% and 3%, respectively, whereas the risk of experiencing a hip fracture is 15% and the risk of dying as a consequence thereof is 1.5% (Grady et al., 1992). Although CHD may be termed a disease of older woman, men are usually affected in middle age.

The cause of the later onset of CHD in women—10–15 years later than in men—may be hormonal in origin. Indirect evidence for this is that premature menopause and premature opphorectomy consistently increase the risk of myocardial infarction in women (Rosenberg, Hennekins, Rosner, Belanger, & Speizer, 1981). The possibility that treatment with estrogen may play a beneficial role in the delayed manifestation of CHD was questioned in the 1970s because of contradictory results from small studies with methodological problems. In addition, these studies included mainly male patients. In one important study (Coronary Drug Project Group, 1970), male patients with myocardial infarction (MI) were given, among other things, high doses of estrogen therapy with thromboembolic and cardiac side effects as a result. In addition, male patients given peroral estrogen as a treatment for prostatic cancer had an increased risk of cardiac complications (Henriksson & Edhag, 1986).

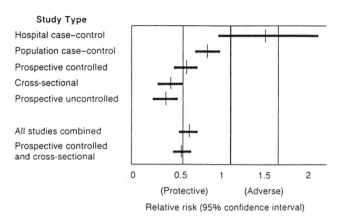

FIG. 12.1. Meta-analysis of observational studies on estrogen use and cardiovascular disease. From Stampfer and Colditz (1991). Reprinted with permission from Academic Press.

During the following years a great number of case control studies, observational analyses, and crossover designed studies have been published where estrogen users were compared with nonusers. In one of the meta-analyses of these studies (Stampfer & Golditz, 1991; see Fig. 12.1) it was concluded that the relative risk of contracting and dying of CHD is reduced with about 50%. The main criticism against these studies has been that there is a selection bias. The included estrogen users have been healthy American women from the middle and upper classes whose cardiovascular prognosis was already favorable.

Furthermore, the investigations mainly involved unopposed estrogens and the role of gestagen addition has not been sufficiently explored. Only recently, the results from the PEPI study (The Working Group for the PEPI Trial, 1995) and the Nurses' Health study (Grodstein, Stampfer, Manson, et al., 1996) in healthy women showed no harmful effect of gestagen addition on cardiovascular risk factors. However, the first study did not study "hard" cardiovascular endpoints and the latter is an epidemiological study. Therefore, as far as primary prevention is concerned, prospective randomized placebo-controlled studies with mortality and morbidity as endpoints have not been yet been published.

There is also a lack of prospective placebo-controlled secondary preventive studies in women with documented CHD. In cross-sectional studies (Gruchow, Anderson, Barboriak, & Sobocinski, 1988; Hong, Romm, Reagan, Green, & Rackley, 1993; MacFarland, Bonitac, Homung, Earnhardt, & Humphries, 1989; Sullivan et al., 1988) a group of estrogen users showed fewer atherosclerotic manifestations than a group of nonusers when coronary angiography was performed (see Table 12.1). We do not think that results

TABLE 12.1
Effects of Estrogens on Coronary Arteriosclerosis as Verified by Angiographic Studies

First author	Year	Study Design	Study Size	Endpoints	Risk Estimates
Hong et al.	(1993)	Cross-sectional	Users = 18 Nonusers = 72	Coronary stenosis	0.13
Sullivan	(1988)	Case-control	Cases = 1.444	≥ 70% stenosis	0.44*
Gruchow	(1988)	Cross-sectional	Users = 154 Nonusers = 779	Severe occlusion Moderate occlusion	0.37* 0.57*
McFarland	(1989)	Case-control	Cases = 137	≥ 70% stenosis	0.50*

$*p < 0.05$.

such as a 50% reduction of morbidity and mortality in CHD can be obtained only by chance. There is also an ever-increasing number of reports from smaller mechanistic studies that give reasonable biological explanations for the long-term and short-term cardiovascular effects. Some of these effects are discussed in this chapter.

In the first section of the chapter we review various mechanisms by which estrogen may be exerting its protective effects. In the second section we present findings from animal and human studies involving the direct administration of estrogen that provide important insights into the protective effects of estrogen. In the third and final section of the chapter we then discuss the implications of research on estrogen and heart disease in women for the primary and secondary prevention of heart disease.

CARDIOPROTECTIVE EFFECTS OF ESTROGENS—POSSIBLE MECHANISMS

Estrogens and Vasomotor Tone

Estrogen exerts a favorable modulating effect on the peripheral, and on the coronary vasotone. Clinical experiments have shown that estrogen increases the peripheral blood flow (Volterrani, Rosano, Coats, Beal, & Collins, 1995) and decreases the peripheral blood flow resistance (Gangar et al., 1991). The different underlying mechanisms—and how estrogen modulates the endothelial function of the vascular system, which seems to be one of the most important mechanisms—is discussed later in this chapter.

The status of endothelial function is of importance for maintaining the vascular tone. The endothelial cells produce many factors that play an important role in controlling the vascular tone, among these nitric oxide (NO), which is important, because besides its role as a potent vasodilating factor, it has antithrombocyte aggregating action and an antimyoprolifera-

%FMD

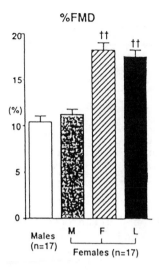

FIG. 12.2. Modulation of the endothelium-dependent flow-mediated
dilation of the brachial artery by
sex and menstrual cycle. From
Hashimoto et al. (1992). Reprinted
with permission. M = Menstrual
phase, F = follicular phase, L =
Luteal phase, FMD = flow-mediated
dilation.

tive effect (Moncada, Palmer, & Higgs, 1991). Thrombocyte aggregation and
smooth-muscle proliferation are essential parts in the process of initiating
atherosclerosis in the arterial wall.

The endothelial function can be studied using a noninvasive method
based on an important physiological mechanism—flow-mediated vasodilation, or the ability of the artery to increase its diameter when blood flow
increases (Celermajer et al., 1992). The stimulus of this dilation is believed
to be a shear stress effect on the vessel wall due to the increased blood
flow. The shear stress effect is thought to stimulate the NO activity or its
release, and probably other undefined endothelial factors (Joannides et al.,
1995). Failure or minimal vasodilation indicates endothelium dysfunction,
which is a risk marker and an early manifestation of arterial atherosclerosis
(Celermajer, Sorenson, Gooch, et al., 1992; Celermajer, Sorenson, Bull, et al.,
1994). A major peripheral artery, usually the brachial artery of the arm, is
used for this purpose (using forearm cuff occlusion and release). The diameter
and flow changes in the artery are studied using ultrasound technique.

There seem to be sex- and age-related differences in the endothelial
function. In men, the endothelium-dependent flow-mediated vasodilation of
the brachial artery decreases gradually after the age of 40, but in women
the picture is different. It starts to diminish after the age of 50, or about the
age of menopause, and at this time it decreases rather abruptly (Celermajer,
Sorenson, Spieghalter et al., 1994). This suggests again that female reproductive hormones may lie behind this apparent physiological difference in
the endothelial function between men and women.

It is interesting to notice that the endothelial function in healthy young
premenopausal women varies in the different phases of the menstruation
cycle (see Fig. 12.2). Flow-mediated vasodilation is greatest during the

follicular phase and the luteal phase, significantly lower in the menstrual and premenstrual phases when estradiol levels are at their lowest (Hashimoto et al., 1995). This could explain why some female patients with angina pectoris (AP) have increased episodes of AP during the premenstrual and menstrual phases.

Estrogens and Lipids

One of the most important effects of estrogens occurs via their lipid-lowering properties. Before menopause, plasma levels of low-density lipoproteins (LDL cholesterol) levels are lower and plasma levels of high-density lipoproteins (HDL cholesterol) levels are higher in women compared with men of the same age. After menopause, LDL cholesterol levels rise, commonly exceeding those of age-matched men, with a shift to smaller, more dense, and potentially more atherogenic particle sizes, and HDL cholesterol levels decline (Sempos, 1993).

Regarding the triglycerides, there is an obvious sex-related difference. Increased plasma levels of triglycerides is not an independent risk factor for cardiovascular disease (CVD) in men and young women, but constitutes an independent risk factor in older, postmenopausal women (Austin, 1988; Castelli, 1986). It is still uncertain whether this is due to a direct effect of the triglycerides, or whether the triglycerides are markers for other atherogenic lipoproteins.

Perorally administered estrogens increase plasma levels of HDL and decrease levels of LDL but, cause an increase in the triglycerides levels or leave it unaffected in postmenopausal women with normal or elevated baseline lipid levels. Transdermally administered 17 β-estradiol has no effect on lipoprotein levels, suggesting that the hepatic effects of estrogen absorbed through the gut are important for changes in lipoprotein levels. The reduction in LDL cholesterol levels is probably a result of accelerated conversion of hepatic cholesterol to bile acids and increased expression of LDL receptors on cell surfaces, resulting in augmented clearance of LDL from the plasma. The increase in HDL levels is due to increased production of apolipoprotein A-1 and decreased hepatic lipase activity, effects that increase levels of HDL_2, the HDL subparticle considered to be most active in reverse cholesterol transport. VLDL levels increase because of enhanced production of apolipoprotein B and triglycerides, but these particles may not be of atherogenic potential.

Estrogen therapy has also been shown to reduce levels of lipoprotein (a), a lipoprotein with structural features of LDL and plasminogen, believed to be proatherogenic and antithrombolytic, that increases the plasma concentration after menopause (Lobo, Notelovitz, Bernstein, Khan, & Ross, 1992). From the Stockholm study in women with coronary artery disease we found

Lp(a) to be an important and independent risk factor for coronary artery disease (CAD) in women (Orth-Gomér et al., 1996). The estrogen-induced, lipid-lowering effect on LDL levels is about 15%, whereas modern cholesterol synthesis inhibitors like statins will reduce LDL as much as 25%. That means that the estrogen reduction in lipoprotein levels are a little less pronounced. Whether there is a syngergistic effect of the combination of the two is still unclear.

Most of the lipid-lowering trials were performed in men. The effects of lipid-lowering drugs in women have therefore been uncertain. In the 1960s and 1970s, three lipid-lowering trials in Europe included both men and women, and in a meta-analysis of these trials, cholesterol lowering was found to be equally beneficial to men and women in terms of reduction of cardiac mortality (Castelli, 1986). Furthermore, it was recently reported in the Scandinavian Simvastatin Study including 700 women (the Scandinavian Simvastatin Study Group, 1994) that female postinfarction patients also benefit from lipid lowering, at least so far as reinfarction and other cardiovascular events are concerned. In summary, the estrogen-induced lipid effects might explain a great proportion of the long-term antiatherogenic results from the aforementioned angiographic studies.

Estrogens and Coagulation Factors

Other important effects are the modulation of the coagulation factors. A *high* oral estrogen dose such as found in the contraceptive pill will increase the production of coagulation factors in the liver, which may cause the status of the coronary arteries to deteriorate. However, the current doses of post-menopausal estrogen-replacement therapy are much lower than those previously used in contraceptive pills. Consequently, dose-dependent pro-coagulant activity by alkylated estrogens has been proposed (Winkler, Koslowski, Schindler, & Schindler, 1991). It has also been reported that estrogens induce an increase in fibrinolytic activity by increasing levels of tissue plasminogen, and decreasing the levels of plasminogen activator-I (Winkler, 1992).

In a comparative study of postmenopausal women (either untreated or estrogen treated) it was found that the levels of procoagulative factors such as fibrinogen, factor VII and PAI-1 were much higher among untreated women (Scarabin et al., 1993). This might indicate an increased coagulation and decreased fibrinolysis in the group of patients not undergoing estrogen treatment. A positive anticoagulative effect on coagulation factors was observed in the group undergoing estrogen therapy. The overall balance between coagulation and fibrinolysis induced by estrogens favors a reduction in thrombosis. Even though some new studies showed a slight increase in thrombolembolic events (Daly, Vessey, Hawkins, Carson, Gough, & March, 1996), others could not show an association (Lowe, Greer, & Cooke, 1992;

Paganini-Hill, Ross, & Hendersson, 1988). Prospective, randomized studies confirming this have not been published, but are on the way; however, negative effects of postmenopausal estrogen replacement therapy on the hemostasis are unlikely.

Estrogens and Blood Pressure Control

High blood pressure is no longer a contraindication for estrogen treatment as it was previously. In most cases, estrogen treatment will decrease blood pressure probably due to peripheral vasodilatation. Sometimes the blood pressure is unaffected, but about 5% of postmenopausal women taking estrogen may react with an increased blood pressure (Mashack & Lobo, 1985). Long-term estrogen or estrogen–gestagen treatment does not affect blood pressure (The Working Group for the PEPI Trial, 1995).

From a recent Norwegian thesis (Nordby, Haaland, & Os, 1992), women with recently debuted hypertension were found to have lower levels of estradiol compared to their healthy controls. The underlying mechanisms are still unknown.

Estrogens, Glucose and Insulin Metabolism

Estrogen-treated women have a lower incidence of diabetes compared with untreated women. Diabetic women have a higher incidence of CHD than diabetic men, which suggests that the sex hormones influence on glucose and insulin metabolism may be of particular significance with regard to the risk of CHD (Stevenson, Crook, Godsland, Collins, & Whitehead, 1994). The carbohydrate metabolism is prone to progressive alteration after the meno-pause—particularly the insulin resistance, which gradually deteriorates at that time (Walton, Godsland, Proudler, Wynn, & Stevenson, 1993).

Elevated insulin concentrations are frequently found in women with CHD and are likely to be due to insulin resistance. Hyperinsulinaemia may in-crease CVD by directly promoting atherogenesis, and insulin propeptide may also be important in this respect. Increased insulin concentrations may adversely effect several risk factors for CHD, and it has been suggested that insulin resistance is a pivotal metabolic disturbance in a constellation of cardiovasular risk factors. In addition, there is an association between hy-perinsuliaemia and hypertension. Increased insulin concentration is also associated with high triglyceride and low HDL, as well as increased small and LDL particles. Obesity is also associated with insulin resistance, and it is the central or android body distribution that correlates with these meta-bolic distrubances. There is commonly an increase in the antifibrinolytic factor PAI-1 in combination with insulin-increased levels. Estrogen and gestagen promote pancreatic insulin secretion, but the former reduces in-sulin resistance whereas the latter increases it. Hence the menopause reduces pancreatic insulin secretion. However, circulating insulin concentrations rise with age in postmenopausal women and this is due to an increasing insulin resistance and hepatic insulin output (Stevenson et al., 1994).

In summary, in many experimental studies estrogen treatment has been shown to increase the pancreatic insulin response to insulin and to reduce insulin resistance (Stevensen et al., 1994). This positive effect varies depending on which type of estrogen is used. Ethinyloestradiol and conjugated equine estrogens may impair glucose tolerance and augment insulin levels and the addition of gestagen may produce certain adverse effects on glucose and insulin metabolism. Even if differences have been observed between various gestagens, more data are urgently needed to clarify this issue.

EVIDENCE FROM ANIMAL AND HUMAN STUDIES

In this section we describe the direct effects of the administration of estrogens on cardiovascular function in various studies in both animals and humans. These studies are important because they provide evidence of the important cardiovascular mechanisms behind the estrogen effects.

Direct Arterial Effects

Estrogens and Peripheral Endothelial Function

Data from our research laboratory shows that iv-conjugated estrogen given to postmenopausal women causes a significant improvement of flow-mediated vasodilation in the brachial artery within 30 min. This was examined in a double-blind crossover designed study in which seven postmenopausal women received placebo, 2.5 mg, and 5 mg conjugated estrogen with a one-week interval between each examination.

Similar results were reported from another group (Gilligan, Badar, Panza, Quyyumi, & Canon, 1995) showing acute improvement in the peripheral endothelial function after acute infusion of 17β-estradiol (achieving physiological premenopausal levels of 17β-estradiol). This was investigated by an invasive method, using acute acetylcholine infusion in the brachial artery, and measuring the blood-flow volume by pletysmography technique. The acetylcholine infusion acts as a stimulator of the endothelial NO activity by endothelial, receptor-mediated vasodilation of the vessels with healthy endothelium and vasoconstriction in the vessels with endothelial dysfunction via a receptor-mediated mechanism in the smooth muscles of the vessel wall. The results could not be reproduced after 3 weeks of daily estradiol transdermal patch therapy.

However, another group showed an improvement in flow-mediated vasodilation in hyperlipidemic postmenopausal women 9 weeks after 1 mg and

2 mg per oral estradiol therapy in a placebo-controlled crossover-designed study (Lieberman et al., 1994). There was no difference in the achieved improvement of FMV between 1 mg and 2 mg per oral estradiol therapy. This was the longest clinical trial showing improvement in endothelial function in postmenopausal women with unopposed HRT.

Estrogens and Coronary Endothelial Function

The aforementioned experiments on the endothelial function of the peripheral circulation most probably describe the endothelial function of the whole systemic circulation including the coronary arteries (Anderson et al., 1995). Four different groups have described the acute effects of different types of estrogens on the endothelial function of the coronary arteries using acute intracoronary infusion of estrogen in postmenopausal women with CAD. Reis et al. (1994) reported that ethinyl estradiol given intravenously in high doses induced acute coronary vasodilation. This type of estrogen and others (17β-estradiol in physiological premenopausal plasma levels) enhanced the acetylcholine-mediated vasodilation in the coronary arteries, indicating improved endothelial function (Collins et al., 1995; Gilligan, Quyyumi, & Canon, 1994). These findings could not be reproduced using intracoronary 17β-estradiol in male patients (Collins et al., 1995). Animal studies performed on apes showed that the favorable acute coronary effects of 17β-estradiol were maintained several months in ovariectomized apes that were put on chronic estrogen treatment (Clarkson, Anthony, & Potvin Klein, 1994).

Estrogens and Nonendothelial Effects

The aforementioned experiments showed a direct effect of estrogen on the endothelial function. Other nonendothelial effects on the vessel wall have also been observed.

17β-estradiol exerts a direct vasodilating effect on isolated coronary artery segments taken from human transplanted hearts of male and female patients (Chester, Jiang, Borland, Yacoub, & Collins, 1995; Mügge, Riedel, Barton, Kuhn, & Lichtlen, 1993). These in-vitro experiments showed that vasodilation starts within 5 min and reaches its maximum after 40 min. The vasodilation was maintained when the endothelium was removed, and was more marked in the female coronary arteries. The mechanism behind this nonendothelium-mediated effect is still unclear.

The Clinical Relevance of the Acute Effects of Estrogens on the Coronary Vascular Reactivity. To come to a conclusion after describing all these studies, there is strong evidence to suggest that acute estrogen administration induces an acute improvement of the peripheral and coronary endothelial function, favorably modulating the vascular tone, and that, at least theoretically, can have a positive impact in the clinical setting of acute coronary insufficiency syndrome. In this unstable clinical condition, there is an increased coronary vascular tone in a lumen segment with superimposed labile nonocclusive thrombus. A slight increase in the vascular tone can have detrimental consequences leading to more myocardial damage by decreasing the vessel lumen and, perhaps, eventually leading to complete vessel occlusion.

Rosano, Sarrel, Poole-Wilson, and Collins (1993) described a positive effect on exercise-induced myocardial ischemia 40 min after acute administration of 1 mg sublingual 17β-estradiol to 11 postmenopausal women with stable angina pectoris (AP) and angiographically documented significant CAD. There was a significant increase in the total exercise time and the time to 1 mm ST-segment depression (1 mm ST-segment depression in an electrocardiographic manifestation of significant myocardial ischemia due to coronary insufficiency) compared to placebo.The estrogen levels reached in this study were above the therapeutical levels attained on regular HRT.

We studied the acute effects of 2 mg sublingual 17β-estradiol on 12 postmenopausal women with the same criteria as the aforementioned study and compared it with placebo and 2.5 mg p.o. nitroglycerine in a double-blind crossover design (Al-Khalili, Schenck-Gustafsson, Eksborg, Landgren, & Rydén, 1996). We found no effect of estrogen on the exercise capacity, nor on the time to ST-segment depression. Nitroglycerine causes a significant increase in time to 1 mm ST-segment depression.

The estrogen levels reached in this study were nearly double the plasma levels reached in the former study. Holdright et al. (1995) studied 16 postmenopausal women with stable AP and CAD one day after conventional estradiol transdermal patch therapy or placebo. No positive effect was shown on exercise capacity or myocardial ischemia when compared to placebo. There was a tendency, although not significant, toward an earlier debut of ST-segment depression after estrogen patch therapy.

The picture of those paradoxical results is further complicated by the results of earlier studies showing increased pathological ST-segment depression in postmenopausal women, with and without AP, that were taking estrogen (Jaffe, 1977). This was believed to be an explanation for the high percentage of so-called false positive stress tests among women. In a retrospective study (Morise, Dalal, & Duva, 1993) it was found that women with normal coronary angiogram and exercise-induced ST-depressions more often used oral estrogen therapy compared to those without ST-segment changes. In these studies it was proposed that estrogen could induce abnormal ST-changes in the ECG by increasing vasomotor tone. It is well known that digitalis (a medicine used for treatment of heart failure and atrial fibrillation) can induce "false" ST-depression during exercise test. As both digitalis and estrogens are steroids, the molecular similarity has been proposed as a possible explanation for the estrogen induced ST-depression.

In conclusion, there is only one study showing modest but significant improvement in exercise capacity and time to appearance of electrographic signs of myocardial ischemia after acute p.o. estrogen administration. Higher and lower (conventional) doses have failed to show a favorable clinical effect, in spite of the fact that they did show improvement in the coronary vascular reactivity in postmenopausal women with CAD.

Long-Term Cardiovascular Effects of Estrogens. We have described the short-term effects of estrogens on the cardiovascular system. Long-term effects have not yet been studied, and we still do not know if the favorable effects of acute administration of estrogen on the vascular reactivity of the peripheral and coronary circulation can be reproduced after long-term conventional estrogens in postmenopausal women. Whether this can account for the beneficial effects of estrogens that were described in the epidemiological studies is still unclear.

We still lack prospective studies showing the long-term effects of estrogen and of combined hormone treatment therapy on the exercise capacity, and silent and stress-induced myocardial ischemia in postmenopausal women with stable coronary insufficiency. A long-term study of the hemodynamic cardiovascular effects of HRT on healthy postmenopausal women using doppler technique of the left ventricular outflow tract showed that the mean acceleration time and the maximal flow velocity of the aortic blood flow was significantly increased 3 months after initiating therapy, and this finding was reproduced when repeating the study 9 months later (Pines et al., 1991, 1992).

Pines et al. correlated these findings to an increased stroke volume, indicating increased myocardial contractility—in other words, a positive inotropic effect of HRT. This effect could be due to an increase in the myofibrillar and Ca^{2+} myosin ATPase activity (Han, Karaki, Ouchi, Akishita, & Orimo, 1995). The effects of long-term HRT in postmenopausal women with depressed left ventricular function has not yet been validated.

Possible Mechanisms

Endothelial Factors

Nitric Oxide (NO). The exact mechanisms behind the vasculoprotective effects of estrogen are still unknown. We have already shown that estrogen modulates the arterial vascular tone mainly through an endothelial mechanism, most probably involving the endothelial activity of *NO, NO synthase,* or both (the latter being the enzyme that is responsible for the oxidation of the guanidine group of the amino acid L-arginine to NO; Kauser & Rubanyi, 1994).

NO induces vascular dilation and inhibits platelet aggregation, leukocyte adhesion, and smooth-muscle proliferation. All this could explain many of the described acute and chronic benefits of estrogen on the vascular physiology and morphology. However, we still cannot describe the exact mechanism by which estrogen modulates NO activity. Is it by increasing its release? Increasing its production? Increasing the endothelial NO synthase activity? By increasing the vascular tissue sensitivity to NO? Reports of decreased basal release of NO in the aorta of ovariectomized rabbits constitutes for evidence for NO-mediated vascular effects (Hayashi, Fukuto, Ignarro, & Chaudhuri, 1992). Collins, Shay, Jiang, and Moss (1994) showed that relaxation of isolated coronary arteries from estrogen-treated and then acutely estrogen-withdrawn rabbits was endothelium and NO dependent because it was abolished by endothelium removal and the NO synthase inhibitor L-NNA.

Concerning the estrogen effects on the NO synthase activity, there is evidence to show that estrogen regulates calcium-dependent endothelial NO synthase (constitutional NO-syntase) activity in cultured endothelial cells, probably through regulating gene expression by transcription changes (Kauser & Rubanyi, 1994). There are also studies showing that pregnancy and estrogen treatment in guinea pigs increases the activity of endothelial NO synthase in many organs, mainly in the uterine artery but also significantly in the heart (Weiner et al., 1994). These changes cannot account for the acute effects of estrogen because it takes about 16–24 hr for estrogen to stimulate the endothelial NO synthase activity in cultured bovine endothelial cells, and it takes days to increase the NO synthase activity in the hearts of guinea pigs. However, it is not known whether the same effects are present in the fresh noncultured human endothelial cells, or whether estrogen affects the nonendothelial NO synthase (inducible NO synthase) in the vessel wall.

Other Factors. The presence of non-NO effects cannot be ruled out (Samaan & Crawford, 1995). There is evidence to show that estrogen increases the production of *prostacycline* in the rat aortic wall (Chang, Nakao, Orimo, & Murota, 1980). Prostacycline is a vasodilator and it inhibits platelet aggregation. Estrogen reverses the *vasopressin*-mediated coronary spasm in rats (Radinno, Manca, Poli, Bolognesi, & Visioli, 1986). Vasopressin is a pituitary hormone known to be a powerful arteriolar vasoconstrictive factor. Estrogen antagonizes the vascular constrictive effects of *Endothelin-1* (a strong constrictive peptide produced by endothelial cells that seems to play a role in the acute myocardial ischemic process; see Jiang, Sarrel, Poole-Wilson, et al., 1992).

Calcium Channel Blocking Effect

Calcium channel antagonistic effect has also been postulated by some groups based on reports from animal studies, which may account for the vasodilatory effects of estrogen (Collins et al., 1993; Jiang, Poole-Wilson, et al., 1992). It has been shown that 17β-estradiol inhibits the influx of calcium currents and reduces the intracellular free calcium in isolated cardiac myocytes.

Receptors

Estrogen and progesterone have been shown to be expressed in the cardiovascular system of animals and humans, and it has been postulated that these receptors are indeed active (Lin, Gonzales, Carey, & Shain, 1986; Lin, McGill, & Shain, 1982; Lngegno et al., 1988), suggesting a classical receptor-mediated vascular effect (genomic effect) of estrogen. Recently Collins (personal communication, 1996) reported the absence of classical intracellular estrogen receptors in the human coronary arteries. This is in accordance with the findings from our laboratory.

The acute vascular effects that were demonstrated experimentally seem to be mediated by nongenomic effect. This is probably through membrane steroid receptor mediated effects inducing vasoactive reactions, which can be due to a potassium or calcium channel mediated effect through these receptors.

Antioxidant and Antimyoproliferative Effects of Estrogens

Antioxidants such as vitamin E, vitamin C, and Coenzyme Q-10 act in the body by eliminating the dangerous free oxygen radicals produced during the process of LDL oxidation in the vessel wall. An antioxidant effect of estrogen has been shown when estrogen was given acutely and after a few weeks of estrogen patch treatment (Sack, Rader, & Canon, 1994). The antioxidants have antiatherogenic effects, which seem to oppose the effects of oxidized LDL in the arterial wall (LDL oxidation is an initial step in the development of arterial atherosclerosis). NO breakdown is enhanced by the toxic free radicals build during the LDL oxidation process (Keany & Vita, 1995). In this way antioxidants can increase the NO activity and by this contribute to the improvement in endothelial function (Keany et al., 1994).

Smooth-muscle proliferation in the vessel wall in response to injury enhances the process of atherosclerosis. Studies have shown *antimyoproliferative* effects of estrogen therapy on artificially injured carotid artery vessel walls of ovariectomized female and male rats (Chen, Huaibin, Durand, Oparil, & Chen, 1996). Estrogen decreases the collagen synthesis and reduces the smooth-muscle hyperplasia according to other earlier animal in-vitro studies (Fisher, Bashey, Rosenbaum, & Lyttle, 1985; Vargas, Wroblewska, Rego, Hatch, & Ramwell, 1993).

IMPLICATIONS FOR PRIMARY AND SECONDARY PREVENTION

Primary Prevention

Several epidemiological, primary preventive studies since the early 1970s have shown that estrogen replacement therapy in postmenopausal women reduces the risk of developing CHD by 30–50% (Stampfer et al., 1991). However, these are observational studies and so far no available data from placebo-controlled randomized prospective studies. Women's Health Initiative is one such controlled study that has recently started in the United States, and plans to include 160,000 women. Another primary preventive study is planned to start 1997 in the United Kingdom and will be sponsored by the British Medical Research Council.

Secondary Prevention

As for secondary prevention with estrogens or estrogens combined with gestagens after myocardial infarction, PTCA, or CABG, the risk reduction might even be more pronounced (Sullivan et al., 1988). Also, in this respect there are no prospective controlled studies. A comprehensive study, HERS, has started in the United States. In this study, equine conjugated estrogens (Premarin) are used in combination with gestagen. An equivalent study will soon be started in Europe.

Hormones to Older Women

It should be pointed out that it is not always easy to introduce hormones to older female patients 10 years after the menopause. Some experience bleeding, others develop breast tenderness, and many are afraid of getting breast cancer. As far as the cancer risks are concerned, the risk for endometrial cancer in patients with an intact uterus is eliminated by the addition of gestagen. In the case of breast cancer, individual risk assessment is absolutely necessary. Overall, however, in patients with high CAD risk, the risk for breast cancer is generally much smaller than the cardiac risk (Grady et al., 1992). It is also of utmost importance to obtain more knowledge about estrogen and gestagen pharmacokinetics and the doses that should be given to older women. Perhaps the doses should be reduced. A summary is found in Table 12.2 where the cardiovascular effects from estrogen replacement therapy are shown.

CONCLUSION

There is an ever-increasing literature showing direct estrogen effects on coronary and peripheral arteries, long-term effects on lipid levels, coagulation factors, body fat distribution, and carbohydrate metabolism. In spite of the obvious positive results from these mechanistic studies showing a probable biological association between female coronary atherosclerosis and female sex hormones, we must still wait for the results from the more comprehensive large prospective studies before we can issue general recommendations to

TABLE 12.2
Cardioprotection by Estrogens: Mechanisms of Action

Metabolism	Vessel Wall	Cardiovasuclar Parameter
HDL cholesterol ⇑	Endothelin(s) ⇓	Blood pressure ⇓
LDI cholesterol ⇓	EDRF (NO) ⇑	Blood flow ⇑
Oxidized LDL ⇓	Thromboxone A₂ ⇓	Vascular resistance ⇓
Triglycerides ⇓	Prostacyclin ⇑	
Insulin ⇓	Calcium channel blocking ⇑	
Coagulation factors ⇓		
Fibrinolysis ⇑		
Anticoagulation factors ⇑		

Estrogen cardioprotection is conceivably mediated via known risk factors for cardiovascular disease. Estrogens have been described to influence a variety of markers for metabolism as well as vessel wall physiology. Only qualitative changes are marked. The importance of each change in quantitative terms vis-a vis cardioprotection remains to be clarified. This table represents only the recognized activities of estrogens and additional mechanisms of importance may well exist.

treat all women having CAD with sex hormones. However, a rationale for treating certain high-risk female patients suffering from CHD already exists. Theoretically, estrogens seem to be the ideal female cardiac drug.

REFERENCES

Al-Khalili, F., Schenck-Gustafsson, K., Eksborg, S., Landgren, B.-M., & Rydén, L. (1996). Acute administration of sublingual 2mg 17β-estradiol shows no effect on exercise induced coronary ischaemia in postmenopausal women with stable angina pectoris [abstract]. *European Heart Journal, 17*(433), 2350.

Anderson, T. J., Gerhard, M. D., Meredith, I. T., Charrbonneay, F., Delagrange, D., Creager, M. A., Selwyn, A. P., & Ganz, P. (1995). Systemic nature of endothelial dysfunction in atherosclerosis. *American Journal of Cardiology, 75,* 71B–74B.

Austin, M. A. (1988). Epidemiological associations between hypertriglyceridemia and coronary heart disease. *Semin Thromb Hemost, 14,* 137–142.

Castelli, W. P. (1986). The triglycerides issue: A review from Framingham. *American Heart Journal, 112,* 432–437.

Celermajer, D. S., Sorensen, K. E., Bull, C., Robinson, J., & Deanfield, J. (1994). Endothelium-dependent dilation in the systemic arteries of asymptomatic subjects relates to coronary risk factoris and their interaction. *JACC, 24*(6), 1468–1474.

Celermajer, D. S., Sorensen, K. E., Gooch, V. M., Spiegelhalter, D. J., Miller, O. I., Sullivan, I. D., Lloyd, J. K., & Deanfield, J. E. (1992). Non-invasive detection of endothelial dysfunction in children and adults at risk of atherosclerosis. *Lancet, 340,* 111–114.

Celermajer, D. S., Sorensen, K. E., Spiegelhalter, D. J., Georggakopoulos, D., Robinson, J., & Deanfield, J. E. (1994). Aging is associated with endothelial dysfunction in healthy men years before the age-related decline in women. *JACC, 24*(2), 471–476.

Chang, W. C., Nakao, J., Orimo, H., & Murota, S. I. (1980). Stimulation of the prostacycline bio-synthetic activity by estradiol in rat aortic smooth muscle cells in culture. *Biochim Biophys Acta, 619*, 107–118.

Chen, S. J., Huaibin, L., Durand, J., Oparil, S., & Chen, Y.-F. (1996). Estrogen reduces myoinitimal proliferation after balloon injury of rat carotid artery. *Circulation, 93*(3), 577–584.

Chester, A. H., Jiang, C., Borland, J. A., Yacoub, M. H., & Collins, P. (1995). Oestrogen relaxes human epicardial coronary arteries through non-endothelium-dependent mechanisms. *Coronary Artery Dis, 6*, 417–422.

Clarkson, T., Anthony, M. S., & Potvin Klein, K. (1994). Effects of estrogen treatment of arterial wall structure and function. *Drugs, 47*(suppl 2), 42–51.

Collins, P., Rosano, G. M. C., Jiang, C., Lindsay, D., Sarrel, P. M., & Poole-Wilson, P. A. (1993). Cardiovascular protection by oestrogen—a calcium antagonist effect. *Lancet, 341*, 1264–1265.

Collins, P., Rosano, G. M. C., Sarrel, P. M., Ulrich, L., Adamopoulos, S., Beale, C. M., McNeil, J. G., & Pool-Wilson, P. A. (1995). 17Beta-Estradiol attenuates acetylcholine-induced coronary arterialvasoconstriction in women but not in men with coronary heart disease. *Circulation, 92*, 24–30.

Collins, P., Shay, J., Jiang, C., & Moss, J. (1994). Nitric oxide accounts for dose-dependent estrogen-mediated coronary relaxation after acute estrogen withdrawal. *Circulation, 90*(4), 1964–1968.

Coronary drug project group. (1970). The Coronary Drug Project: Initial findings leading to modifications of its research protocol. *JAMA, 214*, 1303–1313.

Daly, E., Vessey, M. P., Hawkins, M. M., Carson, J. L., Gough, P., & Marsh, S. (1996). Risk of venous thromboembolism in users of hormone replacement therapy. *Lancet, 348*, 977–980.

Falkeborn, M., Persson, J., & Adams, H. (1992). The risk of acute myocardial infarction after estrogen–progesteron replacement. *British Journal of Obstetric and Gynaecology, 99*, 821–828.

Fisher, G., Bashey, R., Rosenbaum, H., & Lyttle, C. (1985). A possible mechanism in arterial wall for mediation of sex difference in atherosclerosis. *Exp Mol Pathol, 43*(3), 288–296.

Gangar, F., Vyas, S., Whitehead, M., Crook, D., Metre, H., & Campbell, S. (1991). Pulsatility index in internal carotid artery in relation to transdermal oestradiol and time since menopause. *Lancet, 338*, 839–842.

Gilligan, D. M., Badar, D. M., Panza, J. A., Quyyumi, A. A., & Canon, R. O., III. (1995). Effects of estrogen replacement therapy on peripheral vasomotor function in postmenopausal women. *American Journal of Cardiology, 75*, 264–268.

Gilligan, D. M., Quyyumi, A. A., & Canon, R. O. (1994). Effects of physiological levels of estrogen on coronary vasomotor function in postmenopausal women. *Circulation, 89*, 2545–2551.

Golditz, G., Willet, W., Stampfer, M., Rosner, B., Speizer, F., & Hennkens, C. (1987). Menopause and the risk of coronary heart disease in women. *New England Journal of Medicine, 316*, 1105–1110.

Grady, D., Rubin, S. M., Petitti, D. B., Fox, C. S., Black, D., Ettinger, B., Ernster, V. L., & Cummings, S. R. (1992). Hormone therapy to prevent disease and prolong life in postmenopausal women. *Annals of Internal Medicine, 117*, 1016–1037.

Grodstein, F., Stampfer, M. J., Goldhaber, S. Z., Manson, J. E., Colditz, G. A., Speizer, F. E., Willett, W. C., & Hennekens, C. H. (1996). Prospective study of exogenous hormones and risk of pulmonary embolism in women. *Lancet, 348*, 983–987.

Grodstein, F., Stampfer, M. J., Manson, J. E., Colditz, G. A., Willett, W. C., Bernard, R., Speizer, F. E., & Hennekens, C. H. (1996). Postmenopausal estrogen and progestin use and the risk of cardiovascular disease. *New England Journal of Medicine, 335*, 453–461.

Gruchow, H. W., Anderson, A. J., Barboriak, J. J., & Sobocinski, K. A. (1988). Postmenopausal use of estrogen and occlusion of coronary arteries. *American Heart Journal, 115*, 954–963.

Han, S.-Z., Karaki, H., Ouchi, Y., Akishita, M., & Orimo, H. (1995). 17 beta-estradiol inhibits Ca^2 influx and Ca^{2+} release induced by thromboxane A_2 in porcine coronary artery. *Circulation, 91*(10), 2619–2625.

Hashimoto, M., Akishita, M., Eto, M., Ishikawa, M., Kozaki, K., Toba, K., Sagara, Y., Taketani, Y., Orimo, H., & Ouchi, Y. (1995). Modulation of endothelium-dependent flow-mediated dilation of the brachial artery by sex and menstrual cycle. *Circulation, 92*(12), 3431–3435.

Hayashi, T., Fukuto, J. M., Ignarro, L. J., & Chaudhuri, G. (1992). Basal release of nitric oxide from aortic rings is greater in female rabbits than in male rabbits: Implications for atherosclerosis. *Proceedings of the National Academy of Sciences, 89*(23), 11259–11263.

Henriksson, P., & Edhag, O. (1986). Orchidectomy vs oestrogen in patients with prostata cancer: Cardiovascular effects. *BMJ, 293*, 413–415.

Holdright, D. R., Sullivan, A. K., Wright, C. A., Sparrow, J. L., Cunningham, D., & Fox, K. M. (1995). Acute effects of oestrogen replacement therapy on treadmill performance in post-menopausal women with coronary artery disease. *European Heart Journal, 16*, 1566–1570.

Hong, M., Romm, P., Reagan, K., Green, C., & Rackley, C. (1993). Effects of estrogen replacement therapy on serum lipid values and angiographically defined coronary artery disease in postmenopausal women. *American Journal of Cardiology, 69*, 176–178.

Jaffe, M. D. (1977). Effects of estrogens on postexercise electrocardiogram. *British Heart Journal, 38*, 1299–1303.

Jiang, C., Poole-Wilson, P. A., Sarrel, P. M., Mochizuli, S., Collins, P., & Macleod, K. O. (1992). Effects of 17β-oestradiol on contraction, Ca current and intracellular free Ca in guinea-pig isolated cardiac myocytes. *British Journal of Pharmacology, 106*, 739–745.

Jiang, C., Sarrel, P. M., Poole-Wilson, P. A., & Collins, P. (1992). Acute effect of 17B estradiol on rabbit coronary artery contractile responses to endothelin-1. *American Journal of Physiology 263 (Heart Circ Physiol), 32*, H271–H275.

Jick, H., Derby, L. E., Myers, M. W., Vasilakis, C., & Newton, K. M. (1996). Risk of hospital admission for idiopathic thromboembolism among users of postmenopausal oestrogens. *Lancet, 348*, 981–983.

Joannides, R., Haefeli, W. E., Linder, L., Richard, V., Bakkali, E. H., Thuillez, C., & Luscher, T. F. (1995). Nitric oxide is responsible for flow-dependent dilatation of human peripheral conduit arteries in vivo. *Circulation, 91*, 1314–1319.

Kauser, K., & Rubanyi, G. M. (1994). 17Beta-estradiol and endothelial nitric oxide synthase. *Endothelium, 2*, 203–208.

Keany, J. F., & Vita, J. A. (1995). Atherosclerosis, oxidative stress, and antioxidant protection in endothelium-derived relaxin factor action. *Progress in Cardiovasc Diseases, 38*(2), 129–154.

Keany, J. F., Shwaery, G. T., Xu, A., Nicolosi, R. J., Loscalzo, J., Foxall, T. L., & Vita, J. A. (1994). 17 beta-estradiol preserves endothelial vadodilator function and limits low-density lipoprotein oxidation in hypercholesterolemic swine. *Circulation, 89*(5), 2251–2259.

Lieberman, E. H., Gerhard, M. D., Uehata, A., Walsh, B. W., Selwyn, A. P., Ganz, P., Yeung, A. C., & Ceager, M. A. (1994). Estrogen improves endothelium-dependent flow-mediated vasodilation in postmenopausal women. *Annals of Internal Medicine, 121*, 936–941.

Lin, A. L., Gonzales, R., Carey, K. D., & Shain, S. A. (1986). Estradiol-17β affects estrogen receptor distribution and elevates progesterone receptor content in baboon aorta. *Arteriosclerosis, 6*, 495–504.

Lin, A. L., McGill, H. J., & Shain, S. A. (1982). Hormone receptors of the baboon cardiovascular system. *Cir Res, 50*, 610–616.

Lngegno, M., Money, S., Thelmo, W., Greene, G., Davidian, M., Jaffe, B., & Pertschuk, L. (1988). Progesterone receptors in the human heart and great vessels. *Laboratory investigation, 59*(3), 535–556.

Lobo, R. A., Notelovitz, M., Bernstein, L., Khan, F. Y., & Ross, R. K. (1992). LP(a) lipoprotein: Relation to cardiovascular disease risk factors, exercise and estrogen. *American Journal of Obstetrics & Gynecology, 166*, 1182–1190.

Lowe, G. D. O., Greer, I. A., & Cooke, T. G. (1992). Risk of and prophylaxis of venous thromboembolism in hospital patients. *BMJ, 305*, 567–574.

Mashack, C. A., & Lobo, R. A. (1985). Estrogen replacement therapy and hypertension. *J Repro Med, 30*, 805–810.

McFarland, K. F., Bonitac, M. E., Homung, C. A., Earnhardt, W., & Humphries, J. O. (1989). Risk factors and non contraceptive estrogen use in women with and without coronary disease. *American Heart Journal, 117*, 1209–1214.

Moncada, S., Palmer, R. M. J., & Higgs, E. A. (1991). Nitric oxide: Physiology, pathophysiology, and pharmacology. *Pharmacology Review, 43*, 109–142.

Morise, A. P., Dalal, J. N., & Duva, R. D. (1993). Frequency of oral estrogen replacement therapy in women with normal and abnormal exercise electrocardiograms and normal coronary arteries. *American Journal of Cardiology, 72*, 1197–1199.

Mügge, A., Riedel, M., Barton, M., Kuhn, M., & Lichtlen, P. R. (1993). Endothelium independent relaxation of human coronary arteries by 17 B-oestradiol in vitro. *Cardiovascular Research, 27*, 1939–1942.

Nabulsi, A., & al, e. (1993). Association of hormone-replacement therapy with various cardiovascular risk factor in postmenopausal women. *New England Journal of Medicine, 328*(15), 1069–1075.

Nordby, G., Haaland, A., & Os, I. (1992). Evidence of decreased fibrinolytic activity in hypertensive premenopausal women. *Scandinavian Journal of Clinical Laboratory Investigation, 52*, 275–281.

Orth-Gomér, K., Mittleman, M., Schenck-Gustafsson, K., Eriksson, M., Wamala, S., Belkic, K., Kirkeeide, R., Svane, B., & Rydén, L. (1997). Lipoprotein(a) as a determinant of coronary heart disease in younger women. *Circulation, 95*, 329–334.

Paganini-Hill, A., Ross, R. K., & Hendersson, B. E. (1988). Postmenopausal oestrogen treatment and stroke: A prospective study. *BMJ, 297*, 519–522.

Pines, A., Fisman, E., Levo, Y., Averbuch, M., Lidor, A., Drory, Y., Finkelstein, A., Hertman-Peri, M., Moshkowitz, M., & Be-Ari, D. A. (1991). The effects of hormone replacement therapy in normal postmenopausal women: Measurements of Doppler-derived parameters of aortic flow. *American Journal of Obstetrics & Gynecology, 164*, 806–812.

Pines, A., Fisman, E. Z., Shemesh, J., Levo, Y., Aylon, D., Kellerman, J. J., Motro, M., & Drory, Y. (1992). Menopause-related changes in left ventricular function in healthy women. *Cardiology, 80*, 413–416.

Radinno, R., Manca, C., Poli, E., Bolognesi, R., & Visioli, O. (1986). Effects of 17B-estradiol on the isolated rabbit heart. *Arch Int Pharmacodyn, 281*, 57–65.

Reis, S. E., Gloth, S. T., Blumenthal, R. S., Resar, J. R., Zacur, H. A., Gerstenblith, G., & Brinker, J. A. (1994). Ethinyl estradiol acutely attenuates abnormal coronary vasomotor responses to acetylcholine in postmenopausal women. *Circulation, 89*, 52–60.

Rosano, G., Sarrel, P., Poole-Wilson, P., & Collins, P. (1993). Beneficial effect of estrogen on exercise-induced myocardial ischaemia in women with coronary artery disease. *Lancet, 342*, 133–136.

Rosenberg, L., Hennekens, C. H., Rosner, B., Belanger, C., & Speizer, F. E. (1981). Early menopause and the risk of myocardial infarction. *American Journal of Obstetrics & Gynecology, 139*, 47–51.

Sack, M. N., Rader, D. J., & Canon, R. O. (1994). Estrogen and inhibition of LDL postmenopausal women. *Lancet, 343*, 269–270.

Samaan, S. A., & Crawford, M. H. (1995). Estrogen and cardiovascular function after menopause. *JACC, 26*(6), 1403–1410.

Scarabin, P.-Y., Plu-Bureau, G., Bara, L., Bonithon-Kopp, C., Guize, L., & Samama, M. M. (1993). Hemostatic variables and variables and menopausal status: Influence of hormone replacement therapy. *Thromb Haemost, 70*, 584–587.

Sempos, C. T. (1993). Prevalence of high blood cholesterol among US adults, an update based on guidelines from the second report of the national cholesterol education program adults' treatment panel. *JAMA, 269*, 3009–3014.

Stampfer, M., & Golditz, G. (1991). Estrogen replacement therapy and coronary heart disease. A quantitative assessment of the epidemiologic evidence. *Preventive medicine, 20*, 47–63.

Stampfer, M., Willet, W., Golditz, G., Manson, J., Rosner, B., Speizer, F., & Hennekens, C. (1991). Postmenopausal estrogen therapy and cardiovascular disease. Ten year follow-up from the nurses health study. *New England Journal of Medicine, 325*, 756–762.

Stevenson, J., Crook, D., Godsland, I. F., Collins, P., & Whitehead, M. I. (1994). Hormone replacement therapy and the cardiovascular system. *Drugs, 47*(suppl 2), 35–41.

Sullivan, J., Zwaag, V. R., Lemp, G. F., Hughes, J. P., Maddock, V., Kroetz, F. W., Ramanathan, K. B., & Mirvis, D. M. (1988). Postmenopausal estrogen and coronary artherosclerosis. *Annals of Internal Medicine, 108*, 358–363.

The Scandinavian Simvastatin Study Group. (1994). Randomised trial of cholesterol scandinavian simvastatin survival study (4S). *Lancet, 344*, 1383–1389.

The Working Group for the PEPI Trial. (1995). Effects of estrogen or estrogen/progestin regimens on heart disease risk factors in postmenopausal women: The Postmenopausal Estrogen/Progestin Interventions (PEPI) Trial. *JAMA, 273*, 199–208.

Vargas, R., Wroblewska, B., Rego, A., Hatch, J., & Ramwell, P. (1993). Oestradiol inhibits smooth muscle cell proliferation of pig coronary artery. *British Journal of Pharmacology, 109*(3), 612–617.

Volterrani, M., Rosano, G., Coats, A., Beale, C., & Collins, P. (1995). Estrogen acutely increases peripheral blood flow in postmenopausal women. *American Journal of Medicine, 99*, 119–122.

Walton, C., Godsland, I. F., Proudler, A. J., Wynn, V., & Stevenson, J. C. (1993). The effects of menopause on insulin sensitivity, secretion and elimination in non-obese healthy women. *European Journal of Clinical Investigation, 23*, 466–473.

Weiner, C. P., Lizasoain, I., Baylis, S. A., Knowles, R. G., Charles, I. G., & Moncada, S. (1994). Induction of calcium-dependent nitric oxide synthases by sex hormones. *Proc Natl Acad Sci, 91*, 5212–5217.

Winkler, U. H. (1992). Menopause, hormone replacement therapy and cardiovascular disease: A review of haemostaseological findings. *Fibrinolysis, 6*(suppl 3), 5–10.

Winkler, U. H., Koslowski, S. C. O., Schindler, E. M., & Schindler, A. E. (1991). Changes of the dynamic equilibrium of hemostasis associated with the use of low dose oral contraceptives: A controlled study of cyproteroneacetate containing oral contraceptives combined with either 35 or 50 ug ethinyl estradiol. *Advances in Contraception, 7*, 273–284.

13

Social Stress, Reproductive Hormones, and Coronary Heart Disease Risk in Primates

Carol A. Shively
Sheree L. Watson
J. Koudy Williams
Michael R. Adams
Bowman Gray School of Medicine of Wake Forest University

OVERVIEW

Animal models are helpful in clarifying the nature of relationships between risk factors and coronary heart disease (CHD) that are observed in epidemiological studies particularly when addressing risk factors, such as psychosocial stress, to which human subjects cannot be randomly assigned. In this chapter the results of a series of experiments addressing psychosocial, and reproductive effects on CHD risk in female monkeys are reviewed. The effects of experimental manipulation of psychosocial stress on reproductive function and CHD risk are presented. The most important concept to emerge from these studies is the possibility that women's CHD risk later in life may be largely determined during the premenopausal years. This concept is presented as a life-span model of CHD risk for women.

CHD RISK IN WOMEN: A MONKEY MODEL

Clinical and epidemiological studies of CHD often reveal the need for information that cannot be ethically or practically obtained in studies of human beings. Under such circumstances, an appropriate animal model may advance the understanding of the disease process. Cynomolgus macaques

(*Macaca fascicularis*) have several characteristics that make them especially well-suited as animal models of the progression of coronary artery atherosclerosis (CAA). When fed a moderately atherogenic diet, cynomolgus monkeys develop plaques that are similar to those observed in human beings. In Western societies, men are more likely to develop CHD and have more CAA than women (Tejada, Strong, Montenegro, Restrepo, & Solberg, 1968; Vanecek, 1976; Wingard, Suarez, & Barrett-Connor, 1983). Similarly, male cynomolgus monkeys have approximately twice the extent of CAA as female cynomolgus monkeys. Like women, female cynomolgus monkeys are protected against CAA relative to their male counterparts (Hamm, Kaplan, Clarkson, & Bullock, 1983).

Cynomolgus monkeys have menstrual cycles that are similar in length and hormone profile to those of women (Jewett & Dukelow, 1972; MacDonald, 1971; Mahoney, 1970). Following bilateral ovariectomy, female cynomolgus monkeys develop CAA as extensive as that observed in males (Adams, Kaplan, Clarkson, & Koritnik, 1985). Surgically and naturally postmenopausal women are also at increased risk for CHD. Replacement of estradiol and progesterone in physiological levels reinstates "female protection" against CAA in cynomolgus monkeys (Adams et al., 1990). Likewise, CHD risk is decreased in postmenopausal women who receive hormone replacement therapy (HRT; Bush et al., 1987). These findings imply that ovarian function, particularly relating to estradiol and progesterone, is an important factor in the phenomenon of female protection for women and female cynomolgus macaques. Examination of monkey society and its inherent psychosocial stressors may indicate useful approaches to the study of the relationship between psychosocial stress and CHD in human society.

SOCIAL SUBORDINATION STRESS AND CHD RISK

Psychosocial factors may also influence the risk of CHD; however, relatively little is known about psychosocial risk factors for CHD specific to women. Cynomolgus monkeys live in social groups, are dependent on complex social relationships, and are susceptible to social stress effects on health. Monkey societies are organized by social-status hierarchies (Shively, 1985). Socially subordinate and socially dominant females behave differently. Subordinate females are the targets of more aggression, are more vigilant, and spend more time alone than dominant females (Shively, Manuck, Kaplan, & Koritnik, 1990; Shively, Kaplan, & Adams, 1986). Subordinate females are also physiologically different from dominant females. Following dexamethasone suppression, the adrenal glands of subordinate females hypersecrete cortisol in response to an adrenocorticotropic challenge (Kaplan, Adams, Koritnik, Rose, & Manuck, 1986). These behavioral and physiological characteristics of subordinates indicate that they are socially stressed.

Additionally, subordinate females have poor ovarian function compared to dominant females (Adams et al., 1985). Subordinates have lower progesterone concentrations during the luteal phase and lower estradiol concentrations in the follicular phase than dominants (see Fig. 13.1). Moderately low luteal phase progesterone concentrations indicate ovulatory disturbances, and very low luteal phase progesterone concentrations indicate anovulatory cycles (Wilks, Hodgen, & Ross, 1976, 1979). These and studies from other laboratories suggest that social subordination stress causes impaired ovarian function.

Subordinate females with poor ovarian function have lower high-density lipoprotein (HDL) cholesterol concentrations and higher total/HDL cholesterol ratios than dominant females with good ovarian function (Adams et al., 1985). In fact, the lipid profile of subordinate females with poor ovarian function is similar to that of ovariectomized females. Subordinate females with poor ovarian function also have more CAA than dominant females. The CAA extent in these females is similar to that observed in both ovariectomized females and males (Adams et al., 1985; Hamm et al., 1983; see Fig. 13.2).

Among female cynomolgus monkeys, social status has a trait-like quality. That is, females rarely change social position and an individual's status in one social group is a good predictor of social status in other social groups (Shively & Kaplan, 1991). For example, in one experiment 41 females were housed in social groups comprised of 4 to 6 monkeys. The groups were

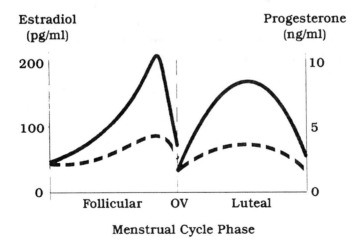

FIG. 13.1. Follicular phase estradiol concentrations and luteal phase progesterone concentrations in dominant females (solid line) and subordinate females (dashed line). From Adams et al. (1985), Shively and Clarkson (1994). © 1985 by and © 1994 by the American Heart Association, respectively. Adapted with permission.

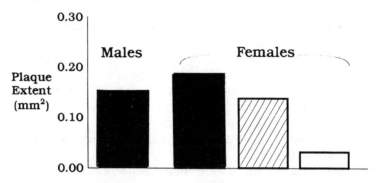

FIG. 13.2. Diet-induced coronary artery atherosclerosis (plaque) extent in male and female cynomolgus monkeys. Ovariectomized females = gray bar; socially subordinate, intact females = hatched bar; and socially dominant, intact females = open bar. From Adams et al. (1985), Hamm et al. (1983). Adapted with permission.

socially reorganized every 3 months. This meant that with every social reorganization, several "strangers" were housed together and social status hierarchies had to be reestablished. In 75% of the social groups, nearly two thirds of the animals that were dominant in the original group were dominant in subsequent groups and, similarly, subordinates in the original group remained subordinate in later groups. Knowledge of a monkey's status in one group allowed prediction of status in other social groups with about 90% accuracy. Thus, the propensity to occupy a given social position appears to be a reliable characteristic of the individual.

Because social status is associated with extent of CAA, we hypothesized that changing the social status of subordinate monkeys might confer on them the resistance to CAA observed in dominant females. Forty-eight adult females were fed an atherogenic diet and socially housed in groups of four for 8 weeks. Social status was determined for each monkey. The social groups were then reorganized so that only previously dominant females were housed together, and only previously subordinate females were housed together in new four-member groups. Because cynomolgus monkeys invariably organize themselves by social status hierarchies, the new social situations dictated that half of the previously dominant animals became subordinate, and half of the previously subordinate females became dominant. Thus, each animal fell into one of four categories: (a) dominants that remained dominant; (b) dominants that became subordinate; (c) subordinates that became dominant; or (d) subordinates that remained subordinate. The monkeys lived in these final social groupings for 26 months.

The results indicated that social status significantly influenced the extent of coronary artery atherosclerosis. As one might predict, the dominant monkeys that became subordinate had much more extensive atherosclerosis than the dominant monkeys that retained dominant status. However, the subordinate monkeys that became dominant also had more extensive atherosclerosis than the subordinates that remained subordinate (see Fig. 13.3). The effects could not be explained by traditional risk factors (e.g., cholesterol concentrations). Moreover, the effects on atherosclerosis were independent of changes in ovarian function. Subordinate monkeys that became dominant and dominant monkeys that remained dominant had relatively good ovarian function, whereas dominants that became subordinate and subordinates that stayed subordinate had relatively poor ovarian function (Shively & Clarkson, 1994). Hence, monkeys that switched social status—in either direction—were the most deleteriously affected. These results suggest that psychosocial stressors exert effects on the progression of CAA that are independent of the influence of ovarian function.

Health-related quality of life may depend to a large degree on congruity or "fit" between the individual and the environment (Levi, 1984). The individual–environment fit is best when there is congruity between abilities and demands, and between expectations and reality. Because social status appears to reflect an intrinsic characteristic of the individual, alteration of social status may have disrupted the individual–environment fit (Levi, 1984; Shively & Kaplan, 1991). Changing social status may have placed demands

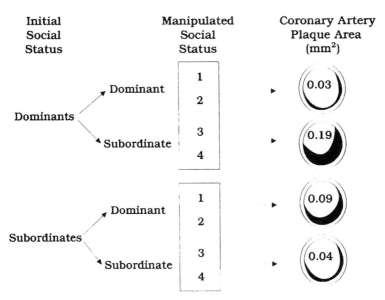

FIG. 13.3. The effects of changing social status on diet-induced coronary artery atherosclerosis extent in female monkeys. Shown are mean values of coronary artery plaque area adjusted for preexperimental predictors of atherosclerosis extent. From Shively and Clarkson (1994). © 1994 by the American Heart Association. Adapted with permission.

on the individuals that could not be met through existing social and behavioral repertoires. The resulting psychosocial dissonance may have contributed to the deleterious health consequences observed.

SOCIAL ISOLATION AND CHD RISK

Nonhuman primate communication relies heavily on tactile cues. When a female monkey spends time alone, she is not in physical contact or within touching distance of another monkey; she is socially isolated. Socially subordinate monkeys spend more time alone and have more extensive atherosclerosis than dominant females. Thus, social isolation may be a psychosocial risk factor for CAA in this species. To test this hypothesis, the coronary arteries of singly and socially housed female monkeys were compared after they had consumed an atherogenic diet for 2 years (Shively et al., 1989). Socially housed females established social status hierarchies. Singly housed females had visual, olfactory, and auditory contact with others, but were unable to touch another monkey. Singly housed animals had four times the CAA of socially housed monkeys. Socially dominant monkeys had the least CAA, socially subordinate females had an intermediate amount of CAA, and singly caged monkeys had the most CAA. Likewise, singly caged females spent the most time alone, social subordinates spent an intermediate amount of time alone, and dominants spent the least amount of time alone. These relationships are reminiscent of observations in human beings which suggest that low social support is associated with increased risk of CHD (Shumaker & Hill, 1991).

CHD RISK FACTORS IN WOMEN
DURING THE PREMENOPAUSAL YEARS

The results of these experiments suggest that psychosocial stress exerts an effect on CHD risk; part of this effect appears to be mediated by ovarian function. In women, difficulties in characterizing menstrual cycle quality over long periods of time hinder studies of stress effects on ovarian function. Nevertheless, several studies support the proposition that social stress can have deleterious effects on ovarian function in women (Barnea & Tal, 1991; Chatterton, 1990; Gindoff, 1989; Matteo, 1987). Furthermore, mechanistic pathways relating social stress to impaired reproductive function in female nonhuman primates have been identified; thus, the hypothesized relationship between social stress and impaired ovarian function is physiologically plausible (Abbott, O'Byrne, Sheffield, Lunn, & George, 1989; Abbott, Saltzman,

& Schultz-Darken, 1992; Biller, Federoff, Koenig, & Klibanski, 1990; Ferin, 1989; Gindoff & Ferin, 1989; Hayashi & Moberg, 1990). The relationship between poor ovarian function during the premenopausal years and CHD risk also is difficult to ascertain due to the double challenge of characterizing ovarian function and detecting an adequate number of clinical CHD events in women. However, there is one report that women with a history of irregular menstrual cycles are at increased risk for CHD (La Vecchia et al., 1987).

Finally, and perhaps most disturbing, it appears that rates of ovarian dysfunction may be quite high among healthy young adult women. In a well-designed study of 66 women, Prior, Vigna, Schechter, and Burgess (1990) studied the relationship between amount of exercise, quality of ovarian function, and bone density in premenopausal women. Subjects were required to have two consecutive ovulatory menstrual cycles. Menstrual cycles were characterized by documenting the occurrence of menses and measuring ovarian steroid concentrations for a year. Of the 66 women preselected for good ovarian function, only 13 (20%) had normal menstrual cycles during the subsequent year. The rest of the subjects had varying degrees of ovarian impairment, and this dysfunction was unrelated to amount of exercise, but was associated with lower spinal bone density. Because ovarian function appears to be an important premenopausal factor mediating CHD risk, more studies of variation in quality of ovarian function are needed to determine the frequency of ovarian dysfunction.

MENOPAUSE AND HORMONE REPLACEMENT THERAPY (HRT)

At menopause, ovarian production of estrogen and progesterone declines dramatically. It is also during this period of a woman's life that rates of clinically detectable CHD begin to accelerate (Kannel, Hjortland, McNamara, & Gordon, 1976; Matthews et al., 1989). Surgically postmenopausal cynomolgus monkeys fed an atherogenic diet have higher concentrations of total plasma cholesterol, lower concentrations of HDL cholesterol, higher total to HDL cholesterol ratios, and more extensive atherosclerosis than their intact counterparts (Adams et al., 1985). Hormone replacement therapy appears to protect surgically postmenopausal females from CAA. Subcutaneous administration of physiologic levels of estradiol, either alone or with progesterone, attenuated the progression of CAA in monkeys fed an atherogenic diet (see Fig. 13.4). The plasma lipid concentrations of the monkeys that received hormone replacement were indistinguishable from untreated monkeys (Adams et al., 1990). These results suggested that estradiol has a beneficial effect on CHD risk independent of its effects on lipid metabolism.

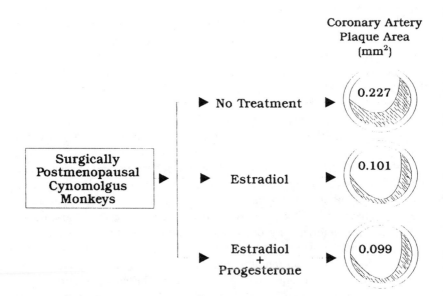

FIG. 13.4. Coronary artery atherosclerosis plaque area in surgically post-menopausal female cynomolgus monkeys fed a moderately atherogenic diet. Monkeys were untreated or treated with physiological levels of either 17β-estradiol or 17β-estradiol plus progesterone administered via Silastic® implants. From Adams et al. (1990). © 1990 by the American Heart Association. Adapted with permission.

SOCIAL STRESS, REPRODUCTIVE HORMONES, AND CORONARY VASOMOTOR FUNCTION

The presence of estrogen may reduce CHD risk by affecting the function of the coronary arteries. In response to neuroendocrine signals, coronary arteries constrict or dilate to regulate the flow of blood to the heart. Coronary vasospasm is a severe or inappropriately timed constriction of the coronary arteries that may contribute to the incidence of myocardial infarction. The effects of ovariectomy and hormone replacement on the vasomotor responses of coronary arteries were assessed using quantitative coronary angiography. In response to intracoronary infusion of the endothelium-dependent dilator acetylcholine, the coronary arteries of ovariectomized females constricted (Williams, Adams, & Klopfenstein, 1990). However, estrogen replacement restored the dilation response of the coronary arteries (Williams, Adams, Herrington, & Clarkson, 1992).

In a subsequent study, the effects of social stress on coronary vasomotor responsivity were determined. In response to intracoronary infusion of acetylcholine, the coronary arteries of dominant female monkeys dilated. A similar infusion of acetylcholine into the coronary arteries of subordinate

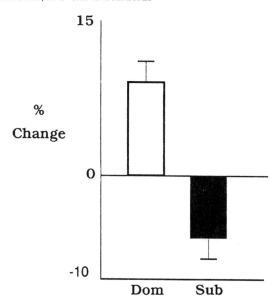

FIG. 13.5. Coronary artery reactivity to intracoronary infusion of acetylcholine (measured as % change from artery diameter at baseline infusion of saline) in socially dominant (dom) or subordinate (sub) female cynomolgus monkeys with diet-induced atherosclerosis. From Williams et al. (1994). © 1994 by the American College of Cardiology. Reprinted with permission.

females, however, resulted in arterial constriction (Williams, Shively, & Clarkson, 1994; see Fig. 13.5). These vasomotor responses were correlated with the quality of ovarian function over the previous 2 years and with estradiol concentrations on the day of the coronary catheterization. These data suggest that, in addition to increasing atherogenesis, estrogen deprivation may increase the risk of CHD in female monkeys by impairing coronary artery function.

SOCIAL STRESS, REPRODUCTIVE HORMONES, AND CHD RISK IN FEMALE PRIMATES: A MODEL

Clinically detectable CHD events occur most frequently after menopause, and CHD is the leading cause of death among women past age 50. Thus, the impact of premenopausal ovarian function on CHD risk may be temporally separate from the clinical manifestation of CHD. However, atherogenesis is a dynamic process that occurs over a lifetime.

Figure 13.6 depicts a hypothesized relationship between ovarian function and arterial changes over the lifetime of female primates under two different conditions. In the first condition (solid line), the premenopausal female

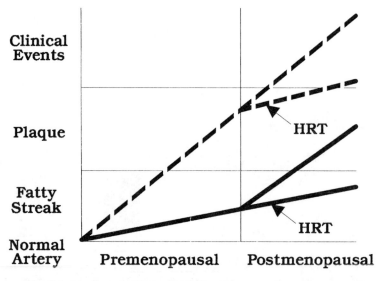

FIG. 13.6. The hypothesized relationship between ovarian status, social stress, and CHD risk in female primates. The horizontal axis describes menopausal status, and the vertical axis depicts atherosclerotic CHD progression. The dashed line = females with high levels of social stress and ovarian dysfunction, and the solid line = females with little social stress and good ovarian function. The graph depicts how hormone replacement therapy (HRT) affects postmenopausal cardiovascular events. From Shively et al. (1994). Adapted with permission.

primate is not stressed and has good ovarian function. In this situation, atherosclerosis never proceeds to the point of a clinical event. Given HRT at the onset of menopause, atherogenesis in this female will continue to be attenuated. In the second condition (dashed line), the premenopausal female has been stressed, ovarian function is impaired, and atherogenesis proceeds at a much greater rate. At menopause, atherogenesis continues at the same accelerated rate as during the premenopausal years when ovarian function was poor. HRT at the onset of menopause in these females may reduce the incidence of clinical events. Thus, premenopausal ovarian function, which is known to be influenced by psychosocial stress, may have a crucial relationship with atherogenesis that affects the rate at which clinically detectable CHD events occur later in life.

CONCLUSIONS

Psychosocial stress has deleterious effects on the ovarian function of female cynomolgus monkeys. Both the stressor, and the stress-induced ovarian dysfunction, are associated with increased CAA and compromised coronary vasomotor reactivity. Manipulation of the stressor ameliorates the ovarian dysfunction, but not the exacerbation of CAA, implying a complex relationship among social stress, physiological stress responses, and disease risk. To the extent that monkeys are similar to human beings, the results of these studies suggest the possibility that women's CHD risk later in life may be largely determined by the amount of social stress and the quality of ovarian function during the premenopausal years. Because the incidence of menses is a poor predictor of the quality of ovarian function, other measures of ovarian function are required to test this hypothesis.

REFERENCES

Abbott, D. H., O'Byrne, K. T., Sheffield, J. W., Lunn, S. F., & George, L. M. (1989). Neuroendocrine suppression of LH secretion in subordinate female marmoset monkeys (*Callithrix jacchus*). In P. H. Eley (Ed.), *Comparative reproduction in mammals and man. Proceedings of the conference of the National Center for Research in Reproduction* (pp. 63–67). Nairobi: Institute of Primate Research, National Museums of Kenya.

Abbott, D. H., Saltzman, W., & Schultz-Darken, N. J. (1992, June). *Hypothalamic switches regulating fertility in primates.* Paper presented at the 14th Congress of the International Society of Primatology, Strasbourg, France.

Adams, M. R., Kaplan, J. R., Clarkson, T. B., & Koritnik, D. R. (1985). Ovariectomy, social status, and atherosclerosis in cynomolgus monkeys. *Arteriosclerosis, 5*, 192–200.

Adams, M. R., Kaplan, J. R., Manuck, S. B., Koritnik, D. R., Parks, J. S., Wolfe, M. S., & Clarkson, T. B. (1990). Inhibition of coronary artery atherosclerosis by 17–beta estradiol in ovariectomized monkeys. *Arteriosclerosis, 10*, 1051–1057.

Barnea, E. R., & Tal, J. (1991). Stress-related reproductive failure. *Journal of in Vitro Fertility and Embryo Transplantation, 8*, 15–23.

Biller, B. M., Federoff, H. J., Koenig, J. I., & Klibanski, A. (1990). Abnormal cortisol secretion and responses to corticotropin-releasing hormone in women with hypothalamic amenorrhea. *Journal of Clinical Endocrinology and Metabolism, 70*, 311–317.

Bush, T. L., Barrett-Connor, E., Cowan, L. D., Criqui, M. H., Wallace, R. B., Suchindran, C. M., Tyroler, H. A., & Rifkind, B. M. (1987). Cardiovascular mortality and noncontraceptive use of estrogen in women: Results from the Lipid Research Clinics Program Follow-up Study. *Circulation, 75*, 1102–1109.

Chatterton, R. T. (1990). The role of stress in female reproduction: Animal and human considerations. *International Journal of Fertility, 35*, 8–13.

Ferin, M. (1989). Two instances of impaired GnRH activity in the adult primate: The luteal phase and "stress." In H. A. Delemarre-van de Waal, et al. (Eds.), *Control of the onset of puberty III* (pp. 265–273). Amsterdam: Elsevier.

Gindoff, P. R. (1989). Menstrual function and its relationship to stress, exercise, and body weight. *Bulletin of the New York Academy of Medicine, 65*, 774–786.

Gindoff, P. R., & Ferin, M. (1989). Endogenous opioid peptides modulate the effect of corticotropin-releasing factor on gonadotropin release in the primate. *Endocrinology, 121*, 837–842.

Hamm, T. E., Jr., Kaplan, J. R., Clarkson, T. B., & Bullock, B. C. (1983). Effects of gender and social behavior on the development of coronary artery atherosclerosis in cynomolgus macaques. *Atherosclerosis, 48*, 221–233.

Hayashi, K. T., & Moberg, G. P. (1990). Influence of the hypothalamic–pituitary–adrenal axis on the menstrual cycle and the pituitary responsiveness to estradiol in the female rhesus monkey (*Macaca fascicularis*). *Biology of Reproduction, 42,* 260–265.

Jewett, D. A., & Dukelow, W. R. (1972). Cyclicity and gestation length of *Macaca fascicularis*. *Primates, 13,* 327–330.

Kannel, W. B., Hjortland, M. C., McNamara, P. M., & Gordon, T. (1976). Menopause and risk of cardiovascular disease: The Framingham Study. *Annals of Internal Medicine, 85,* 447–452.

Kaplan, J. R., Adams, M. R., Koritnik, D. R., Rose, J. C., & Manuck, S. B. (1986). Adrenal responsiveness and social status in intact and ovariectomized *Macaca fascicularis*. *American Journal of Primatology, 11,* 181–193.

La Vecchia, C., Decarli, A., Franceschi, S., Gentile, A., Negri, E., & Parazzini, F. (1987). Menstrual and reproductive factors and the risk of myocardial infarction in women under fifty-five years of age. *American Journal of Obstetrics and Gynecology, 157,* 1108–1112.

Levi, L. (1984). Work, stress and health. *Scandinavian Journal of Work, Environment and Health, 10,* 495–500.

MacDonald, G. T. (1971). Reproductive patterns of three species of macaques. *Fertility and Sterility, 22,* 373–377.

Mahoney, C. J. (1970). A study of the menstrual cycle in *Macaca irus* with special reference to the detection of ovulation. *Journal of Reproduction and Fertility, 21,* 153–163.

Matteo, S. (1987). The effect of job stress and job interdependency on menstrual cycle length, regularity and synchrony. *Psychoneuroendocrinology, 12,* 467–476.

Matthews, K. A., Meilahn, E., Kuller, L., Kelsey, S. F., Caggiula, A. W., & Wing, R. R. (1989). Menopause and risk factors for coronary heart disease. *New England Journal of Medicine, 321,* 641–646.

Prior, J. C., Vigna, Y. M., Schechter, M. T., & Burgess, A. E. (1990). Spinal bone loss and ovulatory disturbances. *New England Journal of Medicine, 323,* 1221–1227.

Shively, C. A. (1985). The evolution of dominance hierarchies in nonhuman primate society. In S. L. Ellyson & J. F. Dovidio (Eds.), *Power, dominance, and nonverbal behavior* (pp. 67–88). New York: Springer-Verlag.

Shively, C. A., Adams, M. R., Kaplan, J. R., Williams, J. K., & Clarkson, T. B. (1994). Social stress, ovarian function, and coronary artery atherosclerosis in primates. In S. M. Czajkowski, D. R. Hill, & T. B. Clarkson (Eds.), *Women, behavior, and cardiovascular disease. Proceedings of a National Heart, Lung, and Blood Institute Conference* (pp. 127–144). Bethesda, MD: National Institutes of Health.

Shively, C. A., & Clarkson, T. B. (1994). Social status and coronary artery atherosclerosis in female monkeys. *Arteriosclerosis and Thrombosis, 14,* 721–726.

Shively, C. A., Clarkson, T. B., & Kaplan, J. R. (1989). Social deprivation and coronary artery atherosclerosis in female cynomolgus monkeys. *Atherosclerosis, 77,* 69–76.

Shively, C. A., & Kaplan, J. R. (1991). Stability of social status rankings of female cynomolgus monkeys, of varying reproductive condition, in different social groups. *American Journal of Primatology, 23,* 239–245.

Shively, C. A., Kaplan, J. R., & Adams, M. R. (1986). Effects of ovariectomy, social instability and social status on female *Macaca fascicularis* social behavior. *Physiology and Behavior, 36,* 1147–1153.

Shively, C. A., Manuck, S. B., Kaplan, J. R., & Koritnik, D. R. (1990). Oral contraceptive administration, interfemale relationships, and sexual behavior in *Macaca fascicularis*. *Archives of Sexual Behavior, 19,* 101–117.

Shumaker, S. A., & Hill, D. R. (1991). Gender differences in social support and physical health. *Health Psychology, 10,* 102–111.

Tejada, C., Strong, J. P., Montenegro, M. R., Restrepo, C., & Solberg, L. A. (1968). Distribution of coronary and aortic atherosclerosis by geographic location, race, and sex. *Laboratory Investigation, 18,* 509–526.

Vanecek, R. (1976). Atherosclerosis of the coronary arteries in five towns. *Bulletin of the World Health Organization, 53*, 509–518.

Wilks, J. W., Hodgen, G. D., & Ross, G. T. (1976). Luteal phase defects in the rhesus monkey: The significance of serum FSH:LH ratios. *Journal of Clinical Endocrinology and Metabolism, 43*, 1261–1267.

Wilks, J. W., Hodgen, G. D., & Ross, G. T. (1979). Endocrine characteristics of ovulatory and anovulatory menstrual cycles in the rhesus monkey. In E. S. E. Hafez (Ed.), *Human ovulation* (pp. 205–218). Amsterdam: Elsevier/North-Holland.

Williams, J. K., Adams, M. R., Herrington, D. M., & Clarkson, T. B. (1992). Short-term administration of estrogen and vascular responses of atherosclerotic coronary arteries. *Journal of the American College of Cardiology, 20*, 452–457.

Williams, J. K., Adams, M. R., & Klopfenstein, H. S. (1990). Estrogen modulates responses of atherosclerotic coronary arteries. *Circulation, 81*, 1680–1687.

Williams, J. K., Shively, C. A., & Clarkson, T. B. (1994). Determinants of coronary artery reactivity in premenopausal female cynomolgus monkeys with diet-induced atherosclerosis. *Circulation, 90*, 983–987.

Wingard, D. L., Suarez, L., & Barrett-Connor, E. (1983). The sex differential in mortality from all causes and ischemic heart disease. *American Journal of Epidemiology, 117*, 19–26.

14

Cardiovascular Reactivity to Mental Stress

Gerdi Weidner
Catherine R. Messina
State University of New York at Stony Brook

One of the most active areas in psychosomatic research has focused on cardiovascular reactivity to mental stress. The underlying assumption of this research is that excessive cardiovascular responses to stress play a role in the development of hypertension and CHD. Although this "reactivity hypothesis" has created some controversy (Pickering & Gerin, 1990), many researchers agree that the supporting evidence is strong and viable (e.g., Light, Sherwood, & Turner, 1992; Manuck, Kasprowicz, & Muldoon, 1990). We begin this chapter with the definition of cardiovascular reactivity, followed by a summary of what we currently know about its diagnostic and prognostic validity. Because studies to date have focused mainly on men, very little is known about the role of excessive cardiovascular reactivity in hypertension and heart disease among women. The second part of this chapter briefly discusses cardiovascular reactivity testing among women and presents the reactivity test protocol from the Swedish Study of Women with Coronary Heart Disease (also see chapter 3 by Orth-Gomér, this volume).

THE CONCEPT OF CARDIOVASCULAR REACTIVITY

Matthews (1986) defined reactivity as "the deviation of a physiologic response parameter(s) from a comparison or control value that results from an individual's response to a discrete, environmental stimulus" (pp. 461–462).

219

That is, cardiovascular reactivity refers to the difference in heart rate, blood pressure, or other measures of cardiovascular function observed between periods of rest and during the presentation of a stressor. This chapter focuses on cardiovascular reactivity measured by noninvasive methods.

The majority of reactivity studies have measured changes in heart rate and blood pressure. Generally, the extent of a person's reactivity on a particular measure, such as blood pressure, is reproducible and relatively stable over time. For example, Steptoe and Vögele (1991) investigated the temporal stability of cardiovascular responses to mental stress in 28 comparisons based on 17 studies with intervals between sessions ranging from one day to more than one year. Most of the comparisons were based on male samples. Systolic blood pressure (SBP) reactions to tasks showed an average weighted z of 0.575 ± 0.034 ($r = 0.52$). For diastolic blood pressure (DBP), the corresponding z value was 0.313 ± 0.035 ($r = 0.30$), and for heart rate (HR), $z = 0.732 \pm 0.031$ ($r = 0.62$). The relatively low values for DBP may be partially due to the fact that the magnitude of DBP responses to mental stress are small compared with SBP. Thus, the low correlations may be due to restriction of range.

Correlation coefficients in studies that report on stability of cardiovascular responses among women separately are of similar magnitude (e.g., Matthews, Rakaczky, Stoney, & Manuck, 1987; Messina, Hutt, & Weidner, 1993). In addition, there is some evidence that measures taken in the laboratory generalize to those in the field when ambulatory measures are used (see review by Turner et al., 1994).

A wide range of stressors have been employed in laboratory research, ranging from the cold pressor test, where participants are asked to place a hand in very cold water, to a variety of mental stressors, such as arithmetic, knowledge quizzes, anagram tasks, or public speaking (see Steptoe & Vögele, 1991). The latter tasks are often labeled "active," whereas the cold pressor test is considered a "passive" stressor. Both women and men evidence cardiovascular reactivity to such tasks. However, the magnitude of response to active stressors seems to be influenced by the nature of the stressor. If the stressor is verbal or requires interpersonal skills, women's cardiovascular responses are rather similar to those of men (cf. Houston, 1988; Weidner, Friend, Ficarrotto, & Mendell, 1989; Weidner & Messina, 1995). This observation is rather intriguing and suggests that perceived relevance of the stressor to one's gender role may play a part in determining the magnitude of cardiovascular responses (cf. Weidner, 1994; Weidner & Messina, 1995).

At present, there is no consensus in the field as to how to analyze reactivity data. As a consequence, we see researchers using change scores (i.e., values obtained during a resting baseline are subtracted from the values obtained during a stressor), sometimes with baseline values as covariates; residualized change scores, analyses of repeated measures, analyses of absolute levels, percentage change score (in relation to baseline value), are used as well. The two most frequently employed statistical techniques appear to be ANOVAs for repeated measures and ANCOVAs of change scores with the baseline score as a covariate.

DIAGNOSTIC VALIDITY OF CARDIOVASCULAR REACTIVITY TESTING

Diagnostic validity refers to the ability of stress reactivity tests to evoke responses that distinguish different clinical groups and discriminate between people with and without disease.

Comparisons of Hypertensives With Normotensives

Several studies comparing cardiovascular responses to stress among normotensives to those of hypertensives have been evaluated in a meta-analysis by Fredrikson and Matthews (1990). Most of the 70 studies examined included data from both men and women. The hypertensives were grouped into three categories: essential hypertensives, borderline hypertensives, and normotensive offspring of hypertensive parents. Only six of the studies in the essential hypertensive category relied on women. Two of the studies on normotensive offspring of hypertensive parents relied on female samples, whereas none did in the borderline hypertensive category. Thus, separate analyses by sex could not be performed. However, Fredrikson and Matthews stated, "We did not find that sex and age influenced the magnitude of the blood pressure and heart rate differences between the case/control groups" (p. 36). Their three major conclusions are:

> First, essential hypertensives exhibit exaggerated blood pressure responses to all stressors, active, passive, and the cold pressor in particular . . . second, borderline hypertensives exhibit exaggerated systolic and diastolic blood pressure and heart rate responses to active stressors mainly, suggesting that an active psychological element is required to elicit elevated responses among mild hypertensives . . . third, normotensive offspring of hypertensive parents show elevated systolic blood pressure and heart rate responses to all stressors and elevated diastolic blood pressure responses to active stressors. (pp. 36–37)

In sum, the diagnostic validity of reactivity testing when distinguishing hypertensives (or persons at high risk for developing hypertension) from healthy controls is quite convincing, especially when the stressor requires active responding. However, given the problem of adequate representation of female samples, the aforementioned conclusions should be viewed as tentative with regard to their applicability to women. We concur with the authors of this meta-analysis that future case/control investigations should emphasize the effects of sex.

Comparisons Involving Heart Disease Patients

Cardiovascular reactivity to mental stress in heart disease patients and controls has been compared in a number of studies (Corse, Manuck, Cantwell, Giordini, & Matthews, 1982; Dembroski, MacDougall, & Lushene, 1979; Krantz et al., 1991; Nolan, Wielgosz, Biro, & Wielgosz, 1994; Schiffer, Hartley, Schulman, & Abelmann, 1976; Sime, Buell, & Eliot, 1980; Valek, Kuhn, Honzak, & Vavrinkova, 1971). Gender composition, type of stressor, and the time elapsed since the last myocardial infarction (MI) are presented in Table 14.1. As can be seen, only very few women were included in these studies.

TABLE 14.1
Studies of Heart Disease Patients and Healthy Controls

Study	Patients	Controls	Stressor	Time Since Last MI[a]
Corse et al. (1982)	24 men (18 MI)	34 men	Concept formation, mental arithmetic, picture completion	4.8 years (median)
Dembroski et al. (1979)	31 men (# of MI patients not reported)	33 men	Structured interview, quiz	not reported
Krantz et al. (1991)	35 men 4 women (# of MI patients not reported)	11 men 1 woman	Mental arithmetic, Stroop color word task, simulated public speaking, reading task	not reported
Nolan et al. (1994)	32 men (all MI patients)	39 men	Serial subtraction, cold pressor test	9-24 months
Schiffer et al. (1976)	20 men 4 women (6 MI patients)	17 men 2 women	IQ-type oral quiz	not reported
Sime et al. (1980)	30 men (all MI patients)	30 men	IQ-type oral quiz	3-15 months
Valek et al. (1971)	30 (sex not reported) (all MI patients)	21 (sex not reported)	Learning names	3.5 years (mean)

[a]Patients only.

Furthermore, results with regard to cardiovascular reactivity are mixed. Some, but not all studies, found evidence for heightened reactivity to mental stress among coronary patients when compared to healthy controls.

In addition, several studies have compared cardiovascular responses to stress among various clinical groups of heart disease patients (Fredrikson & Blumenthal, 1988; Krantz et al., 1981; Langosch, Brodner, & Foerster, 1983; Lowin & DeSilva, 1978; Nestel, Verghese, & Lovell, 1967; Schiffer, Hartley, Schulman, & Abelmann, 1980; Simpson & Shaver, 1991; Specchia et al., 1984; Taylor, Davidson, Houston, Agras, & Debusk, 1982). Four of these are based on men. The remaining studies include a very small number of women, ranging from 1 (Schiffer et al., 1980) to 10 (Specchia et al., 1984). Conclusions about their findings are further impeded by the differences in patient populations studied. There is some indication that cardiovascular reactivity to mental stress may be elevated among more severely ill patients when compared to those with fewer disease manifestations.

Overall, it is difficult to evaluate the findings resulting from studies of patients. Besides the fact that the samples were almost exclusively limited to men, drawing conclusions is difficult for a number of additional reasons: (a) the controls were not always matched in age to the patients; (b) due to small sample sizes, many of the studies did not distinguish between the various clinical manifestations of CHD; (c) some studies did not control for potentially confounding effects of medications, such as beta-blockers; (d) time elapsed since last coronary event differed from study to study.

In spite of these problems, five of the aforementioned patient studies are of further interest, because they are similar with regard to design and methodology to the only study that is currently examining cardiovascular stress reactivity among female patients (see chapter 3 of this volume). Because these studies may facilitate the formation of hypotheses in the Swedish Study of Women with Coronary Heart Disease, they are reviewed in further detail later.

In the study by Dembroski et al. (1979), the 31 male MI patients had higher blood pressure reactivity than the 33 control subjects, but only in response to a quiz (not to an interview). There were no significant differences in HR responses between patients and controls. Most of the patients were on beta-blockers, but no statistical adjustments were made.

Sime et al. (1980) administered a stressful quiz to 30 male MI patients and 30 healthy male controls matched in age and occupation. Results indicated that overall, the patients had lower HR responses than the controls. However, the 12 MI patients who also had angina, hypertension, ECG changes, or any combination thereof had higher DBP reactivity than patients without these symptoms or the controls.

Schiffer et al. (1976) studied 33 executives (14 with angina, 6 with a history of hypertension, 3 with a history of MI, and 19 controls) and 10 nonexecutives with angina (4 with a history of hypertension, 3 with MI). Their sample was predominantly male (37 men, 6 women). A quiz was administered to each participant. Those executives with angina and a history of hypertension had higher blood pressure reactivity than the other groups. Heart rate and blood pressure responses of the nonexecutives were not different from those of the controls. However, nonexecutives had lower HR and SBP responses than executives with angina. These findings suggest that hypertension among coronary patients may be a critical factor in determining their cardiovascular stress reactivity (also see Sime et al., 1980).

Simpson and Shaver's (1991) study also supports the notion that hypertension may play a critical role in the magnitude of cardiovascular stress responses among their sample of 17 male and 7 female coronary patients. In this study, patients with hypertension had greater cardiovascular reactivity (i.e., increases in SBP) to social interaction conditions than nonhypertensive patients.

Finally, the study by Nolan et al. (1994) is similar to the Swedish Study of Women with Coronary Heart Disease because it also includes an assessment of subjective stress responses in addition to cardiovascular stress reactivity. The major reason for examining subjective as well as physiological reactivity to stress is to examine their concordance (i.e., verbal–autonomic response dissociation; cf. Weinstein, Averill, Opton, & Lazarus, 1968). If cardiovascular stress reactivity is accompanied by emotional discomfort, this discomfort can serve as a stimulus to change one's behavior in order to decrease the potentially pathogenic effect of prolonged cardiovascular arousal. In contrast, the experience of very little emotional distress in the presence of cardiovascular arousal may deprive a person of the emotional cues necessary to engage in behaviors that reduce cardiovascular arousal (Kneier & Temoshok, 1984; Kohlmann, Weidner, & Messina, 1995). Nolan et al. (1994) compared cardiovascular and emotional reactivity to psychological stress and the cold pressor test among 32 men who had sustained an acute MI within 2 years with that of 39 healthy male controls. Vasoreactive medications (e.g., beta-blockers) were stopped at least 2 days before laboratory testing and subjects did not smoke for at least one hour before testing. The major finding was that patients showed greater discordance between perceived stress and actual cardiovascular reactivity than the controls during stress and especially during relaxation. For example, patients reported a greater reduction in stress during relaxation, whereas their systemic vascular resistance increased significantly.

Based on the findings from the five aforementioned patient studies, it appears that when hypertension or a history of hypertension is included in the patient diagnosis, differences in cardiovascular reactivity between patients and controls are found. Further, there is some evidence that male patients may show greater discordance between perceived stress and actual cardiovascular reactivity when compared to controls. To the extent that male and female coronary patients show similar cardiovascular and emotional reactions to stress, similar findings may emerge from the Swedish Study of Women with Coronary Heart Disease.

In sum, it appears that diagnostic validity of stress testing is relatively well established when comparing hypertensive to normotensive men. There is some indication that this may apply to female samples as well. However, for coronary patients, the situation is more complicated.[1] Due to many methodological and procedural differences in the studies that have compared mostly male patients to controls, it is difficult to arrive at a more definite statement of whether reactivity testing discriminates between people with and without disease.

PROGNOSTIC VALIDITY OF CARDIOVASCULAR REACTIVITY TESTING

A very important aspect of stress testing is whether it predicts hypertension or CHD among initially healthy people and recurrent events among patients. At the present time, the prospective evidence for a link between cardiovascular stress reactivity and cardiovascular disease is limited because there are not many prospective studies that have included reactivity tests in their protocol. Of those that have, the cold pressor (CP) test was administered and blood pressure and heart rate reactivity were evaluated. The cold pressor test involves immersion of a limb, typically a hand, sometimes a foot, into ice water for a brief duration (1 to 2 minutes).

Reactivity to the Cold Pressor Task, CHD Mortality, and Hypertension

The first study linking heightened cardiovascular responses to CHD was reported by Keys et al. (1971). In this study, DBP reactivity to the CP test predicted CHD mortality in men 23 years later, even when the standard risk factors were statistically controlled. Another study was reported in 1973 by Thomas and Greenstreet, and was based on more than 1,000 male medical

---

[1]Several patient studies have started to employ invasive measures of cardiovascular functioning in response to stress (e.g., radionuclide ventriculography; regional myocardial perfusion and ischemia by measurement of the uptake of rubidium-82 with positron tomography after mental arithmetic and physical exercise). Some interesting findings have emerged. For example, Rozanski et al. (1988) found that mental stress induced silent MI in patients with coronary artery disease (CAD). Also, Tavazzi, Zotti, and Rondanelli (1986) induced arrhythmias with mental stress in patients with CAD. Similarly, Deanfield et al. (1984) showed silent MI in response to mental stress. Krantz et al. (1991) demonstrated that SBP levels during mental stress were highest for the severely ischemic group (CAD patients in this study were categorized as ischemic if significant left ventricular wall motion worsening was induced by any one of the mental stress tasks).

students at Johns Hopkins in classes graduating from 1948 through 1964. In this study, SBP rise to the CP test predicted CHD.

Several other prospective studies evaluated reactivity to the CP with regard to hypertension, or elevated blood pressure levels (Armstrong & Rafferty, 1950; Eich & Jacobson, 1967; Harlan, Osborne, & Graybiel, 1964; Hines, 1940; Menkes et al., 1989; Wood, Sheps, Elveback, & Schirger, 1984). Of these six studies, four were based on men (Armstrong & Rafferty, 1950; Eich & Jacobsen, 1967; Harlan et al., 1964; Menkes et al., 1989), one did not specify gender (Hines, 1940), and one was a 45-year follow-up of 76 boys and 66 girls (Wood et al., 1984). Unfortunately, this latter study did not report findings by sex. Half of these studies support a link between blood pressure reactivity and elevated blood pressure (Hines, 1940; Menkes et al., 1989; Wood et al., 1984). The ones that did not had relatively short follow-ups and other methodological problems.

The strongest study is probably the one by Menkes et al. (1989). This study was a 20- to 36-year follow-up of 910 male physicians. The response rates were very good in this study and the known risk factors of hypertension (i.e., age, body mass index, resting SBP, family history of hypertension, and cigarette smoking) were statistically controlled. Systolic blood pressure reactivity to the cold pressure test remained a significant predictor of hypertension. In sum, the evidence for a prospective link of cold pressor induced blood pressure reactivity to CHD mortality and hypertension among men appears to be strong. We currently lack comparable information on women.

Reactivity to Mental Stress, Hypertension, and Recurrent Events

One problem with stress induced by the CP test is that it is unlike the stressors encountered in daily life. In contrast, mental tasks are often completed under time pressure and involve effort that is a very common element of daily life stressors. In addition to the greater relevance of mental tasks for everyday life, Steptoe and Vögele (1991) stated:

> The specific purpose of mental stress testing is to elicit cardiovascular responses to emotional or behavioral challenges independent of basic reflexes to evaluate the role of the central nervous system in disturbances of cardiac and hemodynamic functions and the involvement of stress mechanisms in cardiovascular disorders. (p. 13)[2]

---

[2]Experimental studies on animals suggest that cardiovascular reactivity to "mental" stress predicts atherosclerosis. For example, individual differences in cardiovascular responsivity to a laboratory threat correlated positively with extent of coronary and cerebral artery atherosclerosis in male and female cynomolgus monkeys fed a cholesterol-containing diet (Kaplan, Adams, Clarkson, & Koritnik, 1984; Manuck, Kaplan, Adams, & Clarkson, 1989; Manuck, Kaplan, & Clarkson, 1983).

Several prospective studies have evaluated cardiovascular reactivity to mental stress as a predictor of elevated blood pressure, or hypertension (Borghi, Costa, Boschi, Mussi, & Ambrosioni, 1986; Falkner, Kushner, Onesti, & Angelakos, 1981; Light, Dolan, Davis, & Sherwood, 1992). The sample of Borghi et al.'s (1986) study was comprised of 34 male and 10 female borderline hypertensives. No gender comparisons were reported. The sample of Falkner et al.'s (1981) study included 27 male and 19 female borderline hypertensive adolescents. Ten females and 18 males developed essential hypertension over a 41-month period; each one of these manifested a high blood pressure, high heart rate, or both in response to mental stress when compared to normotensive controls. However, the remaining borderline hypertensive adolescents who did not develop essential hypertension also evidenced exaggerated cardiovascular reactivity to stress. It is quite possible that—with a longer follow-up period—those may develop essential hypertension as well.

Results from the longest follow-up have been published by Light et al. (1992). Their study links cardiovascular reactivity to a mental stressor (reaction time task involving threat to shock) to stethoscopic blood pressure and ambulatory blood pressure readings in 51 men 10 to 15 years later. The men were 18 to 22 years of age and normotensive at the time of reactivity testing. Heart rate and SBP reactivity were the best predictors of elevated blood pressure levels 10 to 15 years later.

In their review of prospective studies on cardiovascular reactivity as a predictor of hypertension, or elevated blood pressure levels, Light, Sherwood, and Turner (1992) concluded (with respect to mental stress):

> To summarize the available prospective research on reactivity, there have clearly been few studies completed at this time. . . . The results have uniformly indicated that high cardiovascular reactivity is a predictor of higher blood pressure levels and/or hypertension development at follow-up. (pp. 287–288)

At present, we are only aware of two prospective studies that have evaluated cardiovascular responses to mental stress as a predictor of CHD related mortality among heart disease patients. Blood pressure and heart rate reactivity to a videogame (in addition to a variety of psychosocial attributes) were assessed at baseline in 265 patients participating in the Cardiac Arrhythmia Pilot Study (Ahern et al., 1990). These patients were a subset of a larger sample of 502 patients, 83% of whom were male (gender composition of the 265 patients was not reported). Patients had experienced an MI within 6 to 60 days before enrollment. Outcomes were death or cardiac arrest after a one-year follow-up. For the stress reactivity measures, HR reactivity was the only significant predictor (after statistically adjusting for history of prior MI, ejection fraction, beta-blocker or digitalis use [or use of both], presence of transmurality in the qualifying MI, and presence of runs of ventricular premature complexes on the 24-hour ECG at baseline). Results indicated that *diminished* HR reactivity—as well as greater Type B behavior and greater depression—were associated with greater mortality or cardiac arrest. This finding suggests that high-risk post-MI patients are those who have disengaged from life both psychologically as well as physiologically. No gender comparisons were reported.

A pilot study of MI patients has also been published recently (Manuck, Olsson, Hjemdahl, & Rehnqvist, 1992). This pilot study is based on a follow-up of 14 post-MI patients (11 men and 3 women) from Stockholm, who had participated as untreated (placebo) controls in the Stockholm Metropropol Trial (a 3-year postinfarction study). Data were obtained from 13 of the 14 MI patients (one patient refused to take part in the stress session). The gender composition of the final sample was not reported. At the conclusion of the trial, the patients underwent mental stress testing (i.e., a film version of Stroop's color–word interference test) while HR and blood pressure were being monitored. Follow-up ranged from 39 to 64 months. During that time period, five patients had a "clinical event." The main finding was that mean SBP levels and DBP levels during stress testing were higher among those who later succumbed to another event than for those who did not. Baseline values were reported to be similar for the two groups. No differences in heart rate levels were found. It is of interest to note that cardiovascular responses to exercise testing did not differentiate the two groups in this study.

To summarize, prognostic validity of stress reactivity testing among initially healthy individuals is promising, especially with regard to hypertension. This appears to apply to both men and women. The prediction of recurrent events among patients via reactivity testing remains elusive. The report on 13 patients (Manuck et al., 1992) provided initial support for the hypothesis that elevated cardiovascular reactions to mental stress may play a role in the recurrence of clinical events among men. However, this trend may not hold up when data from more patients become available and potentially confounding factors can be taken into account: The data from 265 patients enrolled in the Cardiac Arrhythmia Pilot Study (Ahern et al., 1990) point to *low* heart rate reactivity to mental stress as a predictor of mortality among a predominantly male sample.

CARDIOVASCULAR REACTIVITY TO STRESS AMONG WOMEN

Our current knowledge about the role of cardiovascular stress reactivity in CHD etiology among women is very limited. Most studies that have included women have been done on relatively young, disease-free women and have focused on the influence of Type A behavior and other coronary-prone attributes on cardiovascular responses (Burns, Hutt, & Weidner, 1993; Houston, 1988; Weidner, 1995; Weidner et al., 1989). Based on findings from these studies it appears that women's cardiovascular responses to stress are rather similar to those of men, especially when the stressor is relevant to their gender (cf. Houston, 1988; Weidner & Messina, 1995). That is, interpersonal stressors or verbal stressors (e.g., Stroop's color–word interference test or anagram tasks) are powerful elicitors of cardiovascular stress responses from women in the laboratory.

In addition to gender comparisons, several studies have examined the influence of hormones on cardiovascular responses in women. With regard to menstrual cycle effects, the majority of studies have found little evidence that blood pressure and heart rate reactivity are affected by the menstrual cycle phase (see review by Weidner, 1994). Similarly, in her extensive review of the role of reproductive hormones in both cardiovascular and neuroendocrine function during stress, Stoney (1992) concluded that the relatively small fluctuations in reproductive hormones that occur in normally cycling women do not affect their response to stress. With regard to menopause, studies on the effects of reproductive hormones on reactivity are very few and their findings are mixed. A similar paucity of studies of the effects of reproductive hormones on physiological reactivity during pregnancy has been noted. Furthermore, studies on the effects of exogenous hormones (e.g., estrogen replacement therapy; oral contraceptive use) on cardiovascular stress reactivity are too few to allow for any conclusive remarks.

Cardiovascular Reactivity in the Swedish Study of Women With Coronary Heart Disease

The Swedish Study of Women with Coronary Heart Disease consists solely of women under the age of 65 who are hospitalized within one year with a diagnosis of CAD (angina pectoris or myocardial infarction) in the greater Stockholm area. Each patient is matched to a healthy control subject of the same age and from the same catchment area, randomly obtained from the Stockholm population register. Length of follow-up is scheduled for 3 years. (For more details on this study, see chapter 3 by Orth-Gomér, this volume.) The assessment protocol includes a noninvasive cardiovascular reactivity test for both patients and their controls and is similar to the one employed by Weidner et al. (1989).

Cardiovascular Measures.   Systolic blood pressure, DBP, and HR were measured by an OMRON Auto-Inflation digital sphygmomanometer (model HEM–703C). The microphone was contained in a standard size cuff (or one larger) that was inflated every 60 seconds by the experimenter. After participants had been seated and had received their instructions, a 10-minute baseline of BP and HR readings was taken. The average of the last three readings was taken as the baseline value. Participants were then asked to rate their mood or affect (see the following) and given a list of anagrams to solve while their blood pressure and heart rate were monitored. The average of the two readings obtained during the task was computed to reflect the stress value. After administration of the anagram task, three more measures of blood pressure and HR were taken and averaged to arrive at a resting value. In addition, ambulatory electrocardiogram recordings were obtained from a Holter monitor.

Affect. In order to examine verbal–autonomic response discrepancy (Kneier & Temoshok, 1984; Kohlman et al., 1995), participants were asked to rate to which degree they felt frustrated, angry, anxious, and unhappy. These ratings provided us with their baseline affect. Immediately after the 2-minute anagram task, participants were again asked to rate how they felt now using the same affect dimensions. In addition, they were asked to rate the degree to which they experienced "heart troubles right now." All ratings were made on visual analog scales (100 mm), with one end of the scale indicating the opposite dimension of the other end of the scale (e.g., very angry–not at all angry, etc.).

Stressor. The stressor consisted of 15 anagrams presented on a sheet of paper. Participants were told that they had 2 minutes to solve the anagrams (see Appendix for a copy of the anagrams).

Task Perceptions. Participants were asked to indicate how difficult they felt the experimental task was, how much effort they put into solving it, and how well they thought they solved the task. All ratings were made on 100 mm visual analog scales (e.g., very easy–very difficult, etc.).

Procedure. Reactivity testing took place early in the morning on the second day of the 2-day baseline assessment period. Participants were told that this session was concerned with physiological changes while solving "fairly easy anagrams," and that their blood pressure and pulse would be monitored while they performed the task. When scheduling participants for this session, they were asked to abstain from caffeine-containing beverages and smoking for at least 10 hours before the experiment. All tests were run individually by a female experimenter who was blind to the participant's status. Participants were instructed to sit comfortably on an examination table (leaning against a support, legs straight). The experimenter measured midarm circumference and positioned the appropriate blood pressure cuff over the brachial artery in the upper portion of the participant's nondominant arm. Following brief orienting instructions, an initial blood pressure reading was taken to make sure the equipment was operating properly and to familiarize participants with the procedure. Participants were informed that it was important for them to be in a relaxed state in order to get accurate measures of their blood pressure and HR. The experimenter offered several suggestions to ensure proper relaxation. Participants were told to focus their attention on their breathing. They were also told not to move or talk, because this would raise their blood pressure. The experimenter stated that "some people find it helpful to breathe slowly and think of pleasant things as they relax." The experimenter told the participants that several blood pressure readings would be taken until their blood pressure stabilized. Participants were reminded to remain as relaxed as they could so that stable readings could be obtained, and to focus on their breathing or heart beat to keep thoughts from entering their minds. Systolic blood pressure, DBP, and HR were measured once every minute for a period of 10 minutes. If the last three readings differed by 10 mmHg or more, additional readings were taken until blood pressure stabilized (no more than five additional readings).

Following baseline, participants were introduced to the anagram task and were shown one example. Participants were instructed to remain silent throughout the procedure. Systolic blood pressure, DBP, and HR were monitored once every 60 seconds throughout the anagram task. Following the 2-minute task period, they were told to stop, and indicate how many anagrams they worked on by putting a check mark beside each one. Three measures of task performance were constructed: number of anagrams solved correctly, number of anagrams tried, and the ratio of number of anagrams solved correctly divided by the number of anagrams tried. Finally, participants were asked to fill out the questions regarding their perceptions of the anagrams and to rate their affect again.

Preliminary Results

In order to confirm that the anagrams elicited both physiological and emotional arousal, data from the first 124 participant pairs (patients and their matched controls) were analyzed by ANOVAs for repeated measures. In all analyses performed, there was a significant main effect for assessment time ($p < .001$), indicating that participants were reactive to the anagram task and returned to baseline levels during the resting period. For example, their systolic blood pressure increased by an average of 16 mmHg, and their diastolic blood pressure by 9 mmHg. In addition, participants responded to the anagram task with significant increases in negative affect from baseline levels ($ps < .001$). For example, frustration increased, on the average, by 33.3 points, anger by 14.0 points, anxiety by 10.3, and unhappiness by 10.3. Participants also indicated that the task was challenging. Task difficulty was rated 60 points, on average, and effort involved in solving the task was rated as 65 points (based on a 100 mm visual analog scale). Participants also indicated that they thought they had performed fairly well on the task (mean = 75 points). Thus, it can be concluded that the anagram task was sufficiently challenging to elicit both physiological and emotional arousal. After completion of the baseline period, data for all participants will be analyzed taking into account a variety of variables, such as beta-blocker status, history of hypertension, and patient diagnosis.

SUMMARY

The available research to date supports the notion that cardiovascular stress reactivity plays a role in the etiology of cardiovascular disease (CVD). This is particularly the case for hypertension in men and concerns both diagnostic and prognostic validity (using active and passive stressors). Comparable studies including female samples are very few, but are suggestive of a similar pattern with regard to hypertension.

With CHD as outcome, even fewer studies have included women. The studies on men have many methodological problems, making it difficult to evaluate whether excessive cardiovascular reactivity to mental stress distinguishes patients from controls. Crucial variables that may need to be taken into consideration include history of hypertension and medication. In addition, it appears advisable to assess emotional stress reactions, as their relationship to physiological stress reactions seems to differ between patients and controls.

Prospective evidence linking cardiovascular stress reactivity to heart disease mortality in initially disease-free men is confined to the cold pressor task as a stressor. With regard to the prediction of recurrent events, data from one preliminary study suggest that excessive blood pressure reactivity to mental stress predicts mortality 3 years later, whereas data from the Cardiac Arrhythmia Pilot Study suggest that *diminished* heart rate reactivity predicts mortality one year after assessment.

Although several of the aforementioned findings may encourage an optimistic view of a link between cardiovascular stress reactivity and CVD, it should be kept in mind that we do not know whether distinct cardiovascular responses to stress play a truly causal role in CVD etiology, or whether they are a marker of something else or result from early disease.

The most striking observation is that most studies to date have been conducted with men. The few studies that included women often have not been analyzed for gender differences. Based on studies of younger and healthy women and men, we know that the same stressors that elicit cardiovascular responses among men may not do so among women. Thus, there is a need for the development of standardized tasks that are relevant for both sexes and that can be employed in studies on gender differences in cardiovascular reactivity. Potential gender differences in cardiovascular stress reactivity will have a profound effect on both primary and secondary prevention of cardiovascular diseases for both women and men.

With regard to female coronary patients, the current Swedish Study of Women with Coronary Heart Disease will provide valuable insights into both the diagnostic and prognostic validity of cardiovascular reactivity testing in women. The relatively large number of participants, the inclusion of many medical and psychosocial variables relevant to CHD, and the length of follow-up will contribute to our knowledge of a much neglected problem— that of cardiovascular disease among women.

ACKNOWLEDGMENTS

Correspondence concerning this chapter should be addressed to Gerdi Weidner, Department of Psychology, State University of New York, Stony Brook, NY 11794–2500. Preparation was supported, in part, by grant CRG 921325 from the North Atlantic Treaty Organization (NATO). We would like to thank Dr. M. A. Chesney for her helpful comments on this manuscript, and the staff of the Swedish Study of Women with Coronary Heart Disease for serving as the experimenter (Margita Hogbom) and assisting with data collection (Ingeborg Eriksson and Sarah P. Wamala).

REFERENCES

Ahern, D. K., Gorkin, L., Anderson, J. L., Tierney, C., Hallstrom, A., Ewart, C., Capone, R. J., Schron, E., Kornfeld, D., Herd, J., Richardson, D. W., & Follick, M. J. (1990). Biobehavioral variables and mortality or cardiac arrest in the Cardiac Arrhythmia Pilot Study (CAPS). *American Journal of Cardiology, 66*, 59–62.

Armstrong, H. G., & Rafferty, J. A. (1950). Cold pressor test follow-up study for seven years on 166 officers. *American Heart Journal, 39*, 484–490.

Borghi, C., Costa, F. V., Boschi, S., Mussi, A., & Ambrosioni, E. (1986). Predictors of stable hypertension in young borderline subjects: A five-year follow-up study. *Journal of Cardiovascular Pharmacology, 8*(5), 138–141.

Burns, J. W., Hutt, J., & Weidner, G. (1993). *Behavioral Medicine, 19*, 122–128.

Corse, C. D., Manuck, S. B., Cantwell, J. D., Giordini, B., & Matthews, K. A. (1982). Coronary-prone behavior pattern and cardiovascular response in persons with and without coronary heart disease. *Psychosomatic Medicine, 44*(5), 449–459.

Deanfield, J. E., Shea, M., Kensett, M., Horlock, P., Wilson, R. A., DeLandsheere, C., & Selwin, A. P. (1984). Silent myocardial ischaemia due to mental stress. *Lancet, 2*, 1001–1004.

Dembroski, T. M., MacDougall, J. M., & Lushene, R. (1979). Interpersonal interaction and cardiovascular response in Type A subjects and coronary patients. *Journal of Human Stress, 12*, 28–36.

Eich, R. H., & Jacobsen, E. C. (1967). Vascular reactivity in medical students followed for 10 years. *Journal of Chronic Diseases, 20*, 583–592.

Falkner, B., Kushner, H., Onesti, G., & Angelakos, E. T. (1981). Cardiovascular characteristics in adolescents who develop essential hypertension. *Hypertension, 3*, 521–527.

Fredrikson, M., & Blumenthal, J. A. (1988). Lipids, catecholamine, and cardiovascular responses to stress in patients recovering from myocardial infarction. *Journal of Cardiopulmonary Rehabilitation, 12*, 513–517.

Fredrikson, M., & Matthews, K. A. (1990). Cardiovascular responses to behavioral stress and hypertension: A meta-analytic review. *Annals of Behavioral Medicine, 12*, 30–39.

Harlan, W. R., Osborne, R. K., & Graybiel, A. (1964). Prognostic value of the cold pressor test and the basal blood pressure: Based on an eighteen-year follow-up study. *American Journal of Cardiology, 13*, 683–687.

Hines, E. A., Jr. (1940). Significance of vascular hyperreaction as measured by the cold pressor test. *American Heart Journal, 19*, 408–416.

Houston, B. K. (1988). Cardiovascular and neuroendocrine reactivity, global Type A, and components of Type A behavior. In B. K. Houston & C. R. Snyder (Eds.), *Type A behavior pattern: Research, theory, and intervention* (pp. 212–253). New York: Wiley.

Kaplan, J. R., Adams, M. R., Clarkson, T. B., & Koritnik, D. R. (1984). Psychosocial influences on female "protection" among cynomolgus macaques. *Atherosclerosis, 53*, 283–295.

Keys, A., Taylor, H. L., Blackburn, H., Brozek, J., Anderson, J. T., & Simonson, E. (1971). Mortality and coronary heart disease among men studied for 23 years. *Archives of Internal Medicine, 128*, 210–214.

Kneier, A. W., & Temoshok, L. (1984). Repressive coping reactions in patients with malignant melanoma as compared to cardiovascular disease patients. *Journal of Psychosomatic Research, 28*, 145–155.

Kohlmann, C. W., Weidner, G., & Messina, C. R. (1995). Avoidant coping style and verbal-cardiovascular response dissociation. *Psychology and Health*, 1–15.

Krantz, D. S., Helmers, K. F., Bairey, N., Nebel, L. E., Hedges, S. M., & Rozanski, A. (1991). Cardiovascular reactivity to mental stress-induced myocardial ischemia in patients with coronary artery disease. *Psychosomatic Medicine, 53*, 1–12.

Krantz, D. S., Schaeffer, M. A., Davia, J. E., Dembroski, T. M., MacDougall, J. M., & Schaffer, R. T. (1981). Extent of coronary atherosclerosis: Type A behavior, and cardiovascular response to social interaction. *Psychophysiology, 18*(6), 654–664.

Langosch, W., Brodner, G., & Foerster, F. (1983). Psychophysiological testing of postinfarction patients: A study determining the cardiological importance of psychophysiological variables. In T. M. Dembroski, T. H. Schmidt, & G. Blümchen (Eds.), *Biobehavioral bases of coronary heart disease* (pp. 197–227). New York: Karger.

Light, K. C., Dolan, C. A., Davis, M. R., & Sherwood, A. (1992). Cardiovascular responses to an active coping challenge as predictors of blood pressure patterns 10–15 years later. *Psychosomatic Medicine, 54*, 217–230.

Light, K. C., Sherwood, A., & Turner, J. R. (1992). High cardiovascular reactivity to stress: A predictor of later hypertension development. In J. R. Turner, A. Sherwood, & K. C. Light (Eds.), *Individual differences in cardiovascular responses to stress* (pp. 281–293). New York: Plenum.

Lowin, B., & DeSilva, R. A. (1978). Roles of psychologic stress and autonomic nervous system changes in provocation of ventricular premature complexes. *The American Journal of Cardiology, 41*, 979–985.

Manuck, S. B., Kaplan, J. R., Adams, M. R., & Clarkson, T. B. (1989). Behaviorally elicited heart rate reactivity and atherosclerosis in female cynomolgus monkeys. *Psychosomatic Medicine, 51*, 306–318.

Manuck, S. B., Kaplan, J. R., & Clarkson, T. B. (1983). Behaviorally induced heart rate reactivity and atherosclerosis in cynomolgus monkeys. *Psychosomatic Medicine, 45*, 95–108.

Manuck, S. B., Kasprowicz, A. L., & Muldoon, M. F. (1990). Behaviorally-evoked cardiovascular reactivity and hypertension: Conceptual issues and potential associations. *Annals of Behavioral Medicine, 12*(1), 17–29.

Manuck, S. B., Olsson, G., Hjemdahl, P., & Rehnqvist, N. (1992). Does cardiovascular reactivity to mental stress have prognostic value in postinfarction patients? A pilot study. *Psychosomatic Medicine, 54*(1), 102–108.

Matthews, K. A. (1986). Summary, conclusions, and implications. In K. A. Matthews, S. M. Weiss, T. Detre, T. M. Dembroski, B. Falkner, S. B. Manuck, & R. B. Williams, Jr. (Eds.), *Handbook of stress, reactivity, & cardiovascular disease* (pp. 461–473). New York: Wiley.

Matthews, K. A., Rakaczky, C. J., Stoney, C. M., & Manuck, S. B. (1987). Are cardiovascular responses to behavioral stressors a stable individual difference variable in childhood? *Psychophysiology, 24*(4), 464–473.

Menkes, M. S., Matthews, K. A., Krantz, D. S., Lundberg, V., Mead, L. A., Qaqish, B., Liang, K.-Y., Thomas, C. B., & Pearson, T. A. (1989). Cardiovascular reactivity to the cold pressor test as a predictor of hypertension. *Hypertension, 14*, 524–530.

Messina, C. R., Hutt, J., & Weidner, G. (1993, August). *Oral contraceptive use, parental history of heart disease, and cardiovascular reactivity.* Paper presented at the annual meeting of the American Psychological Association, Toronto, Canada.

Nestel, P. J., Verghese, A., & Lovell, R. H. (1967). Catecholamine secretion and sympathetic nervous responses to emotion in men with and without angina pectoris. *American Heart Journal, 2*, 227–234.

Nolan, R. P., Wielgosz, A. T., Biro, E. S., & Wielgosz, M. B. (1994). Awareness and control of the cardiovascular response to stress among men with and without acute myocardial infarction. *Canadian Journal of Cardiology, 10*(7), 733–738.

Pickering, T. G., & Gerin, W. (1990). Cardiovascular reactivity in the laboratory and the role of behavioral factors in hypertension: A critical review. *Annals of Behavioral Medicine, 12*(1), 3–16.

Rozanski, A., Bairey, C. N., Krantz, D. S., Friedman, J., Resser, K. J., Morell, M., Hilton-Chalfen, S., Hestrin, L., Bietendorf, J., & Berman, D. S. (1988). Mental stress and the induction of myocardial ischemia in patients with coronary artery disease. *New England Journal of Medicine, 318*(16), 1005–1011.

Schiffer, F., Hartley, L. H., Schulman, C. L., & Abelmann, W. H. (1976). The quiz electrocardiogram: A new diagnostic and research technique for evaluating the relation between emotional stress and ischemic heart disease. *The American Journal of Cardiology, 37*, 41–47.

Schiffer, F., Hartley, L. H., Schulman, C. L., & Abelmann, W. H. (1980). Evidence for emotionally-induced coronary arterial spasm in patients with angina pectoris. *British Heart Journal, 44*, 62–66.

Sime, W. E., Buell, J. C., & Eliot, R. S. (1980). Cardiovascular responses to emotional stress (quiz interview) in post-myocardial infarction patients and matched control subjects. *Journal of Human Stress, 9*, 39–46.

Simpson, T., & Shaver, J. (1991). A comparison of hypertensive and nonhypertensive coronary care patients' cardiovascular responses to visitors. *Heart and Lung, 20*(3), 213–220.

Specchia, G., de Servi, S., Falcone, C., Garazzi, A., Angoli, L., Bramucci, E., Ardissino, D., & Mussini, A. (1984). Mental arithmetic stress testing in patients with coronary heart disease. *American Heart Journal, 108*(1), 56–63.

Steptoe, A., & Vögele, C. (1991). Methodology of mental stress testing in cardiovascular research. *Circulation, 83*(4), 14–24.

Stoney, C. M. (1992). The role of reproductive hormones in cardiovascular and neuroendocrine function during behavioral stress. In J. R. Turner, A. Sherwood, & K. C. Light (Eds.), *Individual differences in cardiovascular responses to stress* (pp. 147–163). New York: Plenum.

Tavazzi, L., Zotti, A. M., Rondanelli, R. (1986). The role of psychologic stress in the genesis of lethal arrhythmias in patients with coronary artery disease. *European Heart Journal, 7*(suppl A), 99–106.

Taylor, C. B., Davidson, D. M., Houston, N., Agras, W. S., & Debusk, R. F. (1982). The effect of a standardized psychological stressor on the cardiovascular response to physical effort soon after uncomplicated myocardial infarction. *Journal of Psychosomatic Research, 26*(2), 263–268.

Thomas, C. B., & Greenstreet, R. L. (1973). Psychobiological characteristics in youth as predictors of five disease states: Suicide, mental illness, hypertension, coronary heart disease, and tumor. *Johns Hopkins Medical Journal, 132*, 16–43.

Turner, J. R., Ward, M. M., Gellman, M. D., Johnson, D. W., Light, K. C., & van Doornan, L. J. P. (1994). The relationship between laboratory and ambulatory cardiovascular activity: Current evidence and future directions. *Annals of Behavioral Medicine, 16*(1), 12–23.

Valek, J., Kuhn, E., Honzak, R., & Vavrinkova, H. (1971). Emotions and personality of patients with ischemic heart disease during short-lasting psychical laboratory stress. *Cor Vasa, 13*(3), 165–175.

Weidner, G. (1994). Coronary risk in women. In V. J. Adesso, D. M. Reddy, & R. Fleming (Eds.), *Psychological perspectives on women's health* (pp. 57–81). Washington, DC: Taylor & Francis.

Weidner, G. (1995). Personality and coronary heart disease in women: Past research and future directions. *Zeitschrift für Gesundheitpsychologie, 3*(1), 4–23.

Weidner, G., Friend, R., Ficarrotto, T. J., & Mendell, N. R. (1989). Hostility and cardiovascular reactivity to stress in women and men. *Psychosomatic Medicine, 51*, 36–45.

Weidner, G., & Messina, C. R. (1995). The effects of gender-typed tasks and gender roles on cardiovascular reactivity. *International Journal of Behavioral Medicine, 2*(1), 66–82.

Weinstein, J., Averill, J. R., Opton, E. M., & Lazarus, R. S. (1968). Defensive style and discrepancy between self-report and physiological indexes of stress. *Journal of Personality and Social Psychology, 10*, 406–413.

Wood, D. L., Sheps, S. G., Elveback, L. R., & Schirger, A. (1984). Cold pressor test as a predictor of hypertension. *Hypertension, 6*, 301–306.

APPENDIX

Anagrams (Swedish):

dirao _____

lycek _____

innvak _____

kasav _____

prapep _____

depas _____

nakan _____

aplam _____

glera _____

molbam _____

geles _____

radog _____

kubit _____

vehra _____

lavta _____

15

Blood Pressure Response to Laboratory Challenges and Occupational Stress in Women

Kathleen C. Light
Susan S. Girdler
Sheila West
Kimberly A. Brownley
University of North Carolina, Chapel Hill

To try to understand how and why men and women differ in their physiological responses to the routine demands of daily life at work and at home, and to occasional more intense life stresses, is a daunting challenge. Any efforts to address this theme must consider basic biological differences between the genders (such as reproductive functions and their hormonal components). These efforts also must deal with personality and acquired psychosocial traits that influence how the men and women perceive and respond to the events which impact their lives. In addition, such efforts must retain the flexibility to consider individual differences, which may influence why some women or men respond differently from most others of their gender. Finally, these efforts should begin to consider biologic and psychosocial transitions that occur across different periods of the adult life span.

This chapter selectively reviews some of the recent findings by our research group and others that are focusing on this theme. The review highlights what we have learned about women and their cardiovascular responses to standardized challenges in the laboratory, and to real-life challenges such as a demanding job. First, the review summarizes what is known about gender differences in cardiovascular stress responses. Second, the chapter focuses on the phases of the menstrual cycle in premenopausal women and how hormonal variations over the cycle and across different individuals are associated with differing stress responses. Third, the chapter examines the literature on differences in cardiovascular stress responses before versus after menopause. Finally, it deals with psychosocial factors influencing blood pressure at work, based on data obtained using ambulatory blood pressure monitoring.

GENDER DIFFERENCES IN CARDIOVASCULAR STRESS RESPONSES

From adolescence through early and middle adult years, men demonstrate higher clinic and resting systolic blood pressure (SBP) levels than women. Men also have a higher prevalence of essential hypertension than women within these age groups. This gender difference has led to considerable research directed at clarifying the potential mechanisms responsible for the relative protection from hypertension and other cardiovascular disorders in women under age 55. One line of investigation has derived from the active area of research on cardiovascular reactivity to behavioral stressors. If, as certain proponents have asserted (Manuck, Kasprowicz, & Muldoon, 1990; Obrist, 1985; Schneiderman, 1995), individuals who show large magnitude increases in blood pressure, heart rate, cardiac output, or total peripheral resistance (TPR) are at greater risk of developing hypertension and cardiovascular disease, then greater cardiovascular reactivity in men compared to women may contribute to the observed gender difference in cardiovascular risk. A number of psychophysiological studies focusing on blood pressure and heart rate (HR) responses to standardized behavior stressors have reported that within the 18–50 age range, men indeed do show greater SBP increases to stressors than women, although both genders show similar diastolic pressure (DBP) increases (Matthews & Stoney, 1988; Stoney, Davis, & Matthews, 1987; Stoney, Matthews, MacDonald, & Johnson, 1988; Tischenkel et al., 1989; Weidner, Friend, Ficarotto, & Mendell, 1989). In contrast, several studies have reported that HR increases are greater in women than in men (Girdler, Turner, Sherwood, & Light, 1990; Matthews & Stoney, 1988; Stoney et al., 1987; Tersman, Collins, & Eneroth, 1991; Weidner et al., 1989). Recently, our research group (Light, Turner, Hinderliter, & Sherwood, 1993) attempted to reexamine the issue of gender differences in cardiovascular stress responses within a large biracial sample including 76 men and 79 women. Because certain stressors are thought to differentiate men and women because of their association with traditionally gender-typed behaviors, such as competition and math for men, and emotional expression and communication for women, a broad array of stressors were included in this investigation (see Girdler et al., 1990; Matthews, Davis, Stoney, Owens, & Caggiula, 1991). The tasks included a computerized math task that adjusts problem difficulty according to recent performance, a competitive reaction time task, an active speech task in which subjects must describe their feelings and outward behaviors during a common type of interpersonal conflict with a vendor, a passive speech task in which subjects listen and compare their own performance to another same-gender, same-race subject performing the same speech task, and the forehead cold pressor test. The results of this study indicated that men did show a general pattern of greater SBP increases than women across these stressors, although the magnitude of these differences was modest, averaging 3–5 mmHg depending on the stressor. In addition, women showed greater HR increases than men to one stressor, but that stressor was arguably the most relevant challenge for women, the active speech on the interpersonal conflict. Thus, these findings were generally confirmatory of prior observations, and also point to the importance of gender relevance of tasks.

The study by Light et al. (1993) described earlier also yielded two novel findings. First, through use of impedance cardiography, it demonstrated that independent of race, men show greater vasoconstrictive responses to the forehead cold pressor test than women, all of whom were tested in the follicular phase of the menstrual cycle (see later section on Menstrual Cycle Phase). This task is one shown to evoke pressor responses primarily through increased alpha-adrenergic receptor activity, which results in vasoconstriction. Previously, Freedman, Sabharwal, and Desai (1987) reported that men showed greater vasoconstrictive responses to intravenous administration of alpha agonists than women, indicative of enhanced alpha-receptor sensitivity.

Earlier research in our laboratory by Girdler et al. (1990) compared cardiovascular responses to a series of speech and math tasks in young men and women matched for exceptional levels of academic achievement (medical, dental, and graduate students). In this highly selected sample, there were no differences in blood pressure reactivity to stressors, but men showed greater vasoconstrictive responses than women to all stressors, whereas women showed greater heart rate and cardiac output increases (see Figs. 15.1 and 15.2). More recently, Allen, Stoney, Owens, and Matthews (1993) reported data consistent with the findings of Girdler et al. (1990) after testing women in all phases of their menstrual cycle and using stressors known to evoke greater vasoconstrictive responses, such as the frustrating mirror tracing, the Stroop color–word and the hand-grip tasks. Allen et al. (1993) also found no differences in blood pressure reactivity to any task except the hand grip, but they likewise found that women tended to be greater "cardiac reactors," whereas men tended to be greater "vascular reactors."

Vascular reactivity may in fact be of equal or greater importance than the blood pressure rise itself in enhancing risk of left ventricular hypertrophy and cardiovascular morbidity, because TPR as the central index of

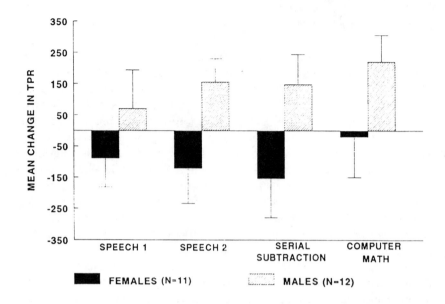

FIG. 15.1. Mean change (+ standard error of the mean or SEM) in total peripheral resistance across all tasks in males and females. From Girdler et al. (1990). © 1990 by the American Psychosomatic Society. Reprinted with permission.

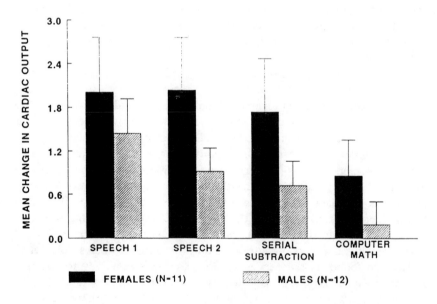

FIG. 15.2. Mean change (+ SEM) in cardiac output across all tasks in males and females. From Girdler et al. (1990). © 1990 by the American Psychosomatic Society. Reprinted by permission.

afterload on the heart is the primary factor influencing increases in left ventricular mass. Increased left ventricular mass index was found in the Framingham studies to be the most powerful predictor other than age of subsequent cardiovascular death (Levy, Garrison, Savage, Kannel, & Castelli, 1990). One of the potential biological factors that may relate to these gender differences in vascular reactivity to stress is the profile of reproductive hormones, with estrogen as the leading focus of current research in women. (See later sections on Menstrual Cycle Phase and Postmenopausal Women.)

A second novel finding from the Light et al. (1993) study involved gender differences in cardiovascular recovery after termination of stressors. Women showed significantly greater recovery of both SBP and DBP after 5 min of recovery than men (see Figs. 15.3 and 15.4). The persistence of the SBP elevation in men might be expected, in view of their greater SBP reactivity during the task. However, both gender groups demonstrated equal increases in DBP during all tasks except the cold pressor, where men showed greater increases, so the lesser recovery of DBP in men after all challenges appears to reflect a process independent of and in addition to their greater task responses. Slower recovery of blood pressure after stress is a potential contributing factor to the greater incidence of hypertension and cardiovascular disease in men versus women prior to age 55. Borghi, Costa, Boschi, Mussi, and Ambrosioni (1986) reported that a failure of blood

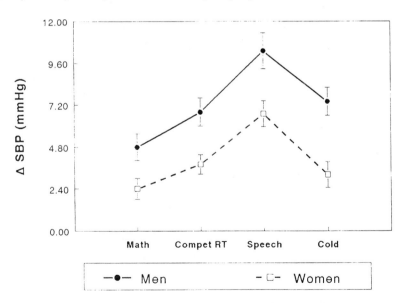

FIG. 15.3. Elevations in mean systolic blood pressure (± SEM) above baseline levels in men and women 5 minutes after the termination of each of four stressors. From Light et al. (1993). © 1993 by the American Psychological Association. Adapted with permission.

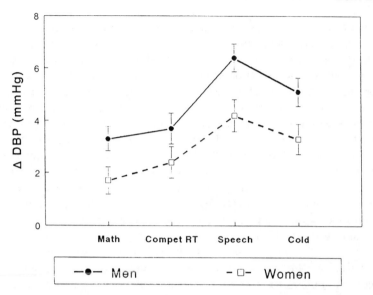

FIG. 15.4. Elevations in mean diastolic blood pressure (± SEM) above baseline levels in men and women 5 minutes after the termination. From Light et al. (1993). © 1993 by the American Psychological Association. Adapted with permission.

pressure to recover to prestress levels 10 min after a mental arithmetic stressor in borderline hypertensive individuals was a strong predictor of the development of sustained hypertension over the next 5 years.

One possible explanation for the greater SBP reactivity to stress in men compared to women was that it resulted from greater increases in sympathetic activity. However, Light, Turner, Hinderliter, Girdler, and Sherwood (1994) reported that plasma epinephrine and norepinephrine responses to these stressors in 67 of the same men and women did not differ during any of the stressors. Instead, the results showed that regardless of gender, subjects with above-average SBP increases to stress associated with high cardiac output increases (presumed to be due to greater beta-adrenergic receptor activity) demonstrated the greatest increases in plasma epinephrine to all tasks except the cold pressor, an alpha-adrenergic challenge. These high cardiac output/high blood pressure reactors included roughly equal numbers of men and women. Norepinephrine responses also tended to be greater in these subjects, although the difference was not significant. Interestingly, Black subjects (both men and women) were found to show significantly greater norepinephrine increases to stressors than White subjects. From these observations, it was suggested that gender differences were probably not due to differences in circulating levels of catecholamines acting on sympathetic receptors. However, it is still plausible that the observed gender differences in stress reactivity and recovery may be due to men having greater sensitivity of both beta- and alpha-adrenergic receptors to agonist activity than women. An alternative explanation is that another humoral factor such as estrogen may be altering cardiovascular responses of women to sympathetic activation in a beneficial way.

MENSTRUAL CYCLE PHASE AND LUTEAL PHASE ESTROGEN LEVELS INFLUENCE VASCULAR RESPONSE

Coronary heart disease (CHD) is the leading cause of death among women as well as men in most industrialized countries. Prior to age 65, however, nearly three times as many men die of coronary causes as women, whereas after age 65, there are approximately equal coronary deaths in both genders (Higgens, 1990). Risk of coronary death also increases after surgical or natural menopause, even after controlling for age (Colditz et al., 1987; Matthews et al., 1989). The increase in CHD after menopause, which cannot be accounted for by other documented risk factors, has led to the view that female reproductive hormones are cardioprotective. This hypothesis is supported by multiple long-term epidemiologic studies showing that prior use of hormone replacement therapy after menopause is associated with markedly decreased risk of cardiovascular death (35–50% less across various studies), and that longer duration of use is directly related to increasing protection against such death (Stampfer & Colditz, 1991; Wolf, Madans, & Finucane, 1991). It is important to note that these are not findings from randomized, placebo-controlled trials of the effects of hormone replacement, such as have recently been initiated in the United States through the Women's Health Initiative, but show differences in risk among women who have and have not elected, with the advice of personal physicians, to use hormone replacement. As a result, these findings on lowered risk are correlational, and despite their impressive apparent strength, do not establish a causal relationship between estrogen and reduced cardiovascular death.

Because there are marked rises and falls in the circulating levels of the primary reproductive hormones, estrogen, progesterone, luteinizing hormone (LH) and follicle-stimulating hormone (FSH) during a typical menstrual cycle in premenopausal women, there has been considerable research directed at evaluating whether cardiovascular and catecholamine responses vary as a function of menstrual cycle phase. In most of the early studies of cardiovascular reactivity across the menstrual cycle, comparisons were made between the midfollicular (preovulatory) phase when all reproductive hormone levels are fairly low, and the late luteal (postovulatory) phase when estrogen and progesterone levels are substantially higher. These studies were weak in several respects, however, including selection of a between-subjects approach rather than making the phase comparison within the same individual, a failure to confirm that ovulation had actually occurred during the cycle, and failure to confirm that levels of the key hormones actually differed between the phases under study. Thus, it is not surprising that these early studies variously observed that blood pressure responses were greater in the luteal phase, were greater in the follicular phase, or did not differ by phase (Hastrup & Light, 1982; Plante & Denney, 1984; Polefrone & Manuck, 1988). More recent studies using a within-subjects comparison and confirming hormonal levels and ovulation have been more consistent, generally indicating that blood pressure and HR responses to stressors do not differ reliably between the follicular and luteal phases of the cycle (Collins, Eneroth, & Landgren, 1985; Girdler, Pedersen, Stern, & Light, 1993; Stoney, Owens, Matthews, Davis, & Caggiula, 1990). One exception is the well-designed study by Tersman et al. (1991), who observed greater SBP reactivity to a cold pressor test in the luteal phase, but this effect appeared primarily due to one subgroup of women—those who were smokers. Recently, use of impedance cardiography has made it possible to examine the TPR and cardiac output responses of women during these menstrual cycle phases. Using this approach in healthy young women where ovulation was confirmed, Girdler et al. (1993) found that TPR responses to stress, after indexing to control for individual differences in body surface area, were significantly lower during the late luteal phase (when estrogen and progesterone levels are increased) compared to the lowest estrogen phase of the menstrual cycle, the early to middle follicular phase (see Fig. 15.5). This observation may be related to the vascular effects of estrogen.

Estrogen replacement, both with and without the addition of progesterone, has been documented to lower total cholesterol and low density lipoprotein (LDL) cholesterol, which is one potential mechanism through which hormone replacement may be lowering cardiovascular risk (Kim, Jang, Cho, & Min, 1994; Lobo, 1991; Sacks, McPherson, & Walsh, 1994; Walsh et al., 1991). However, statistical adjustment for group differences in serum lipid levels reduced but did not eliminate the beneficial effect associated with hormone replacement in the report by Stampfer and Colditz (1991). Most experts agree that the magnitude of CHD risk reduction associated with hormone replacement in postmenopausal women indicates multiple contributing mechanisms, with an estimated 25%–50% of the risk reduction due to improved lipid profiles, and the remainder due to nonlipid mechanisms.

A primary candidate for such a nonlipid mechanism is estrogen's putative action in reducing vasoconstriction and improving peripheral blood flow (Sarrel, 1990). Pines et al. (1991) reported that postmenopausal women on combined estrogen/progesterone replacement therapy for 2.5 months demonstrated increases in blood flow acceleration accompanied by increases

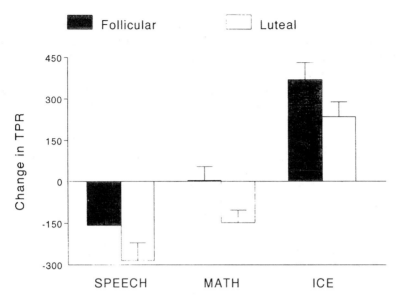

FIG. 15.5. Mean change (+ SEM) in total peripheral resistance during three stressors in healthy young women during the early follicular versus the late luteal phases of their menstrual cycle. From Girdler et al. (1993). © 1993 by the American Psychological Association, Inc. Reprinted with permission.

in stroke volume, suggesting increasing vasodilation together with apparently enhanced inotropic effects on the heart. The specific mechanisms through which estrogen and progesterone replacement may influence vasoconstriction are under intensive study at present. In-vitro studies have shown that estradiol inhibits calcium-mediated vasoconstriction, indicating that estrogen may function as a calcium antagonist (Stevenson, Crook, Godsland, Collins, & Whitehead, 1994).

Equally pertinent to a model of disease pathogenesis focusing on stress and sympathetic nervous system activity is the finding that, in a similar in-vitro study, estradiol inhibited vasoconstriction induced by administration of the alpha-adrenergic agonist phenylephrine and by administration of angiotensin (Ravi, Mantzoros, Prabhu, Ram, & Sowers, 1994). These results suggest that increasing estrogen levels may reduce vasoconstriction during natural sympathetic activity associated with certain types of stress as well. Thus, this mechanism could account for the observation of Girdler et al. (1993) that women show lesser vasoconstriction during stressors during their higher estrogen/progesterone luteal phase than during the follicular phase of their menstrual cycle.

Other preliminary findings by our research group suggest that women who tend to show higher levels of endogenous estrogen during the luteal phase over two menstrual cycles demonstrate a general pattern of lower

TPR compared to women with consistently lower levels of endogenous estrogen (West, Bove, & Light, 1993). In this study, 16 female graduate students aged 23 to 39 who were preparing for their doctoral comprehensive examinations were tested, once during the 2 weeks prior to their examination, and once during a more typical month of graduate activities. Both tests were scheduled on the same luteal phase day of cycles separated by 2 to 5 months. On both testing conditions, cardiovascular responses were monitored during baseline, the forehead cold pressor test, the Paced Auditory Serial Addition Task (PASAT), and a brief interview on current sources of life stress. The primary initial hypothesis under study was that the chronic stress of the comprehensive examination period would be associated with reduced plasma estrogen levels and with adverse changes in vascular responses to stress. No support for this hypothesis was obtained; estrogen levels on average were just as high during the exam as the nonexam test session, and cardiovascular stress responses also did not differ. This was attributed to the fact that subjects did not, in fact, report subjectively greater experience of stress during the exam month, but relatively high stress associated with multiple demands of graduate school and personal life during both test periods.

However, a secondary related hypothesis was that women with consistently high luteal phase endogenous estrogen levels during both the exam and nonexam session would demonstrate reduced vasoconstriction compared to women with consistently low endogenous estrogen. This hypothesis was supported by the data. Vascular resistance index (defined as TPR indexed for differences in body surface area) was higher in the Low Estrogen subgroup than in the High Estrogen subgroup during the baseline and all stressors ($p < .05$), whereas a third subgroup with Intermediate or Inconsistent Estrogen levels showed vascular resistance that was intermediate between the other two groups (see Fig. 15.6). Blood pressure levels did not differ significantly between the Estrogen subgroups, however, because the lower vascular resistance shown by the High Estrogen subjects was compensated for by their significantly higher cardiac index across all baseline and task conditions compared to the Low Estrogen subjects ($p < .05$; see Fig. 15.7).

The High Estrogen group also demonstrated significantly greater HR reactivity (calculated as changes from baseline levels) during the stressful tasks. This greater HR increase to stress and generally higher cardiac index seen in the High Estrogen subgroup may be secondary effects of the reduced vasoconstriction associated with the vascular effects of estrogen. Alternatively, some studies in animal models suggest that estradiol-17-beta may also enhance uptake of calcium in the coronary papillary muscle cells, "thus resulting in a marked shortening of the action potential" (de Beer & Keizer, 1982, p. 228) associated with cardiac contraction, producing increased heart rate and contractility. Furthermore, Pines et al. (1991) observed that hor-

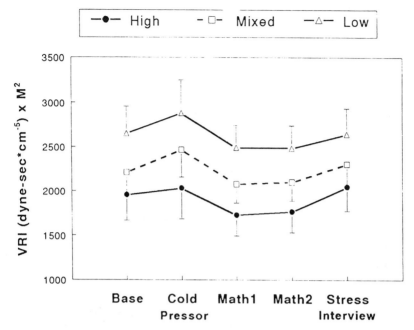

FIG. 15.6. Mean (± SEM) vascular resistance indexed for body surface area during baseline and four tasks in women with high, mixed, or low luteal endogenous estrogen levels assessed over two menstrual cycles. From West et al. (1993).

mone replacement therapy in postmenopausal women not only increased blood flow and flow velocity, but also increased stroke volume significantly, leading these authors to interpret the latter finding as a result of estrogen-induced enhancement of cardiac contractility. Based on these possible mechanisms, it is suggested that both the increased cardiac index and the decreased vascular resistance observed in the High Estrogen women may be primarily related to the actions of estrogen. However, it must be emphasized that progesterone has also been shown to affect both vascular resistance and myocardial contractility, with the direction of its effects opposing that of estrogen. Thus, it may be more accurate to interpret these results as reflecting the net effect of multiple female reproductive hormones and other steroid hormones, including estrogen levels that were directly assessed and progesterone and others that were not assessed.

These potential alterations associated with endogenous estrogen in premenopausal women, together with the lesser SBP and alpha-adrenergically mediated TPR responses to stress and more rapid blood pressure recovery after stress shown by young women relative to men, may indeed relate to the reduced risk of cardiovascular disease among women of this age. With respect to the vascular system and its contribution to cardiovascular risk,

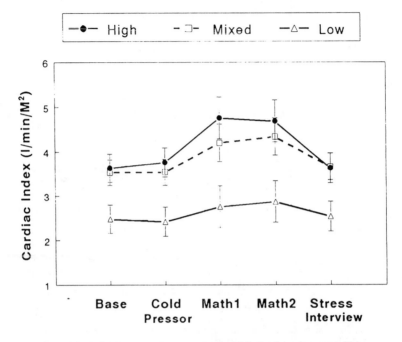

FIG. 15.7. Mean (± SEM) cardiac output indexed for body surface area during baseline and four tasks in women with high, mixed, or low luteal endogenous estrogen levels assessed over two menstrual cycles. From West et al. (1993).

relative dilation of peripheral blood vessels during stress may help to slow or prevent the development of vascular hypertrophy in premenopausal women. In fact, a recent study by our group (Hinderliter, Light, & Willis, 1992) reinforces this possibility. Among the 68 men and 69 women who participated in this study, workday ambulatory blood pressure monitoring (with readings obtained four times per hour throughout a typical working day) and echocardiographic assessment of left structure and function were performed. As expected, men showed higher ambulatory SBP and DBP relative to women (132/83 vs. 123/78, $ps < .0001$). In this healthy young adult sample, where no subject yet demonstrated fixed essential hypertension, left ventricular mass index was nevertheless significantly greater in men than women. This gender difference represented a greater ventricular chamber size, with proportionately greater wall thickness.

Because higher ambulatory blood pressure is known to be associated with increased left ventricular mass index, this result may be viewed as a result of the pressure difference. However, this is not a fully correct view, because the gender difference in left ventricular mass index remained significant even after adjustment for differences in clinic or ambulatory blood pressure, and for differences between men and women in height and body surface area and habitual physical activity. Hinderliter et al. (1992) discussed the possible contributions of both male and female reproductive hormones to this difference. In animal models, gender differences in cardiac size are abolished by orchiectomy and restored by testosterone replacement, suggesting that endogenous androgens may exert a trophic effect on cardiac muscle (Koenig, Goldstone, & Lu, 1982). Estrogen may have the opposite effect, because Garavaglia, Messerli, Schmieder, Nunez, and Oren (1989) reported that gender differences in left ventricular structure among hypertensive patients diminishes after the women pass through menopause.

CARDIOVASCULAR STRESS RESPONSES
IN PRE- VERSUS POSTMENOPAUSAL WOMEN

Relatively few studies to date have addressed the effect of menopause and subsequent use of hormone replacement therapy on physiological responses to stressors. Saab, Matthews, Stoney, and MacDonald (1989) compared blood pressure and plasma catecholamine responses to stress in 15 premenopausal and 16 age-matched postmenopausal women. These investigators observed that HR responses to all mental stressors and both SBP and epinephrine responses to one task, the simulated speech, were greater in the postmenopausal women. Blumenthal et al. (1991) did not replicate this observed cardiovascular reactivity difference, but these investigators did similarly find that postmenopausal women showed greater epinephrine increases to a simulated speech task than premenopausal women. Recently, Owens, Stoney, and Matthews (1993) reported the results of the most extensive study to date, in which they observed that postmenopausal women not using hormone replacement demonstrated: (a) higher 24-hour ambulatory DBP, presumably reflecting greater pressor responses to natural challenges; and (b) greater SBP and DBP increases to a frustrating mirror-tracing task and greater DBP increases to a simulated speech task compared to both premenopausal women and to an age-matched sample of men as well. Isometric exercise, in contrast, did not reveal any reliable group differences (see Fig. 15.8). Interestingly, based on both groups of women, higher plasma levels of FSH and LH were related to greater SBP and DBP increases during the mirror-tracing task, and greater norepinephrine increases during both behavioral tasks. In contrast, higher endogenous estradiol levels were associated with lower SBP, DBP, and norepinephrine responses to these tasks. These results indicate that changes in levels of reproductive hormones during the menopausal period are related to adverse changes in cardiovascular and plasma norepinephrine responses to stressors, which may contribute to the increase in risk of hypertension and cardiovascular mortality seen in the postmenopausal years.

Studies focusing on the effects of hormone replacement therapy and physiological responses to stress are still too limited to yield definitive

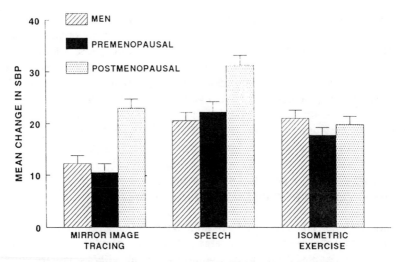

FIG. 15.8. Bar graph showing change in systolic blood pressure in response to three challenging tasks. Data are mean (± SEM) for men, premenopausal women, and postmenopausal women. From Owens et al. (1993). © 1993 by American Heart Association. Reprinted with permission.

results. Collins et al. (1982) reported on the results of a study in which three experimental sessions 6 weeks apart were used to compare responses in two groups of postmenopausal women, those receiving estrogen plus progestin prior to both the second and third sessions, and those receiving placebo before session 2 and then switched to hormone replacement before session 3. In both groups, SBP tended to decrease modestly after receiving replacement hormones, but due to a small sample size ($n = 10$) with complete BP data, these results were apparent only as a trend. Catecholamine and cortisol levels in spot urine collections did not differ after hormone replacement, nor did urinary levels of these hormones obtained during and after mental stressors, although pronounced habituation effects associated with retesting may have obscured any real effect of treatment on these measures or BP responses to stress.

More recently, Lindheim et al. (1992) examined physiological reactivity to stress in 36 postmenopausal women before and after 6 weeks of treatment with transdermal estradiol or placebo. Prior to treatment, the post-menopausal women showed greater SBP responses to a math task and a speech task compared to a group of significantly younger (mean age 37 vs. 56 years) premenopausal women. After treatment, those postmenopausal women on placebo showed the same exaggerated responses as before treatment, whereas those who had used transdermal estradiol demonstrated reduced SBP responses to the stressors that no longer differed from the premenopausal women. The study was somewhat limited in that SBP and

DBP readings were not obtained actually during the stressors, but instead after the events had terminated, thus reflecting primarily differences in early and later recovery, rather than peak responses during the stressors. These investigators also examined plasma levels of corticotrophin, cortisol, norepinephrine, and androstenedione, and after treatment stress-induced increases in these neurohumoral factors were significant for the placebo-treated women, whereas no significant stress-related increases were seen in the estradiol-treated group.

The difference in these results compared to the prior work by Collins et al. (1982) may be due to the route of administration of estrogen, because transdermal estradiol is purported to maintain more constant increases in plasma estradiol levels, or to the lack of progestin treatment in the Lindheim et al. (1992) study, or to other differences in the two protocols, such as the within-subjects versus between-subjects approach, the timing of obtaining blood pressure measurements or other procedures, or both. However, despite the limited nature of the current literature, and the inconsistencies in the available data, the results appear sufficiently provocative to encourage additional research in this area. One very obvious issue that has not yet been addressed is whether TPR responses to stress, previously shown to be influenced by menstrual cycle phase, may be reduced in postmenopausal women by hormone replacement with estrogen alone or with estrogen plus progesterone, the latter being the usual treatment prescribed for women with an intact uterus, in order to minimize any increase in risk of endometrial cancer.

As a result, our research team has recently initiated a randomized, placebo-controlled study to assess the effects of hormone replacement on blood pressure, vascular response, and cardiac index response to stressors after 3 months and 6 months of treatment. Although results at the present time reflect only a small proportion of the final projected sample of 75 participants, the early indications suggest that vascular response to the alpha-adrenergic stressor, the cold pressor test, may indeed be attenuated after hormone replacement (Light, Girdler, et al., 1995). The final data set, which will not be complete until 1997, will provide a clear test of this hypothesis, and will also provide important information on the effects of hormone replacement on pain sensitivity, structural changes in the heart and vasculature, and 24-hour ambulatory blood pressure.

AMBULATORY WORK BLOOD PRESSURE: EFFECT OF PSYCHOSOCIAL FACTORS

Although as a group, women under age 55 have been described earlier as having lower ambulatory work SBP and DBP and lower SBP responses to laboratory stressors compared to men, it is clear that not all women are protected from hypertension and other cardiovascular problems in this age group. For this reason, it seems appropriate to search for those factors that identify special subgroups of women who are more vulnerable than the average woman, and who may exhibit cardiovascular response patterns more similar to men.

In an initial effort to examine psychosocial factors that might relate to increased risk in women, Light, Turner, and Hinderliter (1992) focused on the influence of "job strain" on ambulatory blood pressure at work in a biracial sample of 65 men and 64 women working full time outside the home. Based on the model developed by Karasek and colleagues (Karasek, Baker, Marxer, Ahlbom, & Theorell, 1981), job strain is defined by the joint presence of two relatively independent job characteristics: high psychological demands (the perception of working very hard and fast), and low job decision latitude (low authority and control over job-related matters). Previous investigations employing all-male, primarily White samples had reported that job strain was associated with greater prevalence of hypertension and higher ambulatory blood pressure (Schnall et al., 1990; Schnall, Schwartz, Landsbergis, Warren, & Pickering, 1992). In the Light et al. (1992) investigation, where the average age of subjects was only 32 years, younger than in prior studies, the effect of job strain on men was still seen to be significant. Men with and without high job strain had similar blood pressures in a clinic context, but those with high job strain had significantly higher ambulatory SBP and DBP throughout an 8-hour workday. To control for potential confounding factors, we determined that men who were high and low in job strain did not differ in age, body-mass index, job status, or percentage of readings obtained after exercise or high-stress episodes. Men reporting high job strain did report more readings obtained in the standing posture, but statistical adjustment for this difference did not substantially alter the results. It was also of interest that more Black men than White men studied reported high job strain (30% vs. 18%), suggesting that job strain could potentially contribute to the increased risk of elevated blood pressure in African American men.

In contrast to the men, the women in the Light et al. (1992) sample who reported high job strain did *not* show higher work SBP or DBP. This lack of relationship between job strain and work blood pressure in women has since been replicated by Schwartz and colleagues (Brondolo, Schwartz, Light, & Contrada, 1994). These findings reinforced previous suggestions that psychosocial factors influencing blood pressure are not necessarily similar in women as in men.

Subsequent work with this same sample of subjects focusing on high-effort coping as a behavioral trait extended and confirmed this interpretation of gender differences in response to work. Since the 1970s, laboratory research led by Obrist (Obrist et al., 1978) has indicated that stressful tasks which require a high and sustained level of mental effort will evoke greater and more prolonged elevations of BP than tasks that are easier or cause the subject to give up trying entirely. The predisposition to continue high-effort coping despite all obstacles to success can also be measured as a behavioral trait, using the John Henryism Active Coping Scale developed by James (James, Hartnett, & Kalsbeek, 1983). This scale is designed to assess "the individual's self-perception that he can meet the demands of his environment through hard work and determination" (p. 263). James et al. established the utility of this scale by demonstrating that among African American men living in a rural southern U.S. community, high John Henryism was associated with higher casual blood pressure in those with less than a high school education, presumably because less education meant that even greater coping effort was essential in order to surmount the obstacles to success.

Although the scale, named after an African American folk hero who refused to give up in an unfair battle against a machine (and died as a result), seems to suggest an extreme behavior pattern, the items themselves are in fact not extreme at all, but consistent with the "work ethic." Sample items include the following: "Hard work has really helped me to get ahead in life." "When things don't go the way I want them to, that just makes me work even harder." "I don't let my personal feelings get in the way of doing a job." Because of the previous observations relating high effort to greater sympathetically mediated cardiovascular responses, we hypothesized that persons scoring high in John Henryism would demonstrate higher work blood pressures, if the work context is one that appears to require intense effort in order to achieve career goals.

In our society, a smaller proportion of women and African Americans hold high status occupations, compared to White men, and there is a perception that greater effort and perseverance are required to achieve and retain such jobs if one is female or Black. There are also fewer persons of the same gender and ethnicity to provide workplace social support, a potentially important stress buffer. For example, Farley and Allen (1987) reported that among individuals aged 25 to 64, the percent of persons in executive, administrative, managerial, and professional specialty occupations was 30% for White men, 15% for Black men, 26% for White women, and 19% for Black women.

Thus, we hypothesized that having a high-status job, which has been associated with lower blood pressure in White and Black men (Williams, 1992), might have an adverse rather than a beneficial impact if the individual was predisposed to high-effort coping, and if the individual was in a minority group of those at the high-status job level. Among 143 young adults working full time outside the home, Light and colleagues (Light, Brownley, et al., 1995) reported that the combination of high John Henryism and having a high-status job was associated with significantly higher ambulatory DBP at work in women. Other female subgroups, those low in either John Henryism or job status or both, had mean DBP levels averaged across the 8-hour workday that were significantly lower than men. In contrast, the high-effort, high-job-status women demonstrated work DBP levels that were significantly higher than the other female subgroups, and which did not differ from the men (see Fig. 15.9). Similarly, when the data were reanalyzed examining the influence of ethnic group instead of gender in combination with job status and John Henryism, Light, Brownley, et al. (1995) observed a similar result. Black subjects who were high in both these characteristics had higher mean DBP at work and higher work SBP as well compared to other subgroups of Black workers and to all groups of White workers. Further analyses indicated that 71% of the women and Blacks who had high-status jobs were high-effort copers, whereas only 36% of the White men with high-status jobs reported being high-effort copers (chi-square $p < .05$). This suggests that the trait of high effort coping may make it more likely that a woman or African American man will achieve a high-status job, but it may do so at the cost of blood pressure elevation at work, and in other contexts as well, because these subgroups also had higher blood pressure when studied during baseline and a series of stressors in the laboratory (see Fig. 15.10). These results are

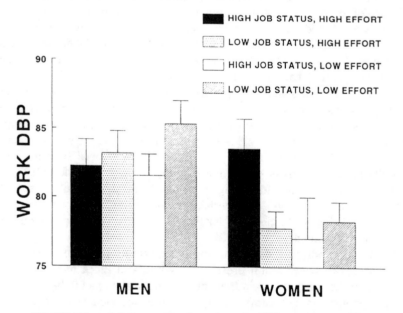

FIG. 15.9. Mean ambulatory diastolic pressure (± SEM) at work in men and women grouped by job status and coping effort (John Henryism). From Light, Brownley, et al. (1995). © 1995 by the American Heart Association. Reprinted with permission.

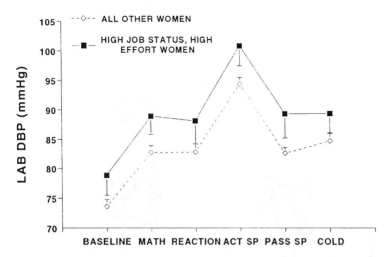

FIG. 15.10. Mean laboratory diastolic pressure (± SEM) in high job status, high-effort coping women versus all other women. Act Sp = Active Speech, Pass Sp = Passive Speech, Cold = Cold Pressor. From Light, Brownley, et al. (1995). © 1995 by the American Heart Association. Reprinted with permission.

intriguing, but it must be recognized that the sample sizes of the Black and female groups with high John Henryism and high-status jobs were small. Thus, these results must be viewed as preliminary until they can be replicated in a larger sample.

It is possible that one factor contributing to the higher work blood pressure of high-effort women and Blacks who have high-status jobs is lesser availability of social support from work colleagues of the same gender and ethnic group. A reanalysis of the data from these same subjects demonstrated a significant stress-buffering effect of social support on blood pressure of persons scoring high in hostility (see Fig. 15.11 and 15.12). Work, home, and clinic blood pressure levels were higher in hostile subjects reporting low social support than in hostile subjects reporting higher support; in fact, blood pressure levels of the hostile subjects with high social support were as low as those of the low hostile subjects (Brownley, Light, & Anderson, 1996). No data were obtained on social support in the workplace, and the potential buffering effect of this factor on high-effort coping at work remains an issue for future research to address.

INTEGRATION AND SUMMARY OF FINDINGS TO DATE

It is widely appreciated that we have recently entered a new era in regard to research in women's health in the United States and elsewhere. Central aspects of this new era include a greater willingness to focus on health

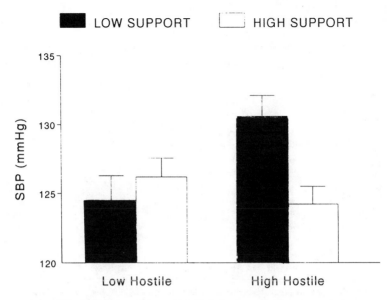

FIG. 15.11. Mean systolic pressure (± SEM) during workday and evening hours in subjects grouped by hostility and appraisal social support. From Brownley et al. (1995). © 1995 by Society for Psychophysiological Research. Adapted with permission.

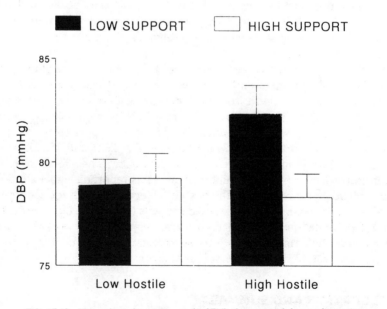

FIG. 15.12. Mean diastolic pressure (± SEM) during workday and evening hours in subjects grouped by hostility and appraisal social support. From Brownley et al. (1995). © 1995 by Society for Psychophysiological Research. Adapted with permission.

concerns that are unique to women, and, when dealing with a health problem like hypertension and cardiovascular disease that is common to both men and women, to acknowledge that biological and behavioral factors influencing the development and management of these disorders will in some cases be different for women. The research summarized previously in regard to cardiovascular responses to laboratory and real-life challenges has underscored some differences that we believe may be potentially relevant to our growing understanding of cardiovascular health and disease in both genders across the adult life span.

In summary, among healthy adults under age 55, men have higher clinic and ambulatory SBP and DBP than women. Men also demonstrate greater SBP increases to certain laboratory stressors (excluding those which capitalize on traditional feminine strengths), greater vasoconstriction to certain stressors including the forehead cold pressor, and they show less complete recovery of both SBP and DBP to prestress levels during the first 5 minutes after a stressful task. In addition, healthy men in this age range show greater left ventricular mass index than women, even after correction for gender differences in body size and ambulatory or clinic blood pressure. All of these gender differences may reflect important contributions of male and female reproductive hormones, and all are potentially relevant to the greater incidence of hypertension and cardiovascular morbidity among men versus women during early adulthood.

Postmenopausal women who are not taking hormone replacement demonstrate higher 24-hour ambulatory blood pressure levels compared to premenopausal women, and have sometimes been observed to show greater SBP and DBP responses to laboratory stressors (particularly those that tend to evoke vasoconstriction) and greater plasma epinephrine response as well. Among healthy premenopausal women, testing in the late luteal phase is associated with greater vasoconstriction and lesser vasodilation responses to laboratory stressors compared to testing in the follicular phase of the menstrual cycle in the same subject. Also, preliminary findings suggest that young women who consistently show higher luteal levels of plasma estradiol exhibit lower vascular resistance and higher cardiac index during baseline and stressors compared to women with consistently lower luteal phase estradiol levels. Altogether, these results are suggestive of a protective effect of female reproductive hormones, and may relate particularly to estrogen's putative effects in attenuating vasoconstrictive responses of sympathetic agonists.

Young adult men appear to show greater adverse effects of job strain on their SBP and DBP levels at work than women. However, women and African American men show greater adverse effects of the combination of high job status and the predisposition to high-effort coping on both laboratory baseline and stress blood pressure levels, and on mean blood pressure throughout an 8-hour workday compared to Caucasian men. Women with high-status jobs who are high-effort copers have higher DBP levels at work than other women, and are the one subgroup tested who did not differ from the men in this respect.

These findings will provide the groundwork for more extensive investigation of the biological and behavioral factors influencing cardiovascular stress responses in women and men over the next decade. They should be viewed as prologue and promise of an exciting period of expansion of knowledge in this very important area of health research.

ACKNOWLEDGMENTS

Much of the research reported in this chapter was supported by NIH grants HL31533, HL50778, and RR00046, and NIMH grant 09885.

REFERENCES

Allen, M. T., Stoney, C. M., Owens, J. F., & Matthews, K. A. (1993). Hemodynamic adjustments to laboratory stress: The influence of gender and personality. *Psychosomatic Medicine, 55,* 505–517.

de Beer, E. L., & Keizer, H. A. (1982). Direct action of estradiol-17b on the atrial action potential. *Steroids, 40,* 223–231.

Blumenthal, J. A., Fredrikson, M., Matthews, K. A., Kuhn, C. M., Schniebolk, S., German, D., Rifai, N., Steege, J., & Rodin, T. (1991). Stress reactivity and exercise training in premenopausal and postmenopausal women. *Health Psychology, 10,* 384–391.

Borghi, C., Costa, F., Boschi, S., Mussi, A., & Ambrosioni, E. (1986). Predictors of stable hypertension in young borderline subjects: A five-year follow-up study. *Journal of Cardiovascular Pharmacology, 8*(suppl 5), S138–S141.

Brondolo, E., Schwartz, J. E., Light, K. C., & Contrada, R. (1994, April). *Ambulatory blood pressure: Effects of job strain and coping style.* Symposium presented at the Society of Behavioral Medicine, Boston, MA.

Brownley, K. A., Light, K. C., & Anderson, N. B. (1996). Social support and hostility interact to influence ambulatory blood pressure in black and white men and women. *Psychophysiology, 33,* 434–445.

Colditz, G. A., Willett, W. C., Stampfer, M. J., Rosner, B., Speizer, F. E., & Hennekens, C. H. (1987). Menopause and the risk of coronary heart disease in women. *New England Journal of Medicine, 316,* 1105–1110.

Collins, A., Eneroth, P., & Landgren, B. (1985). Psychoneuroendocrine stress responses and mood as related to the menstrual cycle. *Psychosomatic Medicine, 47,* 512–527.

Collins, A., Hanson, E., Eneroth, P., Hagenfeldt, K., Lundberg, U., & Frankenhaeuser, M. (1982). Psychophysiological stress responses in postmenopausal women before and after hormonal replacement therapy. *Human Neurobiology, 1,* 153–159.

Farley, R., & Allen, W. R. (1987). *The color line and the quality of life in America.* New York: Oxford University Press.

Freedman, R. R., Sabharwal, S. C., & Desai, N. (1987). Sex differences in peripheral vascular adrenergic receptors. *Circulation Research, 61,* 581–585.

Garavaglia, G. E., Messerli, F. H., Schmieder, R. E., Nunez, B. D., & Oren, S. (1989). Sex differences in cardiac adaptation to essential hypertension. *European Heart Journal, 10*, 1110–1114.

Girdler, S. S., Pedersen, C. A., Stern, R. A., & Light, K. C. (1993). Menstrual cycle and premenstrual syndrome: Modifiers of cardiovascular reactivity in women. *Health Psychology, 12*, 180–192.

Girdler, S. S., Turner, J. R., Sherwood, A., & Light, K. C. (1990). Gender differences in blood pressure control during a variety of behavioral stressors. *Psychosomatic Medicine, 52*, 571–591.

Hastrup, J. L., & Light, K. C. (1982). Sex differences in cardiovascular stress responses: Modulation as a function of menstrual cycle phases. *Journal of Psychosomatic Research, 28*, 475–483.

Higgens, M. W. (1990). Women and coronary disease. Then and now. *Women's Health Issues, 1*, 5–11.

Hinderliter, A. L., Light, K. C., & Willis, P. W., IV. (1992). Gender differences in left ventricular structure and function in young adults with normal or marginally elevated blood pressure. *American Journal of Hypertension, 5*, 32–36.

James, S. A., Hartnett, S. A., & Kalsbeek, W. D. (1983). John Henryism and blood pressure differences among black men. *Journal of Behavioral Medicine, 6*, 259–278.

Karasek, R. A., Baker, D., Marxer, F., Ahlbom, A., & Theorell, T. (1981). Job decision latitude, job demands and cardiovascular disease: A prospective study of Swedish men. *American Journal of Public Health, 71*, 694–705.

Kim, C. J., Jang, H. C., Cho, D. H., & Min, Y. K. (1994). Effects of hormone replacement therapy on lipoprotein (a) and lipids in postmenopausal women. *Arteriosclerosis & Thrombosis, 14*, 275–281.

Koenig, H., Goldstone, A., & Lu, C. Y. (1982). Testosterone-mediated sexual dimorphism of the rodent heart. Ventricular lysosomes, mitochondria and cell growth as modulated by androgens. *Circulation Research, 50*, 782–787.

Levy, D., Garrison, R. J., Savage, D. D., Kannel, W. B., & Castelli, W. P. (1990). Prognostic implications of echocardiographically determined left ventricular mass in the Framingham Heart Study. *New England Journal of Medicine, 222*, 1561–1566.

Light, K. C., Brownley, K. A., Turner, J. R., Hinderliter, A. L., Girdler, S. S., Sherwood, A., & Anderson, N. B. (1995). Job status and high-effort coping influence work blood pressure in women and blacks. *Hypertension, 25*, 554–559.

Light, K. C., Girdler, S. S., Sherwood, A., Miller, S., Steege, J., Lamothe, T., & Hinderliter, A. L. (1995, May). *Estrogen replacement and cardiovascular stress response: Preliminary observations.* Presentation at NIH Meeting on Collaborative Research in Women's Health, Bethesda, MD.

Light, K. C., Turner, J. R., & Hinderliter, A. L. (1992). Job strain and ambulatory work blood pressure in healthy young men and women. *Hypertension, 20*, 214–218.

Light, K. C., Turner, J. R., Hinderliter, A. L., & Sherwood, A. (1993). Race and gender comparisons: I. Hemodynamic responses to a series of stressors. *Health Psychology, 12*, 354–365.

Light, K. C., Turner, J. R., Hinderliter, A. L., Girdler, S. S., & Sherwood, A. (1994). Comparison of cardiac versus vascular reactors and ethnic groups in plasma epinephrine and norepinephrine responses to stress. *International Journal of Behavioral Medicine, 1*, 229–246.

Lindheim, S. R., Legro, R. S., Bernstein, L., Stanczyk, F. Z., Vijod, M. A., Presser, S. C., & Lobo, R. A. (1992). Behavioral stress responses in premenopausal and postmenopausal women and the effects of estrogen. *American Journal of Obstetrics & Gynecology, 167*, 1831–1836.

Lobo, R. A. (1991). Effects of hormone replacement on lipids and lipoproteins in postmenopausal women. *Journal of Clinical and Endocrinological Metabolism, 73*, 925–932.

Manuck, S. B., Kasprowicz, A. L., & Muldoon, M. F. (1990). Behaviorally-evoked cardiovascular reactivity and hypertension: Conceptual issues and potential association. *Annals of Behavioral Medicine, 12*, 17–39.

Matthews, K. A., Davis, M. C., Stoney, C. M., Owens, J. F., & Caggiula, A. R. (1991). Does the gender relevance of the stressor influence sex differences in psychophysiological responses? *Health Psychology, 10*, 112–120.

Matthews, K. A., Meilahn, E., Kuller, L. H., Kelsey, S. F., Caggiula, A. W., & Wing, R. R. (1989). Menopause and risk factors for coronary heart disease. *New England Journal of Medicine, 321,* 641–646.

Matthews, K. A., & Stoney, C. M. (1988). Influences of sex and age on cardiovascular responses during stress. *Psychosomatic Medicine, 50,* 46–56.

Obrist, P. A. (1985). Beta-adrenergic hyperresponsivity to behavioral challenges: A possible hypertensive risk factor. In J. F. Orlebeke, G. Mulder, & L. P. J. van Doornen (Eds.), *Psychophysiology of cardiovascular control: Methods, model and data* (pp. 667–682). New York: Plenum.

Obrist, P. A., Gaebelein, C. J., Teller, E. S., Langer, A. W., Grignolo, A., Light, K. C., & McCubbin, J. A. (1978). The relationships among heart rate, carotid dP/dt, and blood pressure in humans as a function of the type of stress. *Psychophysiology, 15,* 102–115.

Owens, J. E., Stoney, C. M., & Matthews, K. A. (1993). Menopausal status influences ambulatory blood pressure levels and blood pressure changes during mental stress. *Circulation, 88,* 2794–2802.

Pines, A., Fisman, E., Levo, Y., Averbuch, M., Lidor, A., Drory, Y., Finkelstein, A., Hetman-Peri, M., Moshkowitz, M., Ben-Ari, E., & Ayalon, D. (1991). The effects of hormone replacement therapy in normal postmenopausal women: Measurements of Doppler-derived parameters of aortic flow. *American Journal of Obstetrics & Gynecology, 164,* 806–812.

Plante, T. G., & Denney, D. R. (1984). Stress responsivity among dysmenorrheic women at different phases of their menstrual cycle: More ado about nothing. *Behavior Research and Therapy, 22,* 249–258.

Polefrone, J. M., & Manuck, S. B. (1988). Effects of menstrual phase and parental history of hypertension on cardiovascular response to cognitive challenge. *Psychosomatic Medicine, 50,* 23–36.

Ravi, J., Mantzoros, C. S., Prabhu, A. S., Ram, J. L., & Sowers, J. R. (1994). In vitro relaxation of phenylephrine- and angiotensin II-contracted aortic rings by beta-estradiol. *American Journal of Hypertension, 7,* 1065–1069.

Saab, P. G., Matthews, K. A., Stoney, C. M., & McDonald, R. H. (1989). Premenopausal and postmenopausal women differ in their cardiovascular and neuroendocrine responses to behavioral stressors. *Psychophysiology, 26,* 270–280.

Sacks, F. M., McPherson, R., & Walsh, B. W. (1994). Effect of postmenopausal estrogen replacement on plasma Lp(a) lipoprotein concentrations. *Archives of International Medicine, 254,* 1106–1110.

Sarrel, P. M. (1990). Ovarian hormones and the circulation. *Maturitas, 590,* 287–298.

Schnall, P. L., Pieper, C. F., Schwartz, J. E., Karasek, R. A., Schlussel, Y., Devereux, R. B., Ganau, A., Alderman, J., Warren, K., & Pickering, T. G. (1990). The relationship between "job strain," workplace diastolic blood pressure, and left ventricular mass index. *JAMA, 263,* 1929–1935.

Schnall, P. L., Schwartz, J. E., Landsbergis, P. A., Warren, K., & Pickering, T. G. (1992). Relation between job strain, alcohol, and ambulatory blood pressure. *Hypertension, 19,* 488–494.

Schneiderman, N. (1995, March). *Reactivity as a candidate risk factor for hypertension and coronary heart disease: Our servant is dressed modestly.* Paper presented at the Society of Behavioral Medicine, San Diego, CA.

Stampfer, M. J., & Colditz, G. A. (1991). Estrogen replacement therapy and coronary heart disease: A quantitative assessment of the epidemiological evidence. *Preventive Medicine, 20,* 47–63.

Stevenson, J. C., Crook, D., Godsland, I. F., Collins, P., & Whitehead, M. I. (1994). Hormone replacement therapy and the cardiovascular system: Nonlipid effects. *Drugs, 47*(suppl 2), 35–41.

Stoney, C. M., Davis, M. C., & Matthews, K. A. (1987). Sex differences in physiological responses to stress and coronary heart disease: A causal link? *Psychophysiology, 24,* 127–131.

Stoney, C. M., Matthews, K. A., McDonald, R. H., & Johnson, C. A. (1988). Sex differences in lipid, lipoprotein, cardiovascular and neuroendocrine responses to acute stress. *Psychophysiology, 15,* 645–656.

Stoney, C. M., Owens, J. F., Matthews, K. A., Davis, M. D., & Caggiula, A. (1990). Influences of the normal menstrual cycle on physiologic functioning during behavioral stress. *Psychophysiology, 27*, 125–135.

Tersman, Z., Collins, A., & Eneroth, P. (1991). Cardiovascular responses to psychological and physiological stressors during the menstrual cycle. *Psychosomatic Medicine, 53*, 185–197.

Tischenkel, J. J., Saab, P. G., Schneiderman, N., Nelesen, R. A., Pasain, R. D., Goldstein, D. A., Spitzer, S. B., Woo-Ming, R., & Weidler, D. J. (1989). Cardiovascular and neurohumoral responses to behavioral challenge as a function of race and sex. *Health Psychology, 8*, 503–524.

Walsh, B. W., Schiff, I., Rosner, B., Greenberg, L., Ravnikar, V., & Sacks, F. M. (1991). Effects of postmenopausal estrogen replacement on the concentration and metabolism of plasma lipoproteins. *New England Journal of Medicine, 325*, 196–204.

Weidner, G., Friend, R., Ficarrotto, T. J., & Mendell, N. R. (1989). Hostility and cardiovascular reactivity to stress in women and men. *Psychosomatic Medicine, 51*, 36–45.

West, S. G., Bove, A. B., & Light, K. C. (1993). Chronic stress in women: Estrogen and cardiovascular function [abstract]. *Psychosomatic Medicine, 5*, 115.

Williams, D. R. (1992). Black–white differences in blood pressure: The role of social factors. *Ethnicity & Disease, 2*, 126–141.

Wolf, P. H., Madans, J. H., & Finucane, F. F. (1991). Reduction of cardiovascular disease-related mortality among postmenopausal women who use hormones: Evidence from a national cohort. *American Journal of Obstetrics and Gynecology, 164*, 489–494.

CONCLUSIONS AND RECOMMENDATIONS

16

Women, Stress, and Heart Disease: Concluding Remarks

Gösta Tibblin
University of Uppsala, Sweden

Kristina Orth-Gomér
Karolinska Institute, Stockholm, Sweden

WOMEN AND CARDIOVASCULAR HEALTH

The issue of women's health has long been neglected. This statement applies to many medical areas, but it has become most evident in the field of cardiology. Cardiology has traditionally been a medical specialty that seemed to be created by men, for men. Male patients have been visible and dominant in every aspect of cardiology from research to clinical care (e.g., in coronary care units). In this context it is easy to understand why most women believe they will die from cancer rather than from heart disease.

However, this assumption is not true. Heart disease is the leading cause of death for women, as it is for men. Female patients are frequently encountered in the cardiology department, but they are older and seem to get less visibility and attention than do male patients. Because women are temporarily protected against atherosclerosis by their reproductive hormones, heart disease becomes clinically and epidemiologically prominent at a later stage in women's lives. Men are struck by the illness at least 10 years before women.

This issue was the basis for Nanette Wenger's chapter about the status of coronary heart disease (CHD) among women. In a convincing way she showed how cardiologists have neglected female CHD on all levels including prevention, diagnostic procedures, and therapeutic actions. This neglect has occurred despite the fact that CHD is the leading cause of death in women and a major source of disability and psychosocial dysfunction for women

265

who survive a coronary event. The data presented by Wenger also indicated that women fare more poorly than men after their first event. Women have higher mortality rates following myocardial infarction (MI) and generally show more complications than men.

An important aspect of Wenger's presentation dealt with the causes of the myths, the misperceptions, and the missed therapeutic opportunities in the field of women's cardiovascular health. She suggested that misinformed physicians, unaware female patients, and societal stereotypes such as that myocardial infarction is a male privilege may be at the root of the current situation.

One possible cause of the higher female mortality post-MI may be the fact that women are treated less aggressively than men in the coronary care units. Both surgical and thrombolytic therapy have been shown to be used less frequently in female patients (Dellborg & Swedberg, 1993).

In his chapter, Mikael Dellborg (chapter 2) excused doctors' bias for not treating women as often as men with thrombolytic therapy. From his large clinical study using vector-electrocardiography he concluded that men have more pronounced ischemic ST-changes than women during the acute phase of MI. Because fixed magnitudes of ST-deviation are required for initiating therapy, therapeutic programs will favor men. Therefore, different diagnostic standards may need to be instituted for female cardiac patients. A further difficulty often seen in female clinical cardiology cases is the failure to associate CHD symptoms with underlying coronary artery changes.

Although female patients have been previously neglected, there is a burning interest today in women's cardiovascular health. This attention is due more to advances of the women's movement than to the awakening of cardiologists. Earlier experience from Gothenburg confirms cardiologists' lack of interest in female patients, previous Swedish studies of women's cardiovascular health having gained little attention. Ten years ago Saga Johansson presented her thesis entitled *Myocardial Infarction in Women* at the Clinic for Preventive Cardiology in Gothenburg (Johansson, Vedin, & Wilhelmsson, 1983). Although she reported clinical findings similar to those presented here, at that time her work was received with disinterest. In the same city and in the same research group, Calle Bengtsson investigated risk factors for CHD among women in a large prospective population study. Although his group has published important results in international journals, the response has been weak. Their findings address standard clinical risk factors as well as psychosocial predictors of CHD. In a 12-year follow-up of 795 middle-aged, Gothenburg women, Hällström and coworkers found that depressive and mental disorders predict angina pectoris, and that lack of self-assertiveness predicts MI (Hällström, Lapidus, Bengtsson, & Edström, 1986). Caution should be exercised when interpreting these results, because incidence rates in this age group were low, with only 25 cases of angina and

11 cases of MI observed. Nevertheless, the findings are important and they are being confirmed in more recent studies of larger groups of female patients. Here, Wenger reported that women have numerous cardiovascular risk factors, and she recommended preventive actions. Although primary preventive methods for men have virtually failed to prevent the development of new cases of CHD, those for women will hopefully be more advanced. One possible effective preventive strategy is suggested by Chesney and Darbes in chapter 11 concerning social support and heart disease in women. They advocated the integration of traditional health-behavior-related efforts with an extended concept of women's psychosocial needs and problems. They convincingly argued that social and psychological factors are so intimately intertwined with health and disease that they cannot be treated separately.

Chesney and Darbes' important statement underscored the volume's objective of an integrated concept of women's cardiovascular health. Learning more about women's psychological and social situations will facilitate cardiovascular and other health-promotion efforts.

PSYCHOSOCIAL FACTORS IN WOMEN

In modern society both men and women conduct their lives in two scenes, the workplace and the family environment. On these two stages men and women receive applause and rewards, as well as whistles. Here they develop their identity and either build or lose their self-esteem. In relation to cardiovascular health, the work situation has been closely examined in many studies, despite the fact that a rather small amount of time is spent on the job, and that moves from one job to another are frequent.

In contrast, there has been a paucity of studies about what is happening in the family environment. However, this volume presented an excellent and unique piece by Ulla Björnberg (chapter 9) on the psychosocial well-being among employed mothers with preschool children. In Björnberg's study, the mothers did twice as much work at home as did the fathers. Essential to the mental well-being of the family was not only the mothers' work load or the number of children, but also the balance between the job and the family. Ill health was created by a high-conflict index between job and family and by the accompanying lack of parental identity.

In his important contribution, Ulf Lundberg (chapter 4) presented interesting data showing that although an increasing number of women in modern society are becoming employed outside the home, they tend to continue having the main responsibility for household chores and child care. In his study, women reported higher levels of work overload, stress, and role conflicts than men. The gender differences in these levels increased with increasing number of children. Furthermore, women's stress and work load were reflected in elevated physiological arousal during the job, after work, and at home.

In their provocative chapter, Denny Vågerö and Eero Lahelma (chapter 6) used historical data to demonstrate that working outside the home promotes health in women. In their chapter, Vågerö and Lahelma show that entering the labor market for Swedish women was linked to improved survival chances and reduced mortality. They have included age in their analysis and have eliminated most selection mechanisms. Based on their data, they could not directly explain their findings of improved health in working women, but one possible explanation is that work outside the home may have relieved women's social isolation, positively impacting health. Another possible mechanism is the increased economic resources that accompany women's entry into the work force.

In their thoughtful contribution on gender segregation in the labor market, Kate Hunt and Carol Emslie (chapter 7) tested the Kanter concept of *tokenism*, the phenomenon of being a member of a minority group among a dominant majority. These authors studied women in male-dominated jobs and found that women in managerial and professional jobs tended to fare the worst. The concept of tokenism may explain the high suicide rate among female doctors in Sweden.

Olle Lundberg and Lena Gonäs (chapter 5) pointed to the dramatic changes in women's lives as they enter the labor market. From this presentation we note with pleasure that Swedish males seem to be doing more of the housework. More alarming is that high-stress jobs characterized by high demand and low control have increased in Swedish female-dominated professions over the last decade. A particularly sharp increase is found among such work categories as nurses and nurses' assistants.

In a fascinating chapter, Phyllis Moen (chapter 8) explained her concept of the life-course perspective in relation to women's health. This perspective includes historical aspects of change, such as important life transitions of divorce and retirement in an individual context. Furthermore, Moen discussed the importance of multiple roles, referring to several prospective studies showing that multiple roles promote good health and longevity. These multiple roles can influence life patterns and shape life changes, but they can also moderate the impact of stress.

PSYCHOSOCIAL FACTORS AND CARDIOVASCULAR HEALTH IN WOMEN

The Female Coronary Risk Study was presented by its principal investigator, Kristina Orth-Gomér, in chapter 3. The study is the first in which the investigators relate psychosocial factors to clinical findings and to atherosclerotic changes in female coronary arteries.

In light of the preliminary data of the Female Coronary Risk Study, it is evident that women with CHD report more psychosocial strain than do healthy women. CHD women also had less leisure time, more marital conflict and separations, and more problems with children.

In their respective chapters, Susan Czajkowski (chapter 10) and Margaret Chesney and Lynae Darbes (chapter 11) have examined and elucidated the psychosocial strain in the lives of women with CHD. Both have underlined the importance of social isolation, depression, and the interaction between the two. Chesney and Darbes also demonstrated that depression is an important factor in noncompliance.

In her introductory discussion, Wenger pointed out that we lack randomized controlled studies for evaluating the effects of estrogen in preventing CHD among women. The positive results from observational studies can at least partly be explained by selection mechanisms. It is possible that only health-concerned and well-educated women take the drug and have a low risk of developing the disease independent of estrogen intake.

Karin Schenck-Gustafsson and Faris Al-Khalili described the potential benefits of estrogen replacement therapy, particularly in regard to cardiovascular function. Physiologically, there are several pathways by which estrogens may protect against heart disease. These pathways extend from beneficial effects on lipids and coagulation factors, to vasodilation in response to physical and mental stressors. Gerdie Weidner and Catherine Messina (chapter 14) convincingly described the fact that women show the same cardiovascular responses to mental stress as do men. However, very little is known about the prognostic and diagnostic significance of stress reactivity in women. We shall learn considerably more on completion of the follow-up to the Swedish Female Coronary Risk Study, in which all cases and controls were tested for stress reactivity.

Kathleen Light, Susan Girdler, Sheila West, and Kimberly Brownley (chapter 15) explored the relationship between estrogen, psychosocial factors, and cardiovascular stress response. These authors found that postmenopausal women without hormone replacement had higher ambulatory blood pressure and greater catecholamine responses to stress than did premenopausal women. Those premenopausal women whose estrogen levels were consistently higher during the luteal phase had greater evidence of vasodilatation and lower vascular resistance both during baseline and during stressors than women whose estrogen levels were low. Low estrogen levels were correlated with higher anxiety and lower social support. These findings support observations by Carol Shively, Sheree Watson, J. Koudy Williams, and Michael Adams (chapter 13) in stressed subordinate female monkeys, where estrogen levels were low and ovulation absent. When examined for evidence of coronary artery disease (CAD), subordinate female monkeys had more atherosclerosis than dominant ones. The most extended pathological changes were found in monkeys who were housed in single cages and socially isolated for 8 months. It is suggested that psychosocial factors such as social isolation and social subordination contribute to CAD, and that a portion of this effect is mediated by poor ovarian function. In the discussion it was further suggested that female sex steroids may protect against cardiovascular diseases via oxytocine-related effects. Oxytocine is a female sex hormone involved in childbirth and lactation that is found in small quantities in men (Uvnäs-Moberg, 1989). Oxytocine is argued to cause antistress responses and have an almost "valium"-like effect.

INTEGRATION OF CONCEPTS AND FINDINGS

How can we make an attempt to tie all these data together? Many authors have talked about a high incidence of female myocardial infarction—250,000 a year in the United States. However, most of these women are quite old when they get their first MI and have reached a stage where primary prevention may not be applicable.

It is difficult but tempting to translate the animal findings to the human situation. Shively and her coworkers showed that subordinate female monkeys have exacerbated coronary artery atherosclerosis and altered coronary vasomotion, both of which are associated with suppressed ovarian function. In contrast, in their experiments with male monkeys, male social dominants in unstable social groupings have worsened coronary atherosclerosis. These findings suggest gender differences in the etiology of CHD, which may have therapeutic implications. Vågerö, Lahelma and others told us how Swedish women have moved into the workforce, have left the subordinate housewife life, and have taken a more dominant role. As a result, these women's longevity has increased. The proportion of women who work outside home is increasing in most countries and will soon have reached the male level in nations like the United States, Great Britain, the Netherlands, and Scandinavia (Eurostat and United Nations, 1995).

In the workforce, the subordinate women develop CHD. Increasingly, men are exiting the dominant role and, as O. Lundberg pointed out, taking part in the housework, whereby they can use their oxytocine system. Can the monkey studies explain the decrease in CHD among the men? Can equality between the sexes prevent heart disease in both sexes?!

The most stressful monkey situation was social isolation. For both male and female monkey, the worst stressor was to be alone, to have no one to touch, and no one to groom or to play with. In humans, social isolation and lack of social support are closely linked to depression, as Chesney and Darbes pointed out. These factors have been shown to increase cardiovascular mortality risk in both men and women. Providing supportive social networks, strengthening social ties, and improving social competence offer opportunities to counter this stress and improve the quality of life for individuals and society at large.

REFERENCES

Dellborg, M., & Swedberg, K. (1993). Acute myocardial infarction: Difference in the treatment between men and women. *Quality Assurance in Health Care, 5,* 261–265.

Eurostat and United Nations. (1995). *Geneva women and men in Europe and North America.* United Nations, Geneva.

Hällström, T., Lapidus, L., Bengtsson, C., & Edström, K. (1986). Psychosocial factors and risk of ischaemic heart disease and death in women: A twelve-year follow-up of participants in the population study of women in Gothenburg, Sweden. *Journal of Psychosomatic Research, 4*(4), 451–459.

Johansson, S., Vedin, A., & Wilhelmsson, C. (1983). Myocardial infarction in women. *Epidemiologic Reviews, 5,* 67–95.

Uvnäs-Moberg, K. (1989). Physiological and psychological effects of oxytocin and prolactin in connection with motherhood with special reference to food intake and endocrine system of the gut. *Acta Physiologica Scandinavica, 136*(583), 41–48.

Author Index

Subject Index